PENGUIN BOOKS

PERCH HILL

Adam Nicolson is the author of a number of books, including the *National Trust Book of Long Walks*, *Frontiers*, which won the Somerset Maugham Prize in 1985 and *Restoration*, which tells the story of the rebuilding of Windsor Castle. For four years he wrote 'The View from Perch Hill' column in the *Sunday Telegraph* Magazine.

Adam Nicolson lives on Perch Hill with his wife and five children.

Perch Hill

A New Life

Adam Nicolson

PENGUIN BOOKS
IN ASSOCIATION WITH
CONSTABLE & ROBINSON LTD

PENGUIN BOOKS

Published by the Penguin Group
Penguin Books Ltd, 27 Wrights Lane, London W8 5TZ, England
Penguin Putnam Inc., 375 Hudson Street, New York, New York 10014, USA
Penguin Books Australia Ltd, Ringwood, Victoria, Australia
Penguin Books Canada Ltd, 10 Alcorn Avenue, Toronto, Ontario, Canada M4V 3B2
Penguin Books India (P) Ltd, 11 Community Centre, Panchsheel Park,
New Delhi – 110 017, India
Penguin Books (NZ) Ltd, Cnr Rosedale and Airborne Roads,
Albany, Auckland, New Zealand
Penguin Books (South Africa) (Pty) Ltd, 5 Watkins Street, Denver Ext 4,
Johannesburg 2094, South Africa

Penguin Books Ltd, Registered Offices: Harmondsworth, Middlesex, England

First published in Great Britain by Robinson Publishing Ltd 1999
Published in Penguin Books 2000
2

'The Bright Field' by R. S. Thomas reproduced by kind permission of the publisher
J. M. Dent

Extracts from *Puck of Pook's Hill*, *Something of Myself*, 'My Boy Jack', *A Diversity of Creatures* and 'The Way through the Woods', by Rudyard Kipling, reproduced by kind permission of A. P. Watt Ltd on behalf of the National Trust for Places of Historic Interest or Natural Beauty.

Extracts from *In Time of War*, Sonnet XXVII, and *Poems 1931–1936*, XIV (from *The English Auden*, ed. Edward Mendelson) and 'In Memory of W. B. Yeats' (from *Collected Poems*), by W. H. Auden, reproduced by kind permission of Faber and Faber Ltd.

The moral right of the author has been asserted

Printed in England by Clays Ltd, St Ives plc

ACKNOWLEDGMENTS

This whole book is an acknowledgment of what a place, and the people who make it what it is, can do for a person. I hope that those who appear in these pages, and many others lurking just off-stage, realise how deeply grateful I am to them.

The idea of writing about Perch Hill, not quite in this form but covering much of the same ground, was first put to me by Alexander Chancellor at the *Sunday Telegraph*. Although incidents have been elided, and names changed, readers will recognize that parts of this book originally appeared in the *Sunday Telegraph* magazine. Many people at that paper have over the years steered me in a whole series of right directions, none more than Aurea Carpenter, to whom, in effect, most of this book was first written. No one could have asked for a better editor or friend.

At Robinson Publishing, I would like to thank Nick Robinson, Jan Chamier and Krystyna Green for all the care and attention they have devoted to this book. Julia Cady did an exemplary job of copy-editing the typescript, and Ricca Kawai of making the map of the farm and drawings for the beginning of each chapter.

Caroline Dawnay and her assistant Annabel Hardman have given me, as ever, constant and invaluable support and encouragement.

Above all, I would like to thank here the three people who in their different ways have shepherded me out of the gloom in which this story begins: Sarah Raven, Charles

Moore and Robert Sackville West, to the last of whom this book is dedicated, as a small gesture of gratitude for everything he has done for me.

A.N.
Perch Hill
December 1998

To Robert Sackville West

THE BRIGHT FIELD

If I think of the time when we decided to come here, it is a backward glance into the dark.

A summer night. I am walking home from Mayfair, from dinner with a man I fear and distrust. He is my stepfather and I burp his food into the night air. It is sole and gooseberry mousse. His dining-room is lined in Chinese silk on which parakeets and birds of paradise were painted in Macao some years ago. The birds have kept their colours, they are the colour of flames, but the branches on which they once sat have faded back into the grey silk of the sky. On the table are silver swans, whose wings open to reveal the salt. The Madeiran linen, the polished mahogany, the dumb waiter: it's alien country.

My stepfather and I do not communicate. 'It's only worth reading one book a year,' he says. 'The trouble with this country is the over-education of the young.' 'Calling a parcels service "Red Star" is a sign of the depth of communist influence, even now, in England.'

Nothing is given. I leave the house to walk across London to somewhere on the edges of Hammersmith, where I am living with Sarah Raven, the woman for whom, a few months previously, I have left my wife. That is a phrase which leaves me raw. Sarah has gone somewhere else this evening, to have dinner with friends, and won't be back until midnight or later. I have left as early as I can from the Mayfair house and think 'Why not?' A warm night. A walk through London and its glitter in the dark, to expunge that padded house and all its upholstered hostilities.

There are whores in the street outside, bending down like mannequins to the windows of the slowing cars. Some of the women are so tall and so sweetly spoken they can only be men, with long, stockinged calves and a slow flitter to their eyes. One fixes me straight. 'Looking for company?' she asks. 'Thank you, not tonight, thanks,' and we move on.

I walk down Park Lane, where the cars are thick and the night heavy. The lights from the cars blip, blip, blip through the dark. Life is hurried. I pass the Dorchester and the Hilton, down to the corner where the subway drops into ungraffitied neon. Down and up and down again to the upper parts of Knightsbridge. Along there the windows gleam. A friend of mine has opened a shop in Beauchamp Place. It is lacquered scarlet inside and beautiful, with black Japanese furniture standing on the hardwood floor.

On and out, increasingly out, away from the polish of the glimmer-zone, made shinier at night, to the open-late businesses of South Ken, where Frascati and champagne stand cooled in ranks behind glass and the Indian at the till leaves a cigarette always smoking on the ledge beside him. On, out, westwards, where occasional restaurants are all that interrupt the domestic streets now tailing into dark. The pubs have shut. It is nearing midnight.

For a stretch the street lights are broken, perhaps two in a row, and it is darker here. I think nothing of it. My mind is on other things. On what? I was thinking of a place where I have been happy, some kind of mind-cinema of it flicking through my brain: sitting back on the oars in the sunshine in a small boat off the coast of some islands in the Hebrides, where black cliffs drop into a sea the colour of green ink and the sea caves at their feet drive 50 yards or more into pink, coralline depths. I have been there time and again in the pure air streaming in off the Atlantic, alone on these islands which the last inhabitants left at the turn of the century, drinking in the immediacy of the experience, the uncontaminated intimacy with a natural world enriching me through every band of its enormous spectrum.

That night I was thinking of these things, of hauling lobsters and velvet crabs from the sea, picking the dulse from the walls of the caves, scrambling among the hissing shags and peering down the dark slum tunnels where the puffins live, croaking their curious, endearing note, like a heavy door opening on a rusted hinge, lying down in the long grass while the ravens honked and flicked above me and the buzzards cruised. I was day-dreaming of those times – and perhaps this was a sort of delirium – when there seemed to be no gap between me and the world. I was absorbed by it, as if I had no existence apart from it, in the way that the faces of the green men on the bosses of medieval church roofs fade into the background from which they have emerged, a coming and going, a fading back and a growing out, the end indistinguishable from the beginning, and the man the same as what surrounds him. My mind was away there that night.

I must fight a reluctance to describe what followed. I am wearing a suit, an Italian suit I have had for years, with turn-ups to the trousers and pointed tips to the lapels. It is a sharkish, double-breasted thing. The Mayfair whores had seen a businessman inside it and so, I suppose, did the three youths, late teenagers, in the Lillie Road.

The heels of my shoes were striking the pavement too hard, like flints. I tried to soften them by treading on the balls of my feet. Two of the boys were on the inside of the pavement next to the wall. I did not look at them. The other was on the kerb. I walked between the three like an alley and adrenalin shocked into me as I saw their eyes go white in the unlit street. I saw the kerbside boy nod at the others. I thought how contemptible was my *Daily Mail* fear of these people. I was already beyond them, and relieved, when my eyes and mouth stung and burned and there were hurried hands under my armpits pulling and pushing me into the mouth of a passageway leading off the road. My body had hunched over as the ammonia came into my face – bleach squirted from a lemon squeezer – and they knelt me on the gritty pavement, as though I were being unpacked, a bale of stuff, my body and suit a pocketed rucksack, all hurry and hard fingers against my ribs. I said nothing. I tried to get up but they rubbed the bleach into my eyes, oddly without violence, in the way you would pull back on the chain of a dog, simply a control.

I was not a person but a suit with pockets. I was being fleeced, in the way a shepherd might fleece a sheep. My assets were being stripped. I knelt with the grit of the pavement pricking in my cheek while they looked for money and objects in the suit that was no longer mine. They were robbing the suit. The bleach had emptied it of a person. I could not help but regard from a distance this odd, disembodied theft. I was in pain but the burning in my eyes and mouth seemed unrelated to this professional going-over of my clothes, not my clothes, *the* clothes, *some* clothes.

They left, up the passageway. I lay for a moment on the concrete slabs, excited by the reality of what had happened. My eyes were blurry and my tongue was ulcered and raw. I can taste and smell the ammonia now, years afterwards, a chemical thickness to it, a fog of fumes rising from my mouth into my nose. I got up. I dusted the suit off; it was torn. I walked down to the North End Road. There was a fish-and-chip shop open there. I went in and asked the man behind the counter if I could wash my face in his basin. He looked at me. His apron was up around his armpits. 'We've been messing about a bit, have we?'

'No,' I said. 'I've just been fucking attacked.'

He showed me a room which had a basin and a towel

in it. I washed there, deep in the water, holding the water to my face and eyes, wanting to wash the pain away, and the taste of the bleach, and the furry, clogged thickness on my tongue, but feeling, more than anything, broken, hopeless, at the end of a long and hopeless trajectory which, for many months and even years, had curved only down.

I walked to the house. It wasn't far. I sat down on the doorstep. I said to myself I was fine. But I knew I wasn't and eventually ended up in hospital where, at three in the morning, a doctor hosed the ammonia from my eyes, holding them open with his rubber-gloved fingers one by one, so that the water would sluice around the recesses of the eye. It felt like the second rape of the night. By pure chance, the doctor told me, precisely the same thing had happened to him the year before. Some Spurs fans had set upon him, squirted his eyes with bleach, robbed him and left him feeling blurry like this on the pavement. It was his way of consoling me, I suppose.

Only later, in Sarah's bed, deep in the night, with the grey-yellow wash of the London street lights leaking around the edges of the curtains, did I allow myself to cry, to sob out all the held-back reservoir of humiliation and failure whose dam the mugging had broken.

It was not the attack itself for which I wept and sweated that night but for everything of which it seemed, however irrationally, a culmination: the failure of my first marriage the year before, my guilt at my own part in that failure, the effect my leaving would have on my three sons by that marriage, the failure or near-failure of a business I had been involved with for five years, which I had also abandoned, unable to work properly any longer, leaving it in the hands of my cousin and co-director at the one moment he most needed my help. On top of that, a book I had been trying and failing to write had finally collapsed in exhaustion and uncertainty. If I had been a horse I would have been shot. I should have been shot. I had broken down.

The mugging was a catalyst not of change, but of paralysis. I scarcely moved for three months. I lay in bed. Sarah went alone to work and to parties. I saw in her face a terror of what she had allowed into her life. I let everything about me – my own work, my sense of self-esteem, any idea of care or responsibility for others – fall away. Nothing meant anything to me. I could make no decisions. When I met people I knew, they looked into my face as though something were missing there. I woke up tired. I spoke more slowly than before. I saw a psychotherapist and told him that I felt like a sooted chimney, nothing but a dusty black hollow cylinder inside my skin. I felt that my breath polluted the air around me. I dreamed of my children. We were walking in a rocky place like Crete. 'I am sorry,' I told them. 'I must leave you behind,' and without waiting for an answer set off up the side of a mountain which reminded me of Mount Ida, its dry, limestone bulk, its sterility, its demand to be climbed. I arrived at the chapel on the summit, a place of bare rock, and slumped down beside the walls, my face in my hands, my body with every muscle slackened, every limb like a bone in a bag. When I looked up, I saw the three boys coming towards me, easily moving up on to the final rise, a bobbing movement, alive, lightened, untaxed by the journey on which I had deserted them. 'Why do divorced men become obsessed by their children?' I heard a woman ask. I could have told her: because they watch them from what seems like the far side of death.

Sarah and I began a search for a refuge, however naïvely and hopelessly that idea was conceived. It stemmed from no more than a belief in pastoral. 'Are not these woods more free from peril than the envious court?' a figure in *As You Like It* asks the surrounding company. I knew in the past I had been happy in rural places. I knew, or thought I knew, that a rural place would soothe this crisis. I knew, as I walked out in the streets of London, that there was no solace there. Every surface was dead in my eyes. My mind returned constantly to those islands in Scotland which I had been thinking of on the night of the attack. For 15 years I had owned them. My father had bought them 50 years before for £1,200 and he gave them to me when I was 21, as I shall give them to my son Tom when he is 18. Cynics have said that all this was for tax reasons, but it isn't. I think my father gave them to me because, as a very young man, he had felt enlarged and excited by the ownership of a place like that, by the experience of being there alone or with friends, away from the thing that Auden called 'the great bat-shadow of home', the enclosing, claustrophobic, involuntary oppression of a parental place, which makes a bawling, complaining infant of you. He wanted, I think, to give that same enlargement to me, as I do to Tom.

It worked and the gift was this: memories of weeks there, storm-battered, sun-stilled, on which I continue to

draw every day of my life. I know those islands yard by
yard, I know the places to clamber up and slither down, I
know the particular corners where the pair of black
guillemots always nests or where the bull seal hauls
himself out on the seaweedy rock, I know where the fish
congregate in the tidal streams or where the eddies riffle
off a nose of lichened basalt and throw your dinghy out in
a sudden curving arc towards the Lewis shore. I know the
natural arch where the seals swim and where the kelp
gathers in an almost Ecuadorian sun-barred forest beneath your coasting hull.

I was essentially shaped by those island times. Almost
everything else feels less dense and less intense than those
moments of exposure. The social world, the political
world, the world of getting on with work and a career,
all those were for ever cast in a shadow by the raging scale
and seriousness of my moments of island life. That
intimacy with the natural makes the human seem vacuous.

This may be straight Wordsworthianism and I would
want to disown it in favour of a less monolithically
obvious thing, a glitteringly complex attitude to nature
which shimmered like an opal compared with my all-too-
single basalt slab. But I can't. I know nothing bigger or
finer than the feeling that all barriers are down and a full-
blown flood is running to and fro between you and the
rest of the world.

I know all these things and treat them as my touch-
stones and my yardstick. Is this life, I always ask, as good
as that? Does this place measure up to that? That is the
fixture; everything else can only eddy around it.

We began to search for somewhere that might be the equivalent of all that, a place which in its own terms could be an island, around which the cord could be drawn, and where life could in some ways be hidden, or even innocent. It was the search for an Arcadian simplicity in which crisis and breakdown did not and could not occur. Fantasia you might say, but it had then an urgency and reality stronger and more concrete than anything else in the world around us. There was no sense, it seemed to me, of 'getting away'. There was no desire to enter a capsule or satellite suspended above the earth. It felt, if anything, the very opposite of that, a burrowing in, a search for a bed in which the covers could be drawn up and over us. It was, I now see, these five years later, a search for a womb, a place in which you could be protected from damage. It was an infantile need and ferociously demanding because of it.

We roamed England with the template in our minds. It seems curious now that this search might have landed almost anywhere, that anywhere might have provided the bucket into which the love could have been poured. Dorset, Devon, Somerset, Shropshire, Herefordshire, Oxfordshire, Norfolk, Suffolk, even east Kent: all for a time became the zone in which safety might be found. It looks pathetic now, the two of us, in the white 2CV we had at the time, poking about like moles for a burrow, living with a private intensity the common stuff of rural estate agents' offices.

I had no perspective on what we were doing, or at least suspended any perspective I might have had. We were the first to do this. Of course we weren't – we were the last, the heirs and successors of a line that goes back at least to the Roman love affair with the suburban villa, perhaps beyond that to the first urban civilisations of the Near East, where the concentrated demands and sophistication of city life produced, even at the beginning, a dream image of the garden place, the paradise, in which the realities did not impinge, where the commercial and competitive structures of the city were absent. Is Genesis itself, I now wonder, a symptom of a disenchanted urbanity?

I had no desire to delineate, let alone puncture, the bubble. I needed its insulation and a belief in its power and reality. For years I had kept in my mind, as a sort of mantra, a poem by R.S. Thomas:

> I have seen the sun break through
> to illuminate a small field
> for a while, and gone my way
> and forgotten it. But that was the pearl
> of great price, the one field that had
> the treasure in it. I realize now
> that I must give all that I have
> to possess it. Life is not hurrying
> on to a receding future, nor hankering after
> an imagined past. It is the turning
> aside like Moses to the miracle
> of the lit bush, to a brightness
> that seemed as transitory as your youth
> once, but is the eternity that awaits you.
>
> ('The Bright Field', 1975)

Thomas, a parish priest in the Lleyn peninsula in Gwynedd, in the north-west corner of Wales, is playing a fugue on the words of both Exodus and the Gospels. The Authorised Version does indeed speak of Moses 'turning aside' to the burning bush; Christ, talking to the Apostles, describes the Kingdom of Heaven both as the field with the treasure in it and as the pearl of great price. Both, curiously perhaps to us who dissociate so firmly the religious from the financial, use the language of money and merchants. The conditions of paradise, in Christ's own words, can be bought. If only estate agents had cottoned on to this! Sell all that you have, money for paradise, the pearl of great price, turn aside, turn aside, life is neither hurrying nor hankering, the eternity that awaits you. Heaven is waiting, the paradise womb, only look for it and you will see the bush alight beside you. The brightness of youth can be once again to hand.

My own financial state was catastrophic. I was scarcely in a condition to work, or to look for work. A kind of nauseated vertigo gripped me whenever I tried to write anything. I was producing occasional pieces for the *Sunday Times* but they were ground out like dust from a mortar. All fluency had gone. I wrote a book of captions to photographs of beauty spots. I ghosted another on how to take landscape photographs. I researched the illustrations for a book on evolution. Apart from the islands in Scotland, which I would sell only if death were the other choice, I owned nothing. I had given my house and its contents to my first wife. I was paying her virtually everything I earned. At times I didn't earn enough in the month to pay her what I had promised and Sarah, who was working as a doctor, made up the difference. Sarah, who had inherited some money, at least owned her house in London, all save a small mortgage, and that was the lifeboat. That house in west London, with its three bedrooms and a sliver of a garden, would take us where we needed to go.

In that search for a place, nothing much was working. House after house was wrong, wrong in feeling, wrong in its situation, wrong in its price. The more the vision glowed, the less the places we saw came up to it. There were houses drowning in carpets and improvement, their souls erased. There were others in which the road was too near. Others too dour, many too far from Cambridge where my sons were living with their mother. Both Sarah and I felt an instinctive aversion from arable parts of England. We needed grass and wood, the Arcadian savannah, the lit bush, the field illuminated for a while. I knew that when we found the place it would say 'I am here and I am yours. I am the place.' It was a dark time.

Only at the edges, like jottings and little coloured drawings in the margins of a text, were there any points of light: the finding of wild daffodils one day in a Dorset wood; swimming one warm and languorous evening off Chesil Beach where the swell rolled in like a lion's stretch and yawn, over and over, a long slow growling from the shingle; a weekend on the Lizard in a sea of thrift; dawn on the Helford River, anchored in a boat between the woods, where the night rain dropped off the outstretched leaves into water as still as oil. These were bright fields too, illuminations in their way.

Why should it be that beauty can for an instant make sense of a world in which nothing else does? I am not sure. It is an understanding I can act to without knowing why. Maybe it is simply a recognition of pattern, a concordance between you and the world. Here in a chance beautiful thing is something given, neither engineered nor sought, neither curiously made nor elaborately framed, but dropping as a bead of meaning out of a meaningless sky. Its value, its weight, is in your own recognition of its beauty. There is something naturally there which you naturally recognise as good and the ability to see that beauty is a sign that the world is not an anarchy of violence and destruction. You belong to it and it belongs to you.

That was as near as I could come to understanding why I wanted to live and be in a place that seemed beautiful. The world around you in such a place would constantly touch you and speak to you. It would become an existence thick with understanding and that sense of crowding intelligibility might be almost social in its effect, as though you were actually joining the community of the natural. This, in my loneliness and guilt, became a kind of consolation too and I held on to it as a kind of flag of hope, a thought with which I could identify and salvage what remained of my self. There's a sentence in one of Coleridge's notebooks for 1807, when, also with a broken marriage and a career in ruins, he was staying on a farm in Somerset. A ragged peacock walked the yard: 'The molting Peacock with only two of his long tail feathers remaining, & those sadly in tatters, yet proudly as ever spreading out his ruined fan in the Sun & Breeze.' That was me with my faith in redemption by beauty, like the battle-shot colours of a regiment held up to the last.

I was at work in London – I say at work; I was sitting at my desk, looking at the screen, drinking a cup of coffee, considering from a dead mind the identity of the next possible word – and the phone rang. Sarah, in a coinbox, in a pub, breathless: 'You must come. This is the place. I'm not sure. It might be. It's a valley. An incredible valley. It's like the Auvergne. It's like an English Auvergne. Come on sweetheart. You've got to have a look. It might be all right. It might be. I'm not sure. You've got to come though. Please come.'

She was in Sussex, gone to look at a house that we both knew was too small – it was a converted observatory – and in the wrong place, on the top of a hill where nothing would ever grow, even if its views were to the Downs and the sea and a vast dome of observable sky. It was her second visit. She asked the man living there where he usually went for a walk. He mentioned a lane that dropped from this observatory down through the woods to the valley of a little river.

She had gone down the lane, curling between the hedgerows, under the branches of the overhanging trees. It was springtime and the anemones were starry in the wood. Primroses were tucked into the shade of the hedge banks. Catkins hung off the hazels over the lane. And then, at a corner, where to one side the trees opened out to a view down the valley, and from where the pleats of the valley sides folded in one after another into the blue distance of other woods and other farms, four or five miles away, there was a sign hanging out into the lane. 'FOR SALE'.

She took me back there the next day. Slowly the car
went down the lane. The flowers in the verges, the sunlight
in blobs and patches on the surface of the road. The
knitted detail of this wood-and-field place. If anywhere
were ever to look like nurture, privacy, withdrawal, sustenance, love, permanence and embeddedness, this was it.
Sarah had found it. This was the place.

Or at least this was the valley. We turned the corner,
saw the agent's board, the sign on a little brick building
saying Perch Hill Farm and drove in. Almost everything
about the place was as bad, in our eyes, as you could
imagine it to be. The buildings were a horrible mixture
of the improved and the wrecked: yards and yards of
concrete; a plastic corrugated roof to the disintegrating
barn; an oast-house whose upper storey had been
removed during the war; a 1980s extension to the
farmhouse, in the style of a garage attempting to look
like a granary, paid for, I later learned, by selling off the
milk quota. The farmhouse itself was dark and dingy
downstairs. In most of the ground floor rooms I was
unable to stand up. Upstairs there was grey cheap
carpet, gilded light fittings, downlighters and pine
louvred cupboards. A 1940s brick cow shed had been
enlarged with an extension made of telegraph poles and
more corrugated sheeting. Three other sheds – for
calves, logs and rubbish, I was told – lay scattered
around the site looking as if they were waiting to be
tidied up. Various bits of grass were carefully mown.
There was a decorative fish pond the size of a dining-
room table in front of the granary-sitting room. The
truncated oast-house had become a cart shed but was

now in use as an art gallery. There were places for customers to park.

None of this was quite what had been imagined. The smiles remained hanging on our lips. The buildings were raw-edged. Their arrangement was not quite what you would have hoped for, not quite a clustered yard, but a little strung out along the hill. The geese by the farm pond were angry. And a wind blew from the west. *Turn aside, turn aside. I have seen the sun break through* . . . The Bright Field murmurings were no more than faint.

Was it that time we walked around the farm or another? I don't quite remember. We left again, slowly, back up the Dudwell lane, along others. We had lunch on the grass outside the Ash Tree at Ashburnham. I drank a pint of Harvey's bitter and the bees hummed. We were not sure. We went back on other days, again and yet again, taking friends with us. They all thought not. The place was trammelled. Whatever it might once have had was now gone. We heard somehow that John Wells had looked at the place and rejected it: too much to do. We too should look elsewhere. So we did: a large fruit farm near Canterbury, other places, Brown Oak Farm, Burned Oak Farm, Five Oaks Farm, which I occasionally pass in the car nowadays, now the focus of other lives, diverged from ours like atoms that collided for an instant and then bounced on to other paths which would never connect with ours again.

The Perch Hill valley would not go away. It had taken up residence in my mind. I bought the largest-scale map of it that I could find and kept it on my desk. I read it at night before going to sleep, walking the dream place: the extra-

ordinary absence of roads, the isolated farms down at the
end of long tracks, the lobes of wood and fingers of
meadow, the streams incised into creases in the contours,
the enclosed world away from the brutalising openness
which I had felt had reduced me to the condition I was now
in. It is a hungry business, map-reading. It only feeds the
appetite for the real. I had drawn in red biro a line around
the fields and woods that went with Perch Hill Farm. That
red line made an island of significance even in the richness
of everything that surrounded it. The more I looked at the
map the more real my possession of those fields became,
the more that red biro line described the island reality for
which we were both longing. 'Let's go again,' I said to
Sarah. It would be the last time, the last throw, and then I
would push this map away and the place would mean
nothing to us and we could move on to other places and
other obsessions.

It was a summer evening, four months after Sarah had
first wandered down the lane. We went not to the house
but to the fields. We had brought some bread and cheese
with us. We walked around and the light was pouring
honey on the woods. At the end we lay down in the big
hay meadow known as the Way Field and looked across
the valley to the net of hedgy woods and pastures beyond
it, the terracotta tile-hung farmhouses pimpled among
them, the air of unfiddled-with completeness, the haze of
the hay. Owls hooted, two deer and their fawns came out
of the wood into the bottom of the field to graze and look,
graze and look in the pausing, anxious way they do. Graze
and look, graze and look: it was what we had been doing
for too long. We decided there and then: for the sort of

money that could have bought you an extremely nice
house in West London (double-fronted, courteous neighbours, Rosemary Vereyfied garden, a frieze of parked
German cars, chocolate-coloured labradors in pairs on
red leashes) we would buy a cramped, dark old farmhouse,
a collection of decrepit outbuildings and some fields that
would never in a thousand years produce any income
worth having. Was this wise? Yes. This was wise, the right
thing to do, plumping for the lit bush. What else could
money be for?

John Ventnor, the art dealer who owned the place,
wanted what seemed like an outrageous amount for it:
£480,000. We could afford, we thought, after the endless
shuffling of portfolios, the sale of heirlooms, and the
accommodating of 'certain grave reservations' of financial
advisers, no more than £375,000 and that was what we
offered. Not enough. We offered £20,000 more. Not
enough. What would be enough? He was prepared to
countenance a 10 per cent discount on the asking price:
£432,000. Too much. What about £410,000? Not enough.
And there it stuck for months.

We began again to look at other places but none was
right. The vision in the evening field had its hooks in us.
We waited, hoping that the delay would get to work on
him, but it didn't. It became clear that he shared the
freehold with a stepdaughter who no longer lived there.
She wanted him to sell up but he didn't want to leave. He
had no incentive to lower his price any further. We were
in an impasse.

Sarah sold her house in London, our daughter Rosie
was born and we all moved together into a rented base-

ment flat of profound sterility and gloominess. I got a job on a newspaper and we borrowed money on that rather slender foundation. On winter evenings I drew plans and projections on my computer of how we might change Perch Hill, what kind of garden we might make, how we might take the land and farm it in a way that would be more generous towards it. The sliced-off oast-house became whole again on my night-time screen. I took to sitting in front of it with no other light in the room, a silvery brightness emanating from the dark, a possible future set against a present reality. Plantings and vistas criss-crossed the spaces between the buildings on my computer plans. One after another of these schemes I drew up, ever more elaborate, and they all shared the same title: 'Arcadia for £432,000'. *Give everything you have.*

One winter day I went down there again. I had never seen Perch Hill outside its springtime freshness or its hay-encompassed summer glory. This day was different. I was alone; Sarah remained with Rosie in London. A wind was cutting in from the east and for days southern England had remained below zero. All colour had drained out of the landscape. In the valley, the woods were black and the fields a silky grey like my night-time visions of the place. The stones on the track into the farm were frozen and they made no sound as I drove over them. The geese were huddled in the lee of a bank, fingers of wind lifting the feathers on their backs. Even they couldn't bring themselves to run out and attack me. Frost-filled gusts blew across the frozen pond. The buildings were besieged by cold.

I was there to persuade Ventnor that he should sell his

farm to us for something less than the £432,000 at which he had stuck for so long. I had no real tools or levers with which to achieve this, only to suggest that a lower price might be fair. Smilingly, over a cup of coffee, he refused. We sat first in the kitchen and then by the fire. He was polite but adamant. The oak logs burned slowly. To my own surprise, I felt no resentment. I sat there agreeing with every word he said. Why should he leave the embrace of this? Why should the poor man go out into the cold if he did not want to?

He left the room to see a man who had come to the door and as I sat there I began to be embraced by the warmth of the house. I felt it wrap its own fingers around me. If a house could speak, that was the day it spoke, the day I learned this wasn't simply a place where we could come and impose our preconceptions. We couldn't simply land the Bright Field fantasy here and take that as the reality in which we were now ensconced. There was some kind of dignity of place to be respected here. It had a self-sufficiency which went beyond the demands and obsessions of its current occupants. There was a pattern to it, a private rhythm, the deep, slow music to which it had been moving for the four or five centuries that people had lived in it. The two of us men sitting here now in front of the fire, what were we in the light of that? Transient parasites.

I left and we had failed to agree on price but in some other, quite unstated way, I had succumbed. The buildings might be a mishmash of what we wanted and what we didn't. They might confront us with a list of things to do that stretched ten, twenty years into the future. The price that was required might be so high that it left us on the verge of penury for years to come. But all of that was translated that frosty day, or perhaps started to be translated that frosty day, with the hot oak fire glowing as the only point of colour in a colourless world, into something quite different: a commitment to the place as it actually was, with all the wrinkles of its history and its habits, all its failings and imperfections, all its human muddle. Stop fussing, it said. Give yourself over to what seems good. Here – after catastrophe and culpable failure in my own life, after I had witnessed Sarah, now my wife, tending to me as I collapsed – was some kind of signpost towards coherence. Don't look for the perfect; don't be dissatisfied if the reality does not match the vision. Don't insist on your own way. Feed yourself into patterns that others have made and draw your sustenance from them. Accept the other.

'You mean pay him what he wants?' Sarah asked that evening as I put this to her.

'Yes,' I said. And we did.

GREEN FADING INTO BLUE

A cloud was down over the hill and the air was damp like a cloth that had just been wrung out. The buildings came like tankers out of the mist. Had we made a mistake? 'Is it a sea fog?' Sarah asked Ventnor.

'Oh no,' he said languidly, 'it's always like this here.'

Somehow his grief smeared us. He was unshaven; he had been unable to find a razor after he had packed everything. His mind was moving from one thing to another. This and that he talked about, these keys again, the oil delivery again, his own untidied odds and ends, a sort of humility in front of us as 'the owners' which grated as it reached us, as it must have grated as he said it. His eyes had black rings under them, wide panda-zones of

unhappiness. Anyone, I suppose, would have been griev-
ing at the loss of this place. It looked like an amputation.
Even so, I felt nothing but impatience, as though it were
already ours and he no more than an interloper here. He
said nothing about that. What a curious business, this
buying and selling of the things we love. It's like a slave
trade. *Go, go*, I said to him in silence.

His mother-in-law was there with him. She was less
restrained. She showed us pictures of their dogs cavorting
in the wood. I felt like saying 'our wood'. She was still
possessive. 'I'd hate to think of anyone making a mess in
there after what I've done,' she said. I could see her
primping the back of her hair and looking at me as
though I were a piece of dog mess myself. And I suppose
I was, in their eyes, the agent of eviction. *Go on, away with
you.*

I was edged by it all. The house seemed ugly, stark and
poky. I hardly fitted through a single door. Would it ever
be redeemable? I was still standing off, waiting for the
mooring line but Sarah was sublime, confident, already
arrived. 'Why do starlings look so greasy?' I heard myself
asking Ventnor. 'Like a head of hair that hasn't been
washed for weeks. They look like bookies.' He went at
last, his sadness bottled up inside the great length of his
long, thin body.

We waited for the furniture van. The house seemed
inadequate for our lives. I picked some flowers, I looked at
the view from the top field, our summit, and we waited
and waited for the van. At last they called, about midday.
They were in Brightling, lost. Sarah went to guide them
in, while Rosie slept upstairs. The van came. It was too big

to fit around the corner of the track past the oast-house
and so everything had to be carried from the other side,
100 yards further. All afternoon our possessions rolled out
and into the buildings, this clothing of the bones. *Come
on, faster, faster.* The place started to become ours. It was
as though the house were trying on new clothes. Sarah
was worried by the sight of a staked lilac. Was the wind
really that bad?

The removal men went. The oast looked like a jumble
sale and the various rooms of the house half OK with our
furniture. 'Change that window, pull down that extension, put the cowl of the oast back.' I could have spent
£100,000 here that day. Sarah and Rosie went off shopping. Ventnor returned to collect a few more things. I
didn't want to have to deal with him again. 'I see they've
done some damage there,' he said, pointing at the place
where the lorry's wheels had cut into the turf, trying to
get around the sharp corner by the oast-house. I hadn't
even noticed. I listened to his engine as he drove off
towards somewhere else in England, the gears changing
uphill to Brightling Needle, and then down more easily
the far side, the sound, like a boat's wake, slowly folding
back into the trees. We never saw him again.

He had gone, it was quiet and I was alone for the first
time in Perch Hill. I could feel the silence between my
fingertips, the extraordinary substance of this new place,
this new-old place, new-bought but ancient, ours and not
ours, seeping and creeping around me. It was as though I
had learned sub-aqua and for the first time had lowered
myself gingerly into the body of the pool, to sense this
new dimension thickly present around me as somewhere

in which life might be lived and movements made. Until
now all I had seen was the surface of the water, its tremors
and eddies. Now, like a pike, I could hang within it. I
could feel the water starting to flow and ripple between
my fingers.

That evening, as the sun dropped into the wood, I walked
the boundaries, the shores of the island, the places where
the woodland trees reached their arms out over the
pastures. Here and there, the bluebells crept out into
the grass like a painted shadow. Wild garlic was growing
at the bottom of the Slip Field. I lay down in the Way
Field, the field where we had decided to come here all
those months before, a place and a decision which were
now seared into my life like a brand, and as I lay there felt
the earth under my back, its deep solidity, as Richard
Jefferies had done 100 years before on the Wiltshire
Downs. The hand of the rock itself was holding me
up, presenting me to the sky, my body and self moulded
to the contours and matched to the irreducibility of this
hill on this farm at this moment. 'You cannot fall through
a field,' I said aloud.

I took stock. What was this place to which we were now
wedded? It had cost £432,000, plus all the fees. We had
borrowed £160,000 to make that up, on top of the
London house. My father was lending us £25,000. Our
position was strung out and I had ricked my back. I felt as
weak and as impotent as at any time in my life. It was an
intuitive understanding, an act of faith, that the deep
substance of this little fragment of landscape would mend
that lack and make me whole. It was a farm of 90 acres in

the Sussex Weald, about two hours south of London in the usual traffic, but no more than an hour from Westminster Bridge at five on a summer's morning. It was down a little lane, as obscure as one could feel in the south of England, with no sound of traffic and an air of enclosure and privacy. At the edge of the land, by the lane, was the farmyard, with its utterly compromised mixture of bad old and bad new.

Beyond the farmyard itself, things improved. It was indeed one Bright Field after another. The buildings were at almost the highest point and in all directions the land fell away in pleats, like the folds of a cloth as it drops from the table to the floor. The creases were filled with little strips of wood under whose branches small trickly streams made their way towards the River Dudwell. The broad rounded backs of the pleats were the fields themselves, eleven of them, little hedged enclosures. They made up the small island block entirely surrounded by wood. That wood was part of the ancient forest of the Weald, whose name itself, cognate with *Wald*, meant forest. The farmland was cut from it perhaps in the fifteenth or sixteenth century. The house was built in about 1580 and was probably made of the oaks that once grew where it stood. It was poor land, solid clay, high and windy all year, cold, wet and clammy in the winter, hard, heavy and cloddy in the summer.

Because nothing destroys a landscape like money, its poverty had preserved it. We were on the edge of viable agriculture here, one of the last pieces to be cleared from the wood and already in part going back to it. You could see the lines of old hedges, hornbeam and hawthorn,

growing as 40-foot trees in the middle of the woods. Those
were the boundaries of the ghost fields, abandoned and
returning to their natural condition. Because it was so
poor, it had never been worth a farmer's while to drive the
land hard. That's why these fields are as beautiful as any
you could find in Europe, or the world come to that.

There was a line from a poem of Tennyson's which,
from time to time that year, was bumping up into my
conscious mind, and presumably lurking not far beneath
for the rest of it. 'Green Sussex,' it said, 'fading into blue.'
That was this farm in a phrase: the green immediacy, the
plunge for the valley, the stepped ridges of the Weald,
blueing into the distance ten and twelve miles away. This
wasn't a little button of perfection, a cherry perched on a
cake of the wrecked, but part of a larger world and as I lay
in the Way Field that evening all I could think of was the
feeling of extent that ran out from there across the lane,
down into the field called Toyland, beyond that into the
valley of woods running off to the west, to the river down
there, the deer nosing in that wood and the sight I had
that morning, as we were waiting for the van, of the fox
running down through that field, on the wood edge, no
more than the tip of its tail visible above the grasses, a
dancing point like the tip of a conductor's baton . . .

I shall not forget that evening. The spring was going
haywire around me. It was DNA bedlam, nature's opening day. The blackthorn was stark white in the dark and
shady corners. The willows had turned eau-de-nil. Oaks
were the odd springtime mixture of red and formaldehyde
yellow, precisely the colour of old flesh preserved in
bottles. The wild cherries stood hard and white like

pylons in the wood and the crab apples, lower, more crabbed in form, were in full pink flower – an incredible thing a whole tree of that, the most sweetly beautiful flower in England, dolloped and larded all over the branches of a wrinkled, half-decrepit tree. In places nothing was doing better than the nettles and the thistles, but in the wood, there were the wall-to-wall bluebells, pale, almost lilac in the Middle Shaw, that eyeshadow blue: in the half-lit green darkness of the wood, that incredible, glamorous, seductive haze of the bluebell's blue, a nightclub sheen in the low light, the sexiest colour in the English landscape, hazing my eyes, a pool of colour into which, if I could, I would have dived there and then.

There were deer on the top field. The light was catching the ridged knobbles of their spines. I drank it up: this bright sunshine, even late, the bars of it poking into the shadows of the wood; the comfort of the grass; the lane a continuous mass of wood anemones, cuckoo flowers, primroses; and one very creamy anemone up by the gate. Its colour looked to me like the top of the milk.

'These foam-bells on the hidden currents of being', Hugh MacDiarmid once called spring flowers, and that attitude, a slightly dismissive superiority, used to be mine too. Geology, the understructure, the creation of circumstances: those were the things that used to matter to me. I preferred the hard and stony parts of the north and west or the higher places in the Alps where, after the snow has gone, the crests and ridges are left as abused and brutalised as any frost-shattered quarry. Walking across those high, dry Alps, I have seen the whole world in every direction desert-like in its austerity, a bleakness beyond either ugliness or beauty, and thought that life could offer me nothing more. 'I am enamoured of the desert at last,' MacDiarmid wrote, 'The abode of supreme serenity is necessarily a desert.'

I still lusted after that, for all the clean hard-pressure rigour of that alienating landscape, serene precisely because it is so dreadful, because from that point of desiccation there was nowhere lower to fall. But alongside it now, there was this other thing, this undeniable life-spurt in the spring, whose toughness was subtler than the stone's but whose persistence would outlive it. Genes last longer than rocks. They slip through unbroken while continents collide and are consumed. These plants, I now saw, were the world's version of eternity, the lit bush. If you wanted to ally yourself with strength, nothing would be more sustaining than the spring flowers.

Over the following days, we dressed the house as though preparing it to go out. It was like dressing a father or mother. She sat there mute while coats and ribbons were tried on her. 'Oh you look nice like that,' we would say, 'or that, or maybe that.' Rooms acquired meaning, another meaning. In the kitchen, painted on the cupboard door, I found a coat of arms: six white feathers on a blue ground and the motto '*Labore et perseverantia*', By work and perseverance. It looked fairly new. What was it, a kind of d'Urberville story of a noble family collapsed to the poverty of this, to the resolution of that motto against all the odds? It was certainly a failed farm. That was the only reason we were there. We had crept like hermit crabs into a shell that others had vacated.

But I guessed the arms and the motto had no great ancestry. Had Ventnor himself painted them here in the last few years? I knew that he had attempted to farm this farm, to continue with the dairy herd that he had bought with it. But he didn't know what he was doing and had lost a fortune. The last thing he asked me before he left was 'Are you thinking of farming here?' to which I had been noncommittal. With something of a glittery eye, he told me not to consider it. That was a sure route to disaster. Soon stories were reaching me of Ventnor sitting in the kitchen here, his unpaid bills laid out on the table in front of him like a kind of pelmanism from hell, his head in his hands, his prospects hopeless. Every one of these stories ended with the same warning: Don't do it.

The Ventnor experience seemed somehow to stand between us and an earlier past. He was one of us, an urban escapee, a pastoralist, who had turned the old oast-house into an art gallery and put coach-lamp-style lights outside the doors. Where was the contact with the real thing, the real past here? There was a glimmering of discontent in my mind about that gap, still a glass wall between us and the essential nature of Perch Hill. Before Ventnor, I knew, the last farmers here had been called Weekes. Where were they? Had all trace of them disappeared? It wasn't long before we realised that the very opposite was the case: Ken and Brenda Weekes still lived in the cottage 200 yards away across the fields. A day or two after our arrival, Sarah and I went up to see them and from that moment they became a fixed point in our lives.

The boys were here and were shrieking in the new expanse of garden. Sarah and I were anxious and buoyed

up in equal measure at what we had taken on. Across the
fields, we could hear Ken mowing the lawn around his
cottage: the sound of a half-distant mower in early
summer, a man in shirtsleeves and sleeveless jersey, his
dog on the lawn beside him, the sun slipping in and out of
bubbled clouds, and all around us, to east and west,
Sussex stepping away into an inviting afternoon. It was,
in a way, what we had come here for.

We walked up there, not across the fields that first time
but up the lane. The hedge was in brilliant new leaf. Ken
and Brenda came to their garden gate, asked us in, a cup
of tea in the kitchen, Gemma the dog lying by the
Rayburn, and a sort of inspecting openness in them both,
the welcome mixed with 'Who are you? What sort of
people are you?' I shall always remember two things Ken
said. One with his tang of acid: 'You know what they
always said about this farm, don't you? They always said
this was the poorest farm in the parish.' The other with
the warmth that can spread like butter around him:
'That's one thing that's lovely, children's voices down
at the farm again. That's a sound we haven't had for a
long time here.'

To a degree I didn't understand at the time, we had
entered Ken Weekes's world. Perhaps we had bought the
farm, perhaps the deeds were in our name, perhaps we
were living in the farmhouse, perhaps I was meant to be
deciding what should happen to the woods and fields, but
none of that could alter the central fact: Perch Hill was
Ken's in a deeper sense than any deed of conveyance
could ever accomplish.

He had come here in 1942 as a six-year-old boy to live

in the house we were now occupying. His father, 'Old Ron', was farm manager for a London entrepreneur and 'a gentleman, one of the real old gentry', Mr George Wilson-Fox. 'Old Wilson' used to come down with his friends on a Saturday. The Weekeses would all put on clean white dairymen's coats to show the proprietor and his guests the herd of prize pedigree Friesians, spotless animals, their tails washed twice a day every day, the cow shed white-washed every year, a cow shed so clean 'you could eat your dinner off that floor'.

It was a place dedicated to excellence. Wilson-Fox made sure there was never any shortage of money for the farm and Ron imposed his discipline on it. 'The cattle always came first,' Ken remembered. 'Even if you were dying, you had to look after the cows. I remember Old Ron kicking us out of bed to go and milk the cows one morning when I could hardly move – "Come on, you bugger, get out, there's work to do" – and it was so cold in there in the cow shed with a north-easterly that the milk was freezing in the milk-line. But we got it done. It all had to be done by eight in the morning if you wanted to sit down to breakfast. You couldn't have breakfast unless the cattle had been looked after first.'

It is a lost world. Nothing like these small dairy farms exists here any more. They have all gone and Ken has witnessed their disappearance, the total evaporation of the world in which he grew up. About that he seems to feel bleak and accepting in equal measure. Every inch of this farm carries some memory or mark of Ken's life here: the day the doodlebug crashed in the wood at the bottom of the Way Field; those moments in Beech Meadow where

Old Ron, in late June or early July, would pick a bunch of flowers for Dolly, Ken's mother, the signal for the boys that haymaking was about to begin; the day the earth suddenly slipped after they had ploughed it in the field for ever after known as the Slip Field. A farm is a farmer's autobiography and this one belongs to Ken.

When he married Brenda, in 1959, they moved into the cottage across the fields. His mother and brother stayed in the farmhouse. Wilson-Fox died in 1971, but Ken continued farming for the trustees of the estate for another 15 years until, in 1986, the farm was sold, along with its herd of cattle, to John Ventnor who wanted to be a farmer. Ken stayed in the cottage, set the art dealer on his way, helping him for a year or so, but they fell out. 'We had a misunderstanding,' Ken said. For several years after that Ken was not even allowed to walk his dog in these fields.

There was something of a false cheeriness in both of us as we talked. Each of us was guarded against the other. But the afternoon floated on Ken's stories. He could remember seeing the pilots of the Luftwaffe Messerschmitts, low enough for you to see a figure in the cockpit. 'Oh yes, you could see them sitting in there all right.' One evening the Weekeses were all down in the Way Field getting in the hay and there were so many of the German planes that his father said they'd better go in. 'You could never tell, could you? Bastards.' Ken's performance culminated in his favourite story about the hunt. He was out in the Cottage Field, tending to one of the cows that was poorly, when he chanced to look up and see a whole crowd of the hunt come pouring down the trackway that leads off the bridlepath and into the Perch Hill farmyard.

"I say," Ken bellowed at them – 'because they'll only understand you if you talk to them in a way they do understand – "why don't you fucking well bugger off out of there." And,' Ken says, looking round, all smiles, 'do you know what? They did!'

Another piece soon dropped into place. Will Clark came up one day from the village. He had been doing odds and ends on the farm for John Ventnor. Peter, his son, had been working in the wood and mowing the grass. Ventnor had said that there was no one he could recommend more highly. And that's how it turned out. As soon as Will walked into the yard I could see what he meant. His eyes were the colour of old jeans. He swept his hair in a repeated gesture up and over his forehead into a wide long curl that could only be the descendant of a rocker's quiff, 40 years on. He smiled with his eyes and talked with a laugh in his voice. 'We'll be haying soon,' he said. He cuddled Rosie. His taste in shirts was perfect, lime green and tangerine orange, unchanged, I guess, since he was bike-mad in the fifties, when he used to do a ton down the long straight stretch to Lewes called The Broyle, or burn up and down the High Street in the village to impress the girls. He was the only man in Burwash ever to get to Tunbridge Wells in $12\frac{1}{2}$ minutes, or so he told me. He talked broad Sussex: fence posts were 'spiles', working in the mud got you 'all slubbed up', anything that needed doing always involved 'stirring it about a bit,' a sickle was 'a swap'. He had started his working life when he was 14 on a farm at Hawkhurst, just over the border into Kent, looking after the horses. He knew all about machines and wood and wooding and how to get a big ash butt out of a

difficult corner. He was the man of the place and he
would be the man for us. Will had been ill for years – his
kidneys scarcely worked and he had to spend three hours
a day at home on a dialysis machine – and he said that
Peter would have to do the heavy work. 'He's the muscle
man.' And so we plugged in. This other world was closing
over us, some version of pastoral folding us in its lap.

All the same, I was anxious about it all. The stupidity of
what we were doing was brought home, involuntarily or
not, when people we knew from London dropped in.
There was always a vulture in the party, someone who
would unerringly make you sour with a remark. 'Oh yes,'
one of these people said in the early days, nosing around
the ugliness of our horrible buildings, 'it's a very nice *spot*,
isn't it?' A very nice spot: the silent pinchedness of what is
not said. Why do these people wreak destruction? Why do
they do such dishonest damage? I couldn't believe how
soured I felt by those people. I felt they didn't understand,
but that was probably not the case. Could they ever have
understood the way I wanted to wriggle under the skin of
this place so that only my eyes were above the skin of the
turf like a hippo in its river and the bed of green comfort
around me, the osmotic relation to place so that there was
no distinction between me and it, no boundary at the
skin? Of course not, because that is not something that
can be said in polite society. It was that kind of pre-
rational understanding that I was after, like a dog rolling
in muck.

We didn't know what we were doing. We arrived on
this farm as naked as Adam and Eve and we were setting

about making it right. We knew what we wanted – a sense of completeness – and we wanted it with a passion, but we didn't quite know how to get there. All we could do was stumble off into the dark, hoping and trusting that our instincts were right. That was the point, in fact. The whole enterprise was a blunder into truth, wobbling chaotically towards the goal. It was good because it was messy. If it had all been neater, if we had known what we were doing, it wouldn't have had the juice in it. The whole thing would have flattened out in the drear of expertise. As it was, ignorance was the great enabler and incompetence the condition of life. Or so I would say to myself in my storming rage after the nay-sayers had gone.

Sometimes I felt we were surrounded by know-alls. Not the people who lived near us, the Will Clarks, the Ken Weekeses, who approached our efforts with a delicate sense of neither wanting to intrude nor wanting us to come too much of a cropper. No, the real killer know-alls were the partly ruralised urbanites who had acquired the cultural habit of telling other people what to do. It probably stemmed from the prefect system at public schools, compounded by middle-class careers in which the only necessary skill is the ability to disguise bossiness as brains.

You could see them heaving into view a mile away. They were struggling with their mission to inform. They knew they shouldn't. They felt they must. They wished they didn't have to. But they knew they ought to. One has a duty, after all. It's a responsibility to the landscape as a whole. And it would be so sad wouldn't it, if it all came unstuck in the end for Adam and Sarah?

Out came the supercilious smiles. These were the opening, but doomed, attempts at a spirit of generosity. Soon enough they gave way to the barrage of assured, you-really-should-have-asked-me-first, I-want-to-see-you-in-my-study-after-tea, pain-in-the-neck blather. The spirit hit the iceberg and sank. I usually got drunk at this stage.

No area of life was immune. I remember, classically, having our stack of firewood analysed by a man who, from what he was saying, was obviously chief firewood analyst for Deutsche Morgan Grenfell. Not much was right with the way we had done things. The shed was wrong; it needed more air holes, its roof was not very nice, the walls were unsatisfactory and it was in the wrong position. We shouldn't have bothered to put either chestnut or larch logs in the pile because they both spit when they burn and that wasn't good for the kiddies, was it? The oak was useless; it only burned on a massively hot fire, which we would never achieve because the rest of the wood was such rubbish. The ash had been split far too small and would burn too quickly. Sycamore had no calorific value to speak of and what we had was rotten. It would take more energy to start the fire than would be given out by it. And were we two years ahead with our cutting programme? He looked at me in that generous, hesitating way people use to those whose self-esteem they have just bulldozed into a silage pit.

The idea of putting up a building of any kind was a mistake. You would make the windows too small. You would spend too much money on it. You would do something totally out of character. You would create a dreadful ersatz fake ('Tesco's') when people in your position had a responsibility to patronise new architects and architecture. You were living in a retro hell. You would not install the correct insulation/safety features/heating system. Heating systems! May I never, ever have another discussion about heating systems for the rest of my life.

Then there was the chicken question. You were thinking of getting far too many of them. Were you really going to be eating 80 eggs a week? Had you performed the cloacal swab test for salmonella on them yet? You certainly couldn't think of giving eggs away if they had dirty cloacas. Their housing was disgusting and if an RSPCA man should happen by, he would be appalled. You may have heard someone was prosecuted for just this kind of thing the other day. Anyway, they should have been bedded down on sawdust not straw. It was amazing you hadn't found that out for yourself. I don't quite understand why you were going in for these things.

Moving quickly on, children should wear clothes made out of only naturally occurring materials, fed only naturally occurring foods and baked beans should be sugar-free. Trees – these two subjects always somehow elide – should be planted without stakes, or tied only loosely to stakes, or planted without tree-guards or only after a comprehensive drainage system has been installed, or only on M25 rootstock, or only from Deacon's Nursery in the Isle of Wight, or only with local genetic material, gathered from the last of the local orchards and anyway fruit trees were only a pleasure if you have done all the grafting and training yourself. Have you managed to do that, Adam? Or have you ever thought you might be taking on a little much here? Have you had your dog castrated yet? Aaaaaaaargh.

My sons – lovely stage in life – had just then started playing Oasis on their ghetto-blaster at crow-scarer volume. The songs wormed their way into the mind, colonising whole stretches of it. After one particularly gruesome hour or two with a couple of people who came to lunch and knew every damn thing there was to know about the usual subjects – orchards, fire wood, chickens, ducks ('one says, duck, doesn't one, in the plural?') heating systems, woodland management, grants ('We've found we've done quite well out of the whole County Council Heritage Landscape scheme but I'm told, I'm afraid, that they've run out of money now and won't be taking any more applicants at least until fiscal 2000') – I found myself stacking the dishwasher and singing, much too loudly, 'Yer gada roll wiv it / ya gorra take yer time / yer garra say wotya say / dern ledd anybuddy gerrin yer waaaiy . . . / There's nuthin lef for me to saaiy . . .'

The bravado papered over a pit of anxiety. One morning I woke at four and said, aloud, 'I'm worried about the fields.'

'For Christ's sake,' Sarah said without a momentary flicker. She'd heard this sort of thing before and, anyway, was already awake worrying about the garden. We lay there in silence for a moment, travelling through the universe together at 24,000 miles an hour, each in a private little cubicle of hysteria and each thinking the other stupid. 'The fields are fine.'

'They aren't. What's wrong with the garden?'

'It's out of control.'

'That,' I told her, 'is also what's wrong with the fields.'

'I've never heard anything so ridiculous. Fields don't get out of control. That's one of the good things about them. They just sit there perfectly in control for day after day.' Gardens didn't, apparently. Gardens were nature on speed. In fact, you could see them as hyperactive fields. They went mad if you didn't look after them. Anyway the fields were not going to be photographed on Wednesday, were they?'

This was true. Sarah was writing a highly and beautifully illustrated book whose working title was *The Expensive Garden*. From time to time in various parts of the house I used to find half-scribbled lists on the back of invoices from garden centres spread across the south of England, working out exactly how much had been spent on dahlia tubers, brick paths, taking up the brick paths because they were in the wrong place, the new, correctly aligned brick paths, the hypocaust system for the first greenhouse, the automatically opening vent system for the second, the underground electric wiring for the heated cold frames (yes, heated cold frames), the woven hazel fencing to give the correct cheap, rustic cottage look (gratifyingly more expensive than any other garden fencing currently on the market) and the extra pyramid box trees needed before Wednesday.

The consignment of topiary was delivered, one day early that summer, by an articulated Volvo turbo-cooled truck, whose body stretched 80 feet down the lane – it had caused a slight traffic rumpus on the main road just outside Burwash, attempting to manoeuvre itself like a

suppository into the entrance of the lane – and whose
driver with a flourish drew aside the long curtain that ran
the length of its flank, saying 'There you are, instant
gardening!' He must have done it before.

The inside of the lorry was a sort of tableau illustrating
'The Riches of Flora'. It contained enough topiary to re-
equip the Villa Lante. Species ceanothus, or whatever
they were, sported themselves decorously among the
aluminium stanchions of the lorry. The rear section
was the kind of over-elaborate rose and clematis love-
seat-cum-gazebo you sometimes see on stage in *As You
Like It*. Transferred to the perfectly unpretentious vegetable patch maintained by the Weekeses, the disgorged
innards of the Volvo turned Perch Hill Farm, instantly, as
the man said, into the sort of embowered house-and-
garden most people might labour for 20 years to produce.
A visitor the following week congratulated Sarah on what
he called 'its marvellous, patinated effect.' Some patina, I
said, some cheque book.

At that stage, the advance on *The Expensive Garden*
had covered about 15 per cent of the money spent on
making it. If even a tenth of that amount had been spent
on the farm we would already be one of the showpieces of
southern England. 'That point,' Sarah was in the habit of
saying, for reasons I have never yet got her to explain,
'which you always make when we have people to supper,
is totally inadmissible.'

But I was serious about the fields. I wanted the fields,
which were beautiful in the large scale, to be perfect in
detail too. I wanted to walk about in them and think,
'Yes, this is right, this is how things should be. This is

complete.' That is not what I was thinking that summer. In fact, the more I got to know them, the more dissatisfied I became. Hence the 4 a.m. anxieties. The thistles were terrible. Some fields were so thick with thistles that my dear dog, the slightly fearful and profoundly loving Colonel Custard, refused to come for a walk in them. He stopped at the gate, sat down and put on the face which all dog-owners will recognise: 'Me through that?'

In the early hours, I used to have a sort of internal double-dialectic about the fields. It came from an unresolved conflict in my own mind, which could be reduced to this question: was the farm a vastly enlarged garden or was it part of the natural world which happened to be ours for the time being? The idea that it might be a business which could earn us money had never been seriously entertained. We might choose to have sheep, cows, chickens, ducks and pigs wandering about on it, but only in the same way that Sarah might order another five mature tulip trees for a little quincunx she had in mind. I would have animals because they looked nice.

To the question of big garden or slice of nature, I jiggled between one answer and then the other. In part it *was* like a huge, low-intensity garden. We were here because it was heart-stoppingly beautiful and one of the things that made it beautiful was the interfolding of wood, hedge and field. If the distinctions between them should become blurred then a great deal of the beauty would go. The fields must look like fields, shorn, bright and clean, and the woods must look like woods, fluffy, full and dense. Field and wood were, here anyway, the rice and curry of landscape aesthetics. Scurfy fields, as spotty as a week's stubble on an unshaven chin, looked horrible, untended, a room in a mess.

There were other things to think of too. If we simply mowed the fields to keep them bright and green or, horror of horrors, sprayed off the docks and thistles, we would not be attending to other aspects of the grassland which of course are valuable in themselves. There were clumps of dyer's greenweed here, whole spreads of the vetch called eggs and bacon, small patches of the little pink-flowered gentian called field felwort and of the English sage called clary. Sprays would wreck all that and you had to allow those things to set seed and reproduce if they were going to continue. You had to allow them to look messy.

What to do? Obviously I had to learn how to manage grassland properly. I was blundering around in my ignorance. Sometimes the midnight fantasy floated in of buying the perfect field from a lorry that could scarcely fit down the lane, a slice of the meadows under the Jungfraujoch, laid out and cut to size. How did the Swiss make their grass look so pretty?

At last I had a meeting one Saturday morning with the Wrenns, Brian and Stephen, father and son, our farming neighbours from Perryman's, on the other side of the hill. We were all a little shy with each other in the kitchen, too ready to agree with what the other had said.

Brian, sliding the conversation sideways, told me there were nightingales in our woods and nightjars and whea-tears. I knew nothing about these things. We talked about the neutral, the historical, the way that all the farms here face south, their fronts to the warmth, their backs to the wind. How ingeniously the first people to settle here spied out the land. Stephen talked about the poverty of the Weald, the way there is no topsoil, all the fertility poured away down the streams to the southern rich belt, the champaign country of rich southern Sussex. 'This is the poorest, the last bit of ground to be taken,' he said, 'but that's what has saved it.'

Then I said, with the Nescafé in me, we should talk about the real matter in hand. Brian turned businesslike. 'We would certainly like to have all the grass. But it's too late this year to get any nitrogen on for the silage. We'll get some heifers on to graze it later.'

'Of course,' I said, feeling I was about to introduce some urban gaucherie, 'and anyway, from our side, we would like to manage it in as much of a conservationist way as we can.' How I hate that word. To my amazement they lay in happily with that. Even the air between us became somehow emotional at the recognition of shared ideas. Stephen talked about planting some of Perryman's up with willows to provide fuel for a wood-burning power plant. That toboggan feeling developed around the table that we were not such aliens to each other as we might have imagined. The future opened like the curtains of a theatre. We all came to an agreement: they should take some of the grass that year as summer grazing. They would pay £1,000 for that which was better than nothing I supposed, about 1.5 per cent return on capital. The real question was: were we prepared to forego the £3,000-odd pounds we would get from a conventional let for the sake of it looking nice and it being lovely? For saying no to nitrogen and no to high-pressure farming? Were we rich enough for that?

With a new bill-hook, I cut hazels in the wood for
Sarah's cutting patch. The hazel clusters were in stools
eight feet across. The middle of them was a jumble of old
fallen sticks. One stick had rotted entirely on the inside
but the skin had remained whole as an upright paper
tube. There were deer in the wood, their awkward big
bodies breaking the trees they hurried past, and around
my feet tall purple orchids, woodruff and loosestrife. I was
cutting with slashing blunt incompetence at the hazels,
half tearing them away, but I loved their long swinging
creak next to my ear as I carried them home on my
shoulder. I felt the sweat run down my side in single,
finger-sized trickles and I loved the smell next to my ear,
the woody, sweet, bruised, tannic vegetable reeking of the
cut wood. That's what I was here for, the undersense,
those deeper connections, that core of intimacy.

I demolished the fence around the pond, shirt off, sweat
and smell. I sold the tractor on Will's advice and we were
for the moment tractorless. Will was looking for another
more reliable one. I made teepees out of hazels from the
wood and some hurdles out of split chestnut. I tried to buy
a mower but my credit card failed. It was the usual
humiliation in front of a queue of men who were more
interested in that little human drama than anything else.
Rachel the shop girl blushed. I laughed it off, blushing
internally. It felt like a castration. I needed to earn more
money and I had a feeling we were veering, slowly but
quite deliberately, towards a financial crisis.

I loved it here that first spring. I loved the sustenance of
the green, the kestrel that came daily and hung above the
corners of the barns, moving from station to station. I

loved the little seedlings of the oak and aspen sprouting in the grass along the wood edges. I loved the knit of the country, the jersey of it. I loved the sight of the ducks, two wild mallards on the pond, I loved the substance of place, my new fax machine, the gentleness of Will and Peter, Rosie playing in the garden with her new nanny, Anna Cheney, who only years later would dare tell us exactly how horrified she had been at the chaos in which we were living, but how one thing had convinced her to come: the sight of Rosie's face as she sat at the kitchen table, so round and so sweet.

The garden accumulated. I tended to the house as no house before, tidying and hoovering. Sarah and I both had the feeling, if we were honest, that we should have waited to buy a place with more beautiful buildings but there we were, we couldn't say that now. This would be lovely in the slow unnoticed growth of the place around us. Forty years later, as we died, we would look at it and say, 'That was beautiful.' Life would be over, having been lived. The moments of revelation are all there is. This is all there is. This will be the undernote of my life: the making with a purpose, not the drifting of the survivor. Make, and you will be happy.

THE DARTING OF LIFE

That summer burned. The south of England was bleak with heat. Cars along the lane raised a floury dust in their wake. The cow parsley and the trees in the hedges were coated with it like loaves in a bakery. The streams were dry coming off the hill and the river in the trench of the valley was little more than a gravel bed across which a line of damp had been drawn, connecting the shrunken pools.

I spent long days down there in the dark, deep shade of the riverside trees. The valley felt enclosed, a place apart, and secrecy gathered inside it. Rudyard Kipling lived here for the second half of his life – he bought Bateman's, a large seventeeth-century ironmaster's house just below

the last of our fields, in 1902 – and the whole place
remained haunted by his memory. Everywhere you went,
he had already described. It was here, among the hidden
constrictions of the valley where, in Kipling's wonderful
phrase, 'wind prowling through woods sounds like exciting things going to happen,' that I felt most in touch with
where I had come to live. This was the womb.

It was a pathless place, or at least the only paths were the
old deeply entrenched roads, never surfaced, which
dropped from the ridge to the south, crossed the river
at gravelly fords and then climbed through woods again to
the ridge on the other side. They were the only intrusion in
what felt like an abandoned world. The woods were named
– Ware's Wood, Hook Wood, Limekiln Wood, Stonehole
Wood, Great Wood, Green Wood – but it felt as if no one
had been here for half a century. Hornbeam, chestnut, ash
and even oak had all been coppiced in the past but none
had been touched for decades. The marks of the great
combing of the 1987 storm were still there: 80-foot-tall ash
trees had fallen across the river from one bank to the other.
The ivy that once climbed up them now hung in Ama-
zonian curtains from the horizontal trees. Growing from
the fallen trunks, small linear woods of young ashes now
pushed up towards the light.

I stumbled about in here, looking for some kind of
inaccessible essence of the place. The deer had broken
paths through the undergrowth. The clay was scrabbled
away where they had jumped the little side streams. The
fields of underwood garlic had turned lemon yellow in the
shade. And through it all the river wound, curling back
on itself, cutting out promontories and peninsulas in the

wooded banks, reaching down to the underlying layer of
dark, ribbed, iron-rich sandstone. Where it cut into an
iron vein, the metal bled into the stream and the water
flowed past it an almost marigold orange. This too was
Kipling's world, virtually unchanged since he had described it, 90 years before, in *Puck of Pook's Hill*.

> Even on the shaded water the air was hot and heavy
> with drowsy scents, while outside, through breaks in
> the trees, the sunshine burned the pasture like fire . . .
>   The trees closing overhead made long tunnels
> through which the sunshine worked in blobs and
> patches. Down in the tunnels were bars of sand and
> gravel, old roots and trunks covered with moss or
> painted red by the irony water; clumps of fern and
> thirsty shy flowers who could not live away from
> moisture and shade.

As you pushed up through this wooded, private notch in
Sussex, so many miles away from the bungalowed, sign-
posted and estate-agented ridge-top roads, the river
shrank still further to inch-deep pools and foot-wide
rapids where banks of gravel had dammed the flow. In
that clear, shallow water, life was exploding. Midges in
Brownian motion were flashing on and off in the rods of
sunlight that were rammed through the trees. Across the
lazily moving water, insects drifted as slowly as those half-
transparent specks that float across the surface of your
eye. Far below, an inch away on the floor of the stream,
their shadows tracked them, dark, four-petalled flowers
easing across the stones. The dog snapped his chops at the

passing bronze-backed flies. A three-inch-long worm, as thin and as white as a cotton thread, snaked through the water and then under a stone. The stream was full of little shrimps, lying immobile on the gravel or wriggling there like rugby players caught in a tackle or, best of all, jetting around above it as fluidly as spaceships in their fluid medium, the darting of life.

By the middle of July, in all our hayfields, the grass was crisp and it was already late for the haying. That's what they called it here. Not haymaking or the hay harvest, but straightforward 'haying' on the same principle as lambing or wooding. It's the climax of the grass year and, as nothing except grass and thistles will grow on this farm, these few days became the point around which everything else revolved. It was high summer. Even as it was happening you could feel the winter nostalgia for it. You won't get a cattle- or sheep-farmer to talk starry-eyed about haymaking, but there was no doubt, in one sense anyway, that was how they felt. 'Look at that,' one of my neighbours would say to me during the following winter about a bale of his own hay he was trying to sell me. 'You can smell the summer sunshine in it,' and buried his nose in the bale like a wine-taster in the heady, open mouth of his glass.

A friend rang up from London as we were about to start. 'Make hay while the sun shines,' he said to me on the phone, as if there were something original about the phrase. But it hardly needed to be said. Anxiety hovered over the beautiful fields.

They were beautiful. The buttercups and the red tips of

the sorrel gave a colour-wash to the uncut grasses, a shifting chromatic shimmer to the browning fields. The enormous old hedges had thickened into little, banky woods so that the hay, even though it wasn't very thick that year, was cupped in their dark green bowls, a pale soup lapping at the brim.

Ken Weekes had been trying to persuade me all year that what was needed was a good dose of chemicals for the thistles and a ton or two of nitrogen to make the grass grow. We were already squabbling like a pair of old spinsters and I was relying on him for everything I did. Ken told me I needed Fred Groombridge, the sheep man from the village. Fred came down. He looked at me with only one eye, as though permanently squinting at the sun. 'That's because he's thinking with the other one,' Ken said.

I sold most of the hay to Fred as standing grass, £17.50 an acre. I had asked for £30, Fred suggested £15. He budged an inch, I moved a mile, but in return for that absurdly low price, Fred would also cut, turn, row up and bale six acres for me, 500 bales, which I would then have carted into the barn at my own expense. 'Perfect,' Fred said with his left eye, grinning. 'It's only money.'

Fred brought down his wife Margaret – she gave me a cheque before they cut a single blade of grass – and his nephew Jimmy Gray. Ken helped. Will and Peter Clark helped. I cancelled lunches with publishers and meetings in London. Make hay while the sun shines. And for days it did. For the fields, it's the hairdressing moment of the year. When first cut, the hay lies flat and shiny on the razored surface. The sun glints along it like a light on those snips of

wet hair that lie on a barber's floor. To dry it, the grass is
tossed with the tedder – Margaret's job, eight hours at a
stretch, up and down, up and down in the battered old
Ford 4000 tractor, 'stirring it about' and mussing it up, the
shampoo shuffle. Then it is fluffed back into rows for the
baler, the final hairspray and set. What this means is long,
long hours at the wheel of a tractor, looking back over
one's shoulder at the machine that's doing the job, with
such concentration that Fred went past me three times
before he noticed that I was standing there on the edge of
the field waiting to talk to him.

Everything went like a dream and the hay lay soft,
light and 'blue' as Fred called it, a green tinge to the
grey of the drying grasses, in the rowed-up lines on the
field. Not a drop of rain had touched it. This was some
of the best hay anyone had made for years. But then, of
course, things changed. The forecast predicted thunder-
storms that evening and the baler broke. Fred had
bought it from the two old Davis boys who were
retiring from the place over the hill. I only heard this
late in the day, but it was not surprising Fred had kept
the source of the baler a little quiet. That was where,
the year before, the BBC had stumbled on a fragment
of old England, nettles growing through abandoned
horse-drawn hay rakes, fields that looked as if they
had just got out of bed, a farmhouse soft in its long slow
journey towards dilapidation. They had decided to
make their film of Cold Comfort Farm there. God knows
how old the baler was. There was something seriously
wrong with it, but no one could work out what. The
bales it produced were either the size of a handbag or

emerged eight feet long, oozing out with a terrible constipated slowness from the machine's rear vent.

'Neither's any good,' Fred said, and for 15 hours, while the rain threatened, men from various parts of Sussex pored over its innards. The handbook was out on the field. They drank Ribena. Parts were greased, others rubbed down. 'If I never see another Case International baler,' Ken said, 'I won't be sorry.' The weather forecast was getting worse by the hour. In the end, there was nothing for it and the hay was baled in these stupid lengths. As soon as it was done, we stacked it on trailers and carted it into the barn, just as it was, the long and short of it, an acre an hour for six hours of exhausting, dusty, sweaty work. By the time the rain came, my 500 bales were in the barn, perhaps £1,000 worth. We felt delighted. The hay was saved and the barn, filled to the eaves, smelled sweet and musty. I couldn't work out why Fred was looking so pleased with himself too. All his hay was still out in the fields, baled in the modern round jumbo bales, which a highly efficient brand-new machine had been creating all afternoon. They were bound to get a soaking. 'Oh, I don't worry about that,' Fred said through his one eye. 'Rain doesn't hurt jumbo bales. They can stay out there for weeks.' So why on earth had we sweated over our ridiculous salami/sliver-sized bales all afternoon? 'Oh,' Fred said, with a grin the size of the English Channel, 'I thought you wanted to do it up here like we did it in the old days. You didn't want those jumbo bales did you? You wanted something you could get sweaty picking up and putting down so you could feel what it was like to be a real farmer. You did, didn't you?' I

looked up at him as he asked me and saw – one of those
moments of true recognition – that Fred had both of his
eyes, the colour of the sky on a distant, sun-swept
horizon, wide, wide open, as the first drops of rain began
to fall on the bleached and razored fields.

The hay was in, but the trees were suffering. For weeks on
end, from mid-summer onwards, they looked bruised and
battered. A ride on the Northern Line in the evening
rush hour would not have revealed a more exhausted line
of faces than the trees displayed that summer. Our
neighbour from Perryman's, the young dairy farmer,
Stephen Wrenn, who had taken some of the grazing
for his bullocks, came over for a drink one evening, 'I
don't know a farm that's as lucky as this one with its trees.
You'll look after your oaks won't you?'

We had long talks together about what to do with this
land. He had persuaded his father to give up the dairy
herd, rent out the milk quota and turn Perryman's over to
the new short-rotation willow coppice which can be
harvested every couple of years and burned for energy.
So the cows were sold and they were trying to sell his milk
quota. But it had been such a dry year with so little thick
growth in the grass – all top and no bottom, as they say
here – that no one was in the market to take on extra
capacity because feeding the cattle in the coming winter
would cost a fortune. Drought was stalking all of us.

Even at the end of July, the leaves on the trees already
looked used, dirty, in need of replacement. By early
August, some of the hawthorn and hornbeams in the
hedges were already largely yellow. By the end of the

month, the spindle leaves were spotted black and had dried at the edges into a pair of narrow red curling lips. Elders had gone bald before their time and there were ash trees of which whole sections had been a dead manila brown for weeks.

An oak tree 60 feet high and wide may drink about 15,000 gallons of water a day. It is a huge and silent pump, a humidifier of the air, drawing mineral sustenance from these daily lakes of water that pass through it. Where, in a summer like this, could such a tree have got the income it needs?

The truth is, at least with some of the oaks here, they had been running on empty, trying to live through a grinding climatic recession. I was fencing between the Cottage and Target fields – the bullocks had, as ever, been getting through – and I leant on a low oak branch as I unwound the wire. As I pushed against it, quite unconsciously, without any real effort, the branch, perhaps 15 or 20 feet long, came away from the trunk of the tree and dropped slowly to the ground. It had seemed fully alive, decked with leaves and new acorns as much as any other, but it pulled away as softly, as willingly as the wing-bone of a well-cooked chicken. I pushed it into the fence, as an extra deterrent to the cattle.

Two days later, at the top of the Slip Field, I found an enormous branch, full of leaves and acorns, lying on the ground beneath its parent, perhaps 40 feet long, the bulk of a small house or a lorry. It too had been neatly severed at the base, as if the branch had been sacked, ruthlessly dropped for the greater good of the whole.

These living branches rejected in mid-season made me

look at the oaks here in a new light – their scarred bodies, their withered limbs, the usual asymmetry to their outlines, the slightly uneven track taken by each branch as it moves out from the main stem – and started to see each oak not as a thing whole and neatly inevitable in itself, but as the record of its own history of survival and failure, retraction and extension, stress and abundance. Each oak has a visible history. The story it tells is more like the history of a human family than of an individual, forever negotiating hazards, accommodating loss, reshaping its existence.

One afternoon we were all in the kitchen together. We were sitting around the table and Ken as ever was regaling us with stories of past triumphs. Coming over the wood, from the lane that runs down from Brightling Needle towards the valley and on up to Burwash, we suddenly heard the sound of sirens: ambulances, police, fire? We didn't know. It was a rare noise, more troubling here than in any city street. It marked a real person's crisis, someone you knew. We heard that evening. Stephen Wrenn had been killed. A tractor he had been driving toppled over a little bank, no higher than the back of a chair, and crushed his head. He died instantly. He and his new wife had only just returned from his honeymoon. The entire village went into shock over it. Two or three hundred people attended the funeral and the vicar who, a couple of weeks previously, had married him, helped bury him too.

One evening later that summer, when I was taking the children down to the seaside to play on the sands at the mouth of the River Rother, I happened to meet Brian Wrenn, sitting quietly by the river, looking out to sea. I sent the children on down the track and sat down next to him. We talked about Stephen. Brian said he was 'learning to face a different future'. It was as if his whole being was bruised. There is very little to say to a man who has lost his child.

At the edge of our land you could see, across the little side-valley of a stream that runs down to the river, one of the Wrenns' very banky fields. Before, it had been grazed tight, thistly and docky in patches like every bit of land around here, but with a background of new, bright green grass. Now, with the cows gone, and with Stephen gone, it looked different, the hay long and not cut until late, an air of abandonment to it, or at least of other matters on the mind. I looked across at that field and in it saw what had happened to the Wrenn family, the stupid, trivial, devastating disaster, the slice taken out of their lives.

I will always remember Stephen for the grinning optimism of what he said about the trees, the way we were lucky, blessed with the oaks here. 'Look after your trees,' he had said to me, and I will, as a memorial to him if nothing else. Isn't it a habit, in some part of the world, to plant a tree on a person's grave, to fertilise a cherry or an apple with the body? It seems like a good idea. That, anyway, is the picture I now have of Stephen Wrenn, but it is an oak, not a fruit tree, that is springing from his grave, the big-limbed, dark green, thick-boled, spreading, ancient kind of oak, so solid a part of the country here that it is known as the Sussex Weed.

In the aftermath of Stephen's death, we were all rocked back. I took to spending time in the autumn wood. It is, on a quiet day anyway, a pool of calm. All the rush and hurry evaporates in a wood. If you lie down there, nothing happens. There is a sort of blankness, a consoling eventlessness about it. If a pendulum were swinging there, it would be floating as if on the moon, weightlessly falling, weightlessly climbing the far side. A wood distorts and thickens time. Occasionally, a small five- or seven-leaf frond off an ash tree, or a single hornbeam leaf, will spiral towards you. A pigeon, with a chaotic bang-shuffle to its feather noise, will fluster out of the trees.

Those are only the headlines; the body-text is absent. There is no busyness here. The extraordinary patience of these vegetable beings is what defines them. The way in which the trees stand and wait, open-armed, their leaves dangled in the air for sunlight, their roots spread hemispherically beneath them, capable of doing no more than accepting the wetness that might come to hand, this is a form of existence that could not be more alien to our own. The leaning patience of the tree, its long game: that's the beauty and the dignity of it.

This is not the Darwinian picture, in which a wood is a model of the unregulated market in action, a competitive squeezing for space and light, the trunk a necessary support system for the resource-garnering crown, the shade of a wood evidence of how successfully its market space has been filled by the competing members. Even the dominance of mega-structures, the giant beeches, their effortlessly extended limbs, models a human world in which big boys shamelessly and carelessly deny life-juices to their weedier competitors. The lifeless zone beneath their shade, the part we can actually walk about in, is in fact the result of thousands of small vegetable businesses going bankrupt. It's tough at the bottom. If there is any dignity in this free-market wood, it is the smiling, sober-suited, mutual accommodation of directors on the board who would gladly shaft each other if they could.

That Darwinian model, of nature green in twig and leaf, is how we tend to see things now. Dynamism, urgency, competitiveness and the ever-present threat of failure is what colours the modern view of the natural world. In the time-lapse photography of plants on television, all you see is snaking brambles, serpentine stranglers, nodding their heads in speeded-up hunger for space and light – More for me! More for me!

That can seem at the time like a brilliant technical exposure of hidden realities. But that brilliance is a distortion as much as a revelation. It makes plants too similar to us. Lying in the Middle Shaw one morning that autumn, escaping work, fed up with it, haunted by Stephen's death, a sudden squall blew through the trees, unfelt at ground level but caught and noisy in the crowns of the oaks. It was a blast from the west and in that sudden wind, the wood began to knock and cannonade around me; the acorns, of which there were more that year than anyone could remember, were being blown and shaken out of their cups. The wood quite literally was noisy with the oak's seed rain, as the acorns bounced down through the lower branches and spattered on to the leafy floor. This was the seeding moment of the year, the culmination of the year's life. It was as near as a wood could ever come to orgasm.

As the maker of a TV documentary on Middle Shaw, I would certainly have chosen this moment for my film, a real event which needed no time-lapse to dramatise it, the

only moment in fact when trees reach the sort of in-
stantaneousness with which human life is so familiar and
to which it is so addicted. 'Good,' the editor of the series
would have said. 'I see the wood's up to speed.'

But to choose the climax would have been to avoid the
reality. A true film of the rest of the year would have been
grinding in its slowness, a tree equivalent of John Len-
non's famous film of his own genitalia (or was it his
bottom?), filmed by Yoko for hours and hours and hours
in some Scandinavian hotel, a documentary work so
boring it wasn't considered rude. A tree's concurrence
with time, its superbly long rhythms, cannot be captured
in a way that would make people listen to it. The music of
a wood would make Gorecki's Third Symphony look up-
tempo, a snappy little dance-tune. But that is precisely
why the real thing is so much richer than any televised
version could be. Or so it seemed that autumn. The wood
was a balm-bath, a long slow statement, simply, of the
trees' presence and persistence and dignity and life. Of
course groves are sacred.

That was not the way I talked about them to Peter
Clark. He had been wooding for 14 years or so, all his
adult life, and he was expert at it. He used his chainsaw
like a balloon-whisk. A flick here, a zzzzzz there and order
came out of chaos. Our little woods had not been properly
looked after for too long and so Peter started doing
something about them. There was a businesslike air to
the way he approached the semi-derelict tangle of bramble and wind-blown tree. He didn't, as I would have in a
half-hearted, uncertain and rather respectful way, nibble
at the edges, trimming this, pulling away at that. He

waded into the central problem. Confronted with the giant collapsed ash stools, the muddle of elder and bramble and old splintered oak limbs, he attacked them ruthlessly and systematically. The cosmetics were left till later. Meanwhile, the stacks of usable cordwood grew at those points on the edge of the wood where, in a ground-hardening frost, a tractor and trailer would later reach them. His fires consumed the toppings, the useless bits and pieces. Every day that autumn they burned in three or four places at once, positioned so that the smoke could chimney out through a gap between the big trees around them. From a field or two away the wood looked like a small leafy settlement, with the smoke climbing out from the three or four separate hearths and the chainsaw whining and relaxing, whining and relaxing as another fallen thorn or overgrown hazel was sliced and readied.

It was a wonderful sight – in the mind's eye as much as anything else – Peter moulding the wood in the way other people might pick up a lump of clay and shape a pot from it. He was a gentle and not especially gregarious or socially confident man. If there were other people about, he would often decide not to come in for a cup of tea or for lunch. Wooding is a private business, done in private, the results remaining virtually private, the whole event without a public face. And it was there, in that self-contained world, that he excelled. 'Do you like wooding?' I asked him and he replied in the way you might expect. 'It's a job,' he said and lifted his eyebrows into a smile.

We had four patches of woodland on the farm. One, the Way Shaw, was a field that was let go before the war and was now a thicket of bracken and wind-twisted birches.

Ken said the remains of a V-1 doodlebug lay somewhere in there, but nobody knew where. Two of the others, Toyland Shaw and Middle Shaw, are old hornbeam coppices with some big oaks in them. The fourth, the Ashwood Shaw, is a wonderful old ash coppice, with giant stools growing on a steep bank between Great Flemings and Hollow Flemings, some of the stools 12 and 15 feet across, with four or five 60-foot-high trees growing from each divided base.

This, in miniature, is a rich inheritance, an ash wood and a hornbeam wood providing the two necessary materials: one light but strong, making perfect poles for the handles of tools, for rakes and hay forks, the other tough and resistant. Mill cogs were always made of hornbeam wood and whenever I look at them I think of that, the iron hardness lurking under the oddly snake-like bark, the trunks not making good clean poles like the ash but twisted, fixed in a frozen and rather ugly writhing. The ash and the hornbeam, the calm and the perplexed, the classic and the romantic of an English woodland.

I was feeling my way with the wood. Clearing up was obviously the first stage of what to do here, but it wouldn't be enough. That autumn a couple of enormous ash trunks crashed out of the wood and into Hollow Flemings, the field below the shaw. There had been no great winds, nor anything else to disturb them. They had simply grown too big for their foundations. The leverage of the 60-foot trees became too much and they snapped out of their fixings at ground level, leaving a torn stump and exacerbating a weakness which meant that other stems from the same stool would soon go. The only way to save the plants was to cut them down. New growth would spring from the shorn stubs and the interrupted cycle of coppicing, which, judging from the size of the stools, must be many centuries old on that bank, undoubtedly a medieval landscape, would be resumed.

I talked to a local timber man, Zak Soudain, about the wood and he was keen to have it. The bottom end of an ash trunk, where it moves slightly out from the stool then up towards the light, a shape which preserves even in old age the first directions taken by the new stem in the first spring after coppicing, is the most valuable part of all. It is used to make lacrosse sticks. Nothing else will do. The rest, the straight clean lightness of the ash, will go into furniture, probably be stained black and end up in the Loughborough branch of Habitat.

So far, so profitable. But there was a hazard. We were overrun with deer. As we looked out of the bedroom window soon after seven in the morning, there would be eight or ten deer grazing in the field. The fawns in September were still playing with each other in a puppyish, skittish way. There was a stag with a single antler left, walking around lopsided like a car with one headlight out. Deer eat young trees. If we cut the ash down, they would chew off all the new shoots, the stools would die and I would have destroyed a small sliver of the late medieval landscape. But if we didn't cut the ash trees down they would probably collapse in the next big storm and the wood would be destroyed anyway. Deer-fencing was prohibitively expensive and ugly. I wasn't quite sure what to do about this and so I dithered while Peter easily and confidently moved through the fallen mess of things. I

asked him one day what he would do. 'I don't know,' he
said. 'It's not for me to say. You've got to decide Adam.
It's your wood.' I didn't tell him that, as far as I could see,
the wood felt more like his.

That autumn I bought our first sheep: 20 Border Leicester
ewes, which had already been through one year's lambing. They were advertised in the local free-sheet, £600 for
the lot. I knew we had to plunge into livestock and this
was a way of doing it. Will Clark and I drove over to look
at them. Will said he knew about sheep and did quite a bit
of squeezing of the back end of the animals in question. I
certainly knew nothing whatsoever. The woman selling
them, wearing a fetching pair of buckskin chaps, said they
were marvellous. So I bought them.

Carolyn Fieldwick, Will Clark's daughter and wife of
Dave Fieldwick, the shepherd, had a ram to sell us. I
bought him for £100. He was a big stumbling, black-faced
Suffolk and we called him Roger. He arrived on November 5th and started to mosey around our field full of ewes.
If a ewe conceives on Guy Fawkes' Day, Ken Weekes told
me, the lamb will be born on April Fool's Day. Roger
seemed, it must be said, quite cheap at £100, and looked a
little seedy. I could see him in a Dennis Potter play,
snuffling around the ewes' rear ends like a tramp going
through the dustbins at the back of a restaurant. They
didn't much like the look of him or his intentions and
used to move off to eat more grass in some other, less
interfered with part of the field.

It brought back memories of 18-year-old parties, in
which all the girls were pristine, self-sufficient and adult

and I was a grubby, grasping bundle of unattraction, trotting around about two yards behind them. At least I didn't have to wear the sort of thing we put on Roger, a harness that Helmut Newton would have been proud of, holding a large yellow block of crayon wax in the middle of his chest. Whenever Roger managed to corner a ewe, he rubbed this, as a side-effect so to speak, all over her bottom so that we would know she'd been done. After the best part of a week, his score was two yellowed bottoms and one ewe that seemed to have an intensively crayoned left shoulder. Radical misfire or poor sense of geography: whichever it was, nothing could have been more familiar.

What an agony for poor Roger! So many requests, so much rejection. I only caught him in successful action once: a desperate five seconds of up-ended quiver and then down on all fours again, that look of hopelessness flooding back in, a sense of everything being over, a look on his poor, crumpled-ear face of utter bemusement. Why, I said to him, can't we all procreate like the trees? Come for a walk in the wood with me. And of course he looked at me with his own version of withering scorn.

Winter came sidling up on us. By mid-December, with the darkness deeply lowered over the whole place, I found myself reading Donne's great, slow nocturnal on St Lucy's Day, the shortest and the darkest day in the pit of winter. ''Tis the yeares midnight,' are the first seductive words of a funeral march that moves on heavily and softly through the deepest of bass registers:

'Tis the yeares midnight, and it is the dayes,
Lucies, who scarce seaven houres herself unmaskes,
The Sunne is spent, and now his flasks
Send forth light squibs, no constant rayes;
        The worlds whole sap is sunke:

The year's midnight: it's the self-blinding of the year, that terrible lightlessness when all you can do is remember the long lit summer, the after-hay evenings when the fields had a purified cleanness to them, patterned with an odd and unplanned-for regularity in the bales waiting to be collected, each of them throwing its shadow to the next, like a dabbed mark with a broad-bladed pen, while the dog is manically teasing some left-out wisps of hay and the children are playing man-hunt among the bales. What a sudden inrush of lost time that is. Its dropping, vertiginous perspective must be what youth looks like from old age. Perhaps that is the shudder at the heart of winter.

My daughter Rosie, who was two that year, thought the trees were dead. 'The trees are dead,' she said one morning after breakfast, as one might announce that the war in Bosnia was over or Arsenal were third in the Premiership.

'Not dead,' I said, 'just resting.'

'Are they sleepy?'

'Yes, they are, I suppose.'

'Why aren't they lying down then?'

Anyone who doesn't believe in the reality of Seasonal Affective Disorder might learn a thing or two if they took a trip to the Sussex Weald in winter. Our own immediate surroundings that December represented the English winter in excelsis: the sapless, shrunken, dampened sump of sunless gloom. I stayed inside as much as I could and averted my eyes from the windows as I passed. The mud lapping at the walls of the house on two sides had become a glutinated bog decorated with grey-eyed puddles and the semi-mangled remains of the rubbish which something was tearing open at night and distributing among the earth-heaps and trench systems. You could hardly blame the creature; no one could tell that scattering half-consumed, half-rotten rice-puddings and stock bones over what used to be the garden wasn't precisely what we had in mind. Any aesthetically attuned fox/dog/badger could quite happily think that his randomised technique was exactly the principle on which the rest of our landscape was currently designed.

The chickens we had foolishly acquired roamed delightedly among the old-food-encrusted earthwork-play-zone where I let them out every day. They redistributed the mess. None of it ever seemed to disappear.

I had come to hate our chickens. They lurked about in the same murky province as unwritten thank-you letters and work that's late, the guilt zone you'd rather didn't exist. One is meant to love chickens, I know: their fluffy puffball existence, the warm rounded sound of their voices, a slow chortling, the aural equivalent of new-laid eggs, and of course the eggs themselves, gathered as the first of the morning sun breaks into the hen house and the dear loving mothers that have created them cluster purling around your feet for their morning scatter of corn.

Well, I hated them. Before the chickens arrived, I loved them. I sweated for days, building their run with six-foot-

high netting, buried at the base so that the fox couldn't
dig in to get them, with additional electric fencing just
outside the main wire as another fox deterrent. I made a
charming wooden, weatherboarded house for them, the
inside of which I fitted out as though for a page in *Country
Living*. There were some elegant nesting boxes, with
balconies outside them so that the hens could walk
without discomfort to their *accouchements*, ramps towards
those balconies from the deeply straw-bedded ground, a
row of roosting poles so that at night they could feel they
were safe in the branches of the forest trees which the Ur-
memories of their origins in the forests of south-east Asia
required for peace of mind.

When it was finished, I sat down on the rich-smelling
barley straw and smoked a cigarette, thinking that this
was the sort of world I would like to inhabit.

We should have left it at that, but we didn't. We
actually bought some chickens. And a cockerel. He came
in a potato sack and when I tipped him out on to the grass
and dandelions of the new run, he stood there, blinking a
little, surrounded by his harem and I couldn't believe we
had acquired for £8 such a shockingly beautiful creature.
He was a Maran, his white body feathers flecked black in
bold, slight marks as if made with the brush of a Japanese
painter. His eye was bright and his comb and long wattles
the deep dark red of Venetian glass. He seemed huge,
standing a good two feet high, and this fabulous, porce-
lain-figure colouring made a superb and alien presence in
our brick and weatherboarded yard. His chickens, which
he cornered and had with a ruthlessness and vigour we
could only admire, were dumpy little brown English

bundles next to him, heavy-laying Warrens, dish-mops to his Byron. For two days after his ignominious sack-borne arrival, he remained quiet but then began to crow, disturbingly loud if you were near by but, like the bagpipes, beautiful when heard in the distance, down in the wood or with the sheep two fields away.

Within a couple of weeks it was going wrong. My son Ben, who was seven, and I were collecting eggs. It was early evening and the chickens were still out. We didn't realise it but the cock was already in the house and with only the warning of a couple of pecks on my feet, which I didn't recognise for what they were, he suddenly attacked Ben, banging and flapping against his trouser legs in a terrifying explosion of feathers and movement and noise. Ben and I scrambled out of the hen house, him in tears, me shaken.

It worsened over the next few weeks. We were all attacked in turn until one Sunday morning found the entire family cowering behind the glass of the back door, checking to see if Terminator, or Killer Cock as he was also called, was out on the prowl. He had come, I am sure, to sense our fear and was now certain of his place as Cock of the Walk. He had to go. Of course, there was no way I could bring myself to capture him and so we hired a professional to take him away. We thought there might be the most horrifying execution scene in a corner of the yard. What actually happened was a lesson in the psychology of dominance. Alf Hoad is a man with enormously hairy arms. He lives in the village and shoots deer. He was our chosen executioner. Alf arrived in his Land Rover, stepped out of it carrying a sack, walked up to the cock and put him in it. My manliness rating dropped like a stone. The children now look on Alf as something of a god. He took the cock away alive and used him as a guard dog to protect his pheasant chicks against foxes.

It was a relief when Killer went. We could walk about again outside without fear of a rake up the back of the legs, but, without their man, our ugly little brown chickens suffered a drop in status. I looked at them and saw only the slum conditions in which they lived – my fault, they didn't have enough room – and their scrawny appearance – nature's fault, as they were going through the moult – and I blamed them for both. They stopped laying with the days shortening, and so we didn't even have any eggs. In fact, we were quite pleased about that because we had come to think eggs disgusting.

All I could see when I looked at a chicken was its weirdness. There is no expression in a chicken's eye. It's about as warm or responsive as a 100-watt bulb. And there is something in the way they move, a jerky, interrupted urgency, which is deeply unsympathetic. It is as though the chicken has a problem with its synapse firing mechanism, ticking over at the same sort of rate you hear the cylinders going in a dumper truck. Chug, chug, chug, chug, chug: that's a chicken's brain in fifth and flooring it. And that Groucho walk! Why can't a chicken take a step forward without moving its head? It can't even make a single step with anything like a smooth or fluid motion. It picks up a leg, squeezes its foot into a tight little package under its armpit and then chucks it forward, spreading its toes as it does so in a histrionic gesture which, if you had to live with it, would drive you mad within the week.

People, I now understood, had got completely the wrong idea about chickens: they are not the soft, burbly things they always appear to be in pictures and advertisements. They are utterly and profoundly manic. This whole short history has taught me an important lesson. There is something about the chicken which invites maltreatment. No one, I think, would ever have tolerated the idea of battery ducks, even if that were possible. People have caged billions of chickens in the most intolerable conditions because everything about them tells you that they have no soul.

The chickens somehow made the winter worse, its awful unshaven stubbliness. The whole of Sussex looked as if it had been in bed with 'flu for a week. Its skin was ill and a sort of blackness had entered the picture, as if it had been over-inked. No modern descriptions of winter ever put this clodden, damp mulishness at the centre of things. People always talk about ice and frost and glitter and hardness and crispness and freshness and brightness and sparkle and brilliance and tingle. It's all nonsense. England is at sea and has sea-weather, a mediated dampness. That winter it entered our souls.

Why, I wonder, do people pretend that winter is so much icier than it is? Because we can't all have houses in southern Europe to retreat to and so want to doll up the thing we are stuck with at home? Perhaps. Because drama, the extremeness of ice outside and fires within, is in itself alluring? Probably. But I think it may be largely because that hardness, brightness and coldness are all the qualities of the American winter for weeks if not months on end and the modern, particularly commercial iconography, is derived from there. So we do not nowadays share Donne's deep and beautifully gloomy vision but instead console ourselves with a brighter, harder, brittler thing, which is less oppressive and so perhaps, in some strange way, poorer for that. At Perch Hill, in a sea of unglittery mud and damp prospects, with things unfinished, never unpacked or never started all round us, we huddled over our fires. Visiting friends were amazed at the mess. Our first year had come to an end. Was it, I still wondered silently, a mistake? Did we belong here? What were we doing here? Were we going to be happy here? Had we swapped one sort of unhappiness for another?

PATROLLING
THE BOUNDARIES

I became obsessed by Kipling that winter. Bateman's, his house, a mile from ours across the fields, now belongs to the National Trust and I asked them if I could write the text to a new guidebook they wanted there. They agreed. I didn't tell them how much I had come to see Kipling's own position as parallel to mine: almost exactly my age, 36, when he came here, in retreat from the world, in grief over lost children – his six-year-old daughter Josephine dead from pneumonia, my sons severed from me, or part-severed anyway, by divorce – and both of us looking for the sustenance an ancient landscape can provide.

The boys came here often, regularly, and I longed for them to think of this as home. But I was under no illusion: some gap, like the cracks that open in drying clay, had appeared between us. My home was no longer their home. Sitting for those weeks in Kipling's study, at his desk, investigating and exploring his books, handling his objects, walking his land that all but bordered with mine, reading into it the moral and emotional structure of his stories, I was wrapping myself in this Sussex Kipling, not the drum-banging imperialist but the haunted man in whom so much of my own predicament seemed to be prefigured.

Morning after morning, I walked over the hill to Bateman's. It is down in the valley, away from the road, away from the village, surrounded by hedges and high walls. Even though the Kiplings knew it to be a gloomy house, already with the air of sadness it still has in its rooms even on a sunny day, it looked in 1902 like the haven they needed, almost a fortress, stony-faced, protective, and they jumped at it. It was a house in which they could pull up a drawbridge behind them.

There was more to it than simple anti-sociability. A passage in *Something of Myself*, Kipling's late autobiography, provides the key. He is describing his own magical practices as a lonely boy, suffering in a boarding house in Southsea, separated from his parents and his beloved *ayah*, still in India:

> When my father sent me a *Robinson Crusoe* . . . I set up
> in business alone as a trader with savages . . . in a
> mildewy basement room . . . My apparatus was a

coconut shell strung on a red cord, a tin trunk, and a piece of packing case which kept off any other world . . . If the bit of board fell, I had to begin the magic all over again. I have learned since from children who play much alone that this rule of 'beginning again in a pretended game' is not uncommon. The magic, you see, lies in a ring or fence that you take refuge in.

That last sentence could be a description of Bateman's itself, of the place of this valley in Kipling's imagination and of what it meant to me too. It is the magical zone into which others do not intrude and whose power and secret relies on a vigilant patrolling of the boundaries, of a perceived isolation in which the richness of privacy can flower. His American wife Carrie ('a hard, capable little person', Henry James called her) was the Keeper of the Gate and there is a story remembered in Burwash, and told to me by Graham Jarvis, the butcher there, from the Kiplings' later years which dramatises particularly sharply that exclusion of the world.

One of the Bateman's calves was to be slaughtered not for its meat but for its thymus gland, which is at its largest in young animals and is still thought by some to contain life-enhancing, vitality-inducing juices. After John Kipling went missing at the Battle of Loos in 1915, his father suffered repeated and acute gastric pain. The calf's thymus may have been intended to alleviate this. After the gland had been extracted from the animal, Carrie insisted that the rest of the body should not be used for meat. It was to be buried, not on the farm but inside the garden and the ground over it raked to a fine tilth which would show any disturbance. After that tilth had been prepared, she signed the raked ground with her own name.

This is an odd and disturbing image: the life-giving calf, dead and signed for in the garden, locked away from the rest of the world by a mother who had seen the death of two of her three children and shown no public pain. It seems like an unconsciously magical and demonic act, a sacrifice in a Sussex garden, a thousand miles from the world of Burwash and the straightforward use of animals for meat but rather near to the world of Kipling's own poetry and its sense of the enigmatic undercurrents flowing everywhere beneath the surface of the ordinary, to all the bruised and desperate qualities of the poem he wrote for his dead son.

> 'Have you news of my boy Jack?'
> *Not this tide.*
> 'When d'you think that he'll come back?'
> *Not with this wind blowing, and this tide.*
>
> ('My Boy Jack', 1916)

The more I read, the more it became clear that Carrie's protectiveness was also obsessive. In the later years she would not let a single piece of Kipling's handwriting leave the house; everything he wrote had to be typed out by the secretary. When she found the manuscript of *The Irish Guards in the Great War*, Kipling's long careful testament to the men in whose company his son was killed, about to be sent to the publisher with some last-minute handwritten alterations by the author, she insisted that the entire text be retyped. Kipling himself had to apologise to the secretary.

But Carrie's ferocity was an act of love. It allowed

Kipling, among many other things, to explore, in private and in all its ramifications, the place where they lived. The landscape and those whom he saw bound to it, became the heroes of the stories he wrote at Bateman's, at the long walnut desk where I sat reading them. Stone mullioned windows look out on two sides, one eastwards along the pastures of the valley where this author-landowner would have seen his two herds of conker-red Sussex beef cattle and the Guernsey dairy cows, the other, to the right, over the woods that clothe the sides of the valley, the woods from which Puck emerges in the stories like an earthman-impresario to conjure magic for the children, and into which, at the end of each story, he melts wordlessly away.

The figure of Hobden, the hedger and ditcher, the archetypal Sussex man, whose generations have been there for ever, and who knows everything there is to know about the place, is Puck's human equivalent. He is Sussex made flesh, the ancestor of all the Clarks, Groombridges and Weekeses who were also peopling my world. Kipling, as he wrote in a poem, may claim to be the proprietor of a wide stretch of the Dudwell valley, he may hold the deeds, but Hobden, even Hobden the poacher, *possesses* it:

I have rights of chase and warren, as my dignity
    requires.
I can fish – but Hobden tickles. I can shoot – but
    Hobden wires . . .
Shall I summons him to judgment? I would
    sooner summons Pan.

('The Land', 1917)

Kipling, the valley and I clustered together. We became each other's. He put his mark on it, in field after field, at the corners of woods and the twisting of the river, at farms and at cottages now already in ruins and mossed over. In return, the valley shaped his imagination. I trudged after them both. More and more that winter I walked in Kipling's world. The words he used to describe his relationship to it were 'wonder and desire', twin attitudes, one distant and admiring, the other distant and longing. Those were mine too. Working it out with map and text in hand, I found where Hobden's cottage and his forge had been. An alder carr now grows over what must always have been their sludgy, boggy site. At 'the sadder darker end' of the wood, further along the valley, I found what he had described in *Puck of Pook's Hill*: 'an old marlpit full of black water, where weepy, hairy moss hangs round the stumps of the willows and alders. But the birds come to perch on the dead branches, and Hobden says that the bitter willow-water is a sort of medicine for sick animals.' I, too, found myself there, suddenly surprised one day by this: ' "Hst!" he whispered. He stood still, for not twenty paces away a magnificent dog-fox sat on his haunches and looked at the children as though he were an old friend of theirs.'

For the whole Kipling performance here, Puck, the little brown pointy-eared earth god, is the master of ceremonies. He acts as the compère, smoothly and coolly emerging from the leafy wings, presenting the children with the astonishingly immediate and real past, and then just as deftly slipping back into invisibility. In his hands, the boundaries between the real and the imagined are dissolved, the strange and the alien are slickly wafted into concrete existence and with equal panache swept away. Each story ends with that quiver of closure and each new one begins with a sudden unapologised appearance of the strange.

There were multiple layers in this valley for Kipling and he provided another for me. It became for him, as it had for me, a sort of reservoir of the English spirit which can emerge from the leafy shadows for an hour or two and then slide back into them, a place where the gates are down between the landscape, the idea of history and the sense of other lives and other spirits inhabiting the world we call ours. I have walked the abandoned roads with Kipling's most famous lyric in my mind:

> There was once a road through the woods
>   Before they planted the trees.
> It is underneath the coppice and heath,
>   And the thin anemones.
>   Only the keeper sees
> That, where the ring-dove broods,
>   And the badgers roll at ease,
> There was once a road through the woods.
>
> Yet, if you enter the woods
>   Of a summer evening late,
> When the night air cools on the trout-ringed pools
>   Where the otter whistles his mate . . .
> You will hear the beat of a horse's feet
>   And the swish of a skirt in the dew . . .
> As though they perfectly knew
> The old lost road through the woods . . .
>   But there is no road through the woods.
>
>   ('The Way through the Woods', 1910)

That is still there too: the numinous haze above the leaf-litter on the wood floor; the moss-walled trenches of the old lanes dropping to the river where the shallow gravel turns it into fords; the black pools over which the willows and alders curve their long, flexed limbs like the struts of a tented dome; the knowledge of something having just passed, its scent hanging there in the way the smell of fox stays on in a sheltered hollow; and that fearful sensation when you find yourself flicking your head around behind you, knowing you are alone but sensing something else, a crack of a twig, a movement in the trees unexplained by the wind, the moaning creak of one trunk against another. All that is there, in fragments, and never more than at those marginal times, the early, dewy winter mornings and the ever-earlier evenings, as the sun comes in low and pale, its colour diluted by the damp in the air, washing the inside of the wood with sunlight it hasn't seen all year.

I relished all that privacy, the protectiveness, secrecy and subtle explorations of 'the things that are beyond the frontier', but I wondered too if the shut-awayness, the closure, the brusqueness of the Kiplings' dealing with the rest of the local world, whether that was really enough. The story of the buried calf, lurking in my mind for the weeks after I heard it, changed the way I saw that part of the valley. It coloured the landscape like a stain. It somehow drained it of blood. It denied one of the best and richest things about living here: the neighbourliness of it, the net of people we had already become connected to, a net which existed like a map overlying the physical map. Ken Weekes, Fred Groombridge, the Clarks, Nipper Keeley, the timber merchant, the Fieldwicks, the Wrenns: these are people we had come to know and rely on now. You could tell from their names that they were all what they called themselves, 'Old Sussex'. On the farm, each of them would tell me what to do and how to do it, how not to and what I had done wrong so far. There was a form of decorous, reticent generosity about the advice these men gave. They didn't want to tread on toes, but what they said always came with a slight and joshing twist on the end of it.

In one of these conversations with Ken Weekes that winter – it was about whether to put nitrogen on the grass – Ken turned to me and said 'You know, Adam, it's very nice that you've come to live here.'

'Oh,' I said, 'why's that, Ken?'

'Because it looks like you've got money to burn.'

For all that, Ken was a stalwart, helping us out time and time and time again. Neighbourliness is central to the way he is. Remembering his deep and social generosity of spirit, you turn to the cold picture of the dead calf buried in the garden, the anti-neighbourliness, the grief in it, and Bateman's no longer seemed to belong to the country in which it was set. It had become a disconnected anomaly. 'England is a wonderful land,' Kipling wrote to a friend just after arriving at Bateman's. 'It is the most marvellous of all foreign countries I have ever been in.' That remained true of his place in Sussex: never at home, in the way the Weekeses are, but consciously and repeatedly searching for a home, for a feeling of embeddedness in the place. The very search set him apart. Perhaps he was no more than an early forerunner of all those of us who have left cities to find a rural place. As soon as you start to feel the conscious need to look for it, you are bound, perhaps, never to find it. You bring your turmoils with you. Is pastoral of necessity burdened with its own failure?

The cord could be drawn too tight; it might actually strangle you in the end. Could there really be any happiness without elasticity, without an open, fluid relationship with those around you? The natural world, even with all those supernatural, Kiplingesque ghosts wafting constantly through it like a shoal of half-seen fish in the green murk of an abandoned water tank, would that, in the end, be any sustenance at all?

With Ken Weekes one day, as the whole Kipling phase was nearing its end, the neighbourliness between us took a step forward. He had a gun for sale and I bought it, an impulse. It was a 12-bore Silver Sabel De Luxe Side Lock Ejector made by a Spanish gunsmith called Gorosabel. 'That's £1800 new,' Ken said. 'You can have it for £540, seeing as you don't know what you're doing.' I'm not sure why it was £540 but I'm putty in Ken's hands and so I said yes and for the first time in about 20 years I had a gun of my own.

Guns smell delicious: mineral, acrid, serious, not pretty, not part of any cocktail party scene. The smell of a gun is uncompromised. There isn't a soft edge to it. Someone should think of marketing gunsmell as an aftershave.

My Sabel De Luxe was a beautiful thing for the few days that I had it – chased on the silver plate that covers the side lock mechanism, the stock polished, dense, rich, reliable, the opening mechanism sharp, the pleasure of cameras in the precision of its click open and its snap shut. It combined the best of furniture and jewellery, intricacy and solidity, designed for a purpose, moulded to the body, made for me. Of course a gun is a glamorous thing.

I went out with it early one morning, late that February. It was strangely warm and the grass was growing as though it were May. Custard's snout was dripping from the dew bath, like a boxer with his sweat up. Every time he shook his face, the wet flew off it in a halo.

Noises in the distance are more audible first thing in the morning. There was the traffic on the Burwash–Heathfield road along the ridge; jets into Gatwick; pheasants over in Leggett's Wood, a cousin noise to our own stupid chickens clucking; the hollow knocking of a sledge-hammer on a chestnut fence post down near Bateman's; the Coxes' tractor at Sheepshaw Farm, grumbling and farting into life; the spatter of something falling in High Wood on to the leaf floor below the trees.

There I was, standing in the middle of this near-silence, with the sunshine breaking in bars on to the grass of the Slip Field, the warming, smooth-skinned gun in my hand and the dog, obedient, wet and bored at my feet. I stood in the shadow of an ash tree and waited for the rabbits to emerge. I had seen them here before and throughout the grass of this little wood-lined sliver called Hollow Flemings are the nibbled patches and the scattered droppings they had left behind. If there was going to be a Perch Hill killing field, this was the one.

When I was a boy I had a series of guns: a BSA air rifle, with which I shot out the windows of the granary next to the barn at home and killed a robin at three yards on Christmas Day; a .410 shotgun; and then a Holland and Holland 16-bore, a beautiful, slim and elegant thing, more like a walking cane than a shotgun, with which I felt completely at home. I stalked about the fields of my stepfather's farm in Hampshire with my pockets full of cartridges and my heart full of blood-lust, popping off at this and that for the hell of it, enjoying the jolt into the shoulder and the *ding* in one's ears afterwards. It might be a rabbit one day, some pheasants or pigeons or squirrels the next. I wasn't much interested in the bodies or the eating of them. It was the shooting that counted.

This was the time we were all having to read *Les Caves du Vatican* for French 'O' level, with Gide's thrilling idea of the *acte gratuit* – one never translated the phrase – an entirely gratuitous action, for some reason always violent and nasty, to show that you were one of the cool gang, *les subtils*, not subject to the dreary rigidities of conventional moral life which the others, *les crustacés*, suffocated under. In the book the *subtils* shoved strangers out of train doors at 80 miles an hour; I murdered animals. My mother thought I was learning country lore and the Ways of Nature; I knew I was living out the fantasies of a gay French intellectual half a century earlier. Life in the Home Counties had never been so authentic. If I'd been born to different parents in a different class, I would have been sent to Borstal.

The last thing I shot on my teenage grumblings around the Hampshire fields was a hare. It sprang up 15 yards away, out of the footings of a hedge, one December morning. I swung round on to it and shot it once. The shot had no effect and the hare went tearing on across the wide spaces of the field. I watched it for a while and then turned away, to put a new cartridge in the gun. Just as I did that, I saw or thought I saw the hare stutter and tumble over, as though a wire had tripped it. I walked over to the far side of the field and there it was lying on the grass. I touched its eye. The hare was dead. When we came to eat it, there wasn't a single pellet in its body. I'd missed it, but the noise of the gun going off had been enough. The hare had died of shock. I don't remember taking the gun out of my stepfather's cupboard again.

All that was 20 years before. In the meantime, I had shot a single stag, out of curiosity and after a long and beautiful stalk through the hills near Rannoch Moor, but that ended in absurdity too. It was a warm day and the herd of deer was sitting calmly on the cheek of hillside below the stalker and me, 100 yards away. Whispering, he told me that the stag I was to shoot was the one in the middle, 'the hummel'. A hummel is a eunuch, with no antlers. It had never been like this in John Buchan. Not only was my stag a castrato, it was fast asleep, dozing in the autumn sunshine. The stalker began by whistling softly to make it stand up. No good. A light clap of the hands – nothing. Finally, after some banging and shouting, the other deer got up and walked away but my chosen hummel, my sweet fat little eunuch, continued his afternoon dreaming. 'Ach, there's nothing for it,' the stalker said. 'Shoot it where it is.' So I did, through the neck, severing the vertebral column. The hummel never woke for his death; his head slumped forward on to his chest and from a distance there was no telling he had died.

These were the scenes running through my mind that

morning as I stood in the fringes of the wood with Ken's gun in my hand. The sun climbed higher, the rabbits came out into the field but I didn't raise the gun to meet them. 'What is the point?' I said to the dog and we walked back up to Ken's to return the gun. 'I know what you mean,' he said. 'I only shoot clay pigeons myself nowadays. I don't know why, but I don't like the other any more.'

Another killing question loomed up: the hunt. Kipling had banned it from his land and we did too. It was casually done. They asked if they could and we said they couldn't. I wonder now, years later, if this was too casual on our part. I didn't think carefully enough about it, the casual disruption to other people's lives which our casual refusal involved. Dislike of the hunt was largely a gut reaction, founded, absurd as it might sound, on a dislike of horses. There is something in particular about a horse's bottom which makes it difficult to take the horse world seriously. Horses are not alone in this. Different styles of bottom will always colour the way in which you see different parts of the animal kingdom: the encrusted chaos at the back end of a sheep, usually the farmer's fault, too rich a diet, but essentially sheepy nonetheless; the pert neatness with which the rear of the cat meets the outside world; and the way dogs divert one's attention from the bottom itself with the wonderful flag-waving gesture of the tail, leading one's eye up and away to the tip-of-the-wag point of delight. That is the difference between a cat and a dog: one is a take-it-or-leave-it, I'm-no-one-to-make-any-form-of-social-compromise sort of animal, the other nothing but love and diversionary tactics. Unless, as we had, you fail to house-train your dog properly, there is no reason to suspect a dog even has a bottom.

Horses, though, are the apotheosis of the bottom. I cannot help thinking of them as mainly bottoms with a head stuck on the front. And what heroically enormous bottoms they are! That pair of huge round buttocks, a couple of Brobdingnag conkers, sheened up by their owners like a schoolboy with his cherished, oven-hardened seventy-sevener, so full, so fleshy, so bottomy, even when at rest: that is the essence of the horse.

Prizes are awarded on racecourses to the stable-lads who devise the most elaborate chequer pattern in the coat of the horses' bottoms – called 'quarters' in this context – and that, I think, is some recognition of the importance of the bottom to the whole being of the horse. But it is when they set off on their first trot of the morning that the horse-bottom comes into its own. This is the rhythmic, stomach-easing, first stretching out after the gases have been accumulating all night and it is then that the massive bums, the most buttocky buttocks in the animal world, like a chorus of podgy ballerinas performing to a loving audience in front of them, breathe a series of little synchronised farty kisses into the morning air. Squeeze, squeeze, squeeze, fart, fart, fart: it's the flagship gesture of the horse's existence. And the farts, of course, are only the preliminary to another synchronised movement, the flopping out of those steaming piles of Loden-green dung, flop flop, flop, one after another. How the horse manages to make them look as if they have been created by some kind of internal ice-scream scoop, I have no idea. It is one of the miracles of nature.

Riders, I think, know this instinctively about the horse and the bottom. It is why, in their manner, they attempt somehow to compensate for the inherent absurdity of their position. The sillier the bum, the more serious the person on top of it. The pretence doesn't work. To anyone not on a horse, anyone on a horse looks stupid. And the more they try to look dignified, modelling themselves on the equestrian statue of Marcus Aurelius that used to stand in the Campidoglio or whatever it might be, the more you see some idiot looking like the cherry on a Bakewell tart. And if the horse then goes into its early morning intestinal exercises, the effect is worse.

This, I think, may be at the heart of the difficulties that hunting is going through. It is nearly impossible to take someone who is up on a horse seriously, and if you can't take them seriously you can't really accept the idea that they should be horrible to foxes, even when foxes had been as horrible to your ducks and chickens as they have to ours.

That January, the fox had already nabbed a couple of ducks and a day or two later had got at the chickens. In the morning we had eleven, poking around the mist-sodden winter fields and looking happier than they had for a long time. Freedom suited them, to a degree anyway. By the afternoon, I could only see seven. Quite often in the cold, they used to go into the barn and shuffle about in the mad Burmese jungle-fowl style their genes instruct them to adopt, flicking at the hay and pretending they are deep in the tropical rain forest. I did find two in there but two were still missing.

Up in Jim's Field, our best and biggest hay field, I found the other two dead in the grass. Dave Fieldwick's sheep, with his hideous, expensive, Tyson-lookalike Texel rams, were ignoring the two dead animals in their midst. I don't know if a fox had done it. Perhaps a dog had taken and dropped the chickens here. The grass had been pulled at and tufted by the sheep so that it had the look of hair first thing in the morning, a chaotically mussed pelt. Only spring would restore a sleekness to it.

On the grass, whose colour was now halfway between green and tawny, the two dead chickens lay, ten yards apart. One was whole. I couldn't see a mark on it. The other had a big deep gash down its chest, a cut that laid back the flesh in the way that a butcher's knife would scoop the raw chicken breast back from the raw chicken bone. Chest or breast? The sight in front of me hovered between the two. It was shocking somehow, and I was surprised to be shocked, that the actual cut body of the dead chicken looked like 'chicken', the stuff you see in the supermarket chill cabinets, sitting in its polythene tent on its expanded polystyrene tray, its leaking juices being mopped up by its pinkish poly-something nappy. Of course I knew 'chicken' came from chicken, but I had never had the fact pushed in my face before. I eat 'chicken' all the time, but the idea of eating these recently murdered things seemed, in a way I can't quite fathom, impossible.

I picked the bodies up by their smooth and scaly legs, that part of a bird that makes its reptile relatives seem so near to hand, and flung them into the edges of the wood, up over the fringing hawthorns and into the oak and hazel scrub beyond. Let the foxes feed, I said to the corpses arcing outward through the air, and turned for home. The bodies thumped to earth behind me. Their sisters were fluffing up their feathers into powder-puffs against the cold, those little legs sticking out below them like the wire stands on which shoes are sometimes displayed in high-class Bond Street shops. For the first time, I felt sorry for the chickens, victim-creatures, the huddled mothers of children they would never see, not really at home here, their genes pining for the jungle where they belong. Perhaps, I thought, I should take our chickens to some stretch of Javanese wilderness and release them there. It might be the sort of adventure *Horizon* would love to make a TV programme about.

Despite that experience, I had no animus against the fox – of course I preferred foxes to chickens – and no love for the hunt. A week or two later, we had our first slight problem with them. They met just a mile away, next to the 19th-century obelisk known as Brightling Needle. It was a cold morning with mist in the valleys and everything was as it should be. Bottoms emerged from boxes, superbly bottomly, farting as they descended the ramps. Men in tweed jackets smoked Benson and Hedges at 7.30 in the morning – a hard drag followed by the classic Terry Thomas teeth-clench – and square-jawed women appeared in bowler hats. These ladies' heads were perfectly symmetrical about the bowler-hat brim, a living version of those drawings by Rex Whistler which look exactly the same if you turn them upside down.

The traditional two policemen were there in two police

cars. Parked on the side of the road was the traditional ageing, navy-blue Austin Maestro, slightly rusting on the sills, containing the traditional three antis, one with the traditional part-orange, part bleached hair, one with the traditional row of earrings up the rim of his ear and one with a slightly innovative Barbour and tweed cap. I crouched down next to the fugged-up driver's window. It was a sign of the maturity of social life in East Sussex that the man with earrings said that the antis had 'a very good relationship with the hunt' and that things had gone 'very well so far this season'. It sounded positively parliamentary.

One of the policemen took down the number of the car and the occupants sat inside smiling at him. The riders, some of whom I knew anyway to be nice, generous, open, subtle and supple people, looked stiff and stupid on their horses. Has anyone in the saddle ever managed to address anyone on the ground without exuding the whole 'my good man' aura that irritates and alienates so much?

I went home when the field plop-plopped off down the lane, with the hounds effortlessly elegant and dignified in front of them. Mid-morning we had the problem. There was a man on a horse standing next to the farm gate. I stood there looking up at him on his shiny bum and I felt like Wat Tyler at the gates of London with the men of Kent at my back. 'I am *so* sorry,' he said, that 'so' quivering with three more syllables in it than usual. 'We've had a great time and some of us seem to have got *so* overexcited that they just didn't see the electric fencing you've got up for the sheep and I'm afraid they smashed *straight* through it. I'm *so* sorry. We've put it all back together and it's fine now and the sheep of course they're fine, but God how stupid can you be.'

Poor man. He was trying as hard as he could, but there was a structural problem here. It was toff up/peasant down, a spatial metaphor of everything you most resent. It was a medieval moment. Endless hours spent reading about bastard feudalism and town charters could teach you less about the Middle Ages than this simple confrontation. The horse creates an appetite for democracy and whatever the facts, the *feel* of hunting on horses is not democratic. Few people have felt the same sort of loathing for fishing and shooting – those crucially horseless versions of rural killing. The horse is to blame for the condition in which hunting finds itself. Everyone hates being talked down to.

One day soon afterwards I was summoned to London for lunch with a man who wanted to convince me that hunting was not what I imagined it to be at all. Rules, the delicious restaurant in Covent Garden which is usually full of fat red men in suits drinking claret, makes something of a cult out of eating wild animals. A little brochure sits on each of the tables to tell you why this is a good idea. Its basic sermon is this: wild animals are good for you because they spend most of their lives in the gym, migrating here and there, running this way and that, lean, not fatty like your lazy old farm slobs. Wild animals are more admirable than that, always on the go, never taking time for a proper lunch, lean achievers, career creatures who make Elle Macpherson look like a pig that has junked out on pork scratchings.

'Wild salmon will have swum the Atlantic,' it says exhaustingly, 'and so will have firm muscles, less fat and a varied natural diet.' No spare tyre on a wild salmon. All nature is a workout, with the best possible organic niblets as the reward. Wild duck are 'truly free-range birds', sea trout eat only the finest pink shrimps, grouse taste of heather and snipe of bog or, as this brochure put it, 'sweetly rotting wild mushrooms'.

These animals are what they eat, you are what you eat too and so if you eat them, in a sort of apostolic succession, you will become an elk. Magic. There is no need to think of anything as disruptive as actually taking any exercise yourself. You can stay in Rules, you can go red in the face, you can tuck into a capercaillie on fried bread, larded with strips of woodcock freshly braised in goose fat, and you will still be as slinky as a well-hung fox. It's a religious event, the communion for the 90s: eat me, I am your lunch.

I did, and it was delicious too: potted shrimps, a tiny little teal with excellent muscle-tone, scarcely cooked, oozing blood as though it were gravy, and half a bottle of claret. The other half, the other teal and the other shrimps were eaten by Robin Hanbury-Tenison, who was paying. He was Chief Executive of the British Field Sports Society. They could not have a more charming advocate and we ranged happily all over the environment, society, ethics and politics as though we were old friends. It is a curious fact that animal killers are usually nice and Mr Hanbury-Tenison was obviously one of those people who have a certain ease because they are able to countenance hunting and killing. Always trust a huntsman.

We talked about cruelty. Didn't he mind the suffering of the fox as it was chased? Wasn't that unkind? There

were two things about that, he said. A fox, or a hare come
to that, either escaped a hunt or was killed. A hunt never
wounded an animal which then crept away to die in pain.
In that sense hunting was quite different from, and better
than, shooting. Any number of hunts, particularly har-
rier packs, pick up animals that have been wounded with
guns.

Yes, but what about the chase itself? It is the drawn-out
threat of death that many people find most difficult to
stomach. That, he said, swig of claret, lovely smile, is the
second thing, and where they are wrong. He then told a
story about a rat in a cage with a snake. His brother kept a
snake in the Caribbean. It needed its daily live rat and
every morning this is what happened. The snake is lying
curled in the corner of the cage. He twirled his hand
beside the bread rolls to demonstrate the curled snake.
The rat is popped in at the other end of the cage. Other
hand pops in and sits neatly next to the bottle of wine.
The snake then thinks 'Ah, breakfast.' Snake hand
slithers along the table. Rat thinks, 'Here I am in a cage
with a snake. No problem. I can deal with this in a hop
and a skip.' Rat hand hops and skips over the table, easily
and delightfully escaping the open mouth of the snake
hand arching towards it in its gyrations.

The rat is not, as we might imagine it would be, because
we ourselves might be, in terrified paralysis in the corner
waiting for death to come. Not at all. This situation is
only a slightly heightened version of everyday life for the
rat. The rat is always in 'dynamic tension' with its
environment. It is always thinking either 'Oh heavens,
that's going to kill me' or 'Oh good, I think I can kill that.'

That is the substance of rat life and its busy little bright-ness is a product of it.

So the snake stays slithering and the rat keeps hopping while this explanation of its psychology is made. Rat is happy; snake is hungry. Then, suddenly, the snake hand, somehow fused at this point with the hugely open-eyed face of Mr Hanbury-Tenison the other side of a table which I hadn't realised was quite this small until now, rises up in a surge of hunter-gatherer energy and – glup – swallows the rat whole.

A quivering little pause as the disaster sinks in. 'That,' he said, his hands human again now and back on the knife and fork, cutting another slice from the breast of teal, 'is exactly what it is like for the fox.' Such was the realism of the enactment, and the passionate conviction of the mise-en-scène, that anything I might have said in response became immediately redundant. Hunting was nothing to do with red-faced men on big-bottomed horses farting their way across the English countryside. It was the far more charming sight of Robin Hanbury-Tenison's left hand suddenly swal-lowing his right hand whole, the laws of nature in action. Perhaps.

Back home, away from the sluicing of claret and teal-blood, I retreated, as ever, into the privacy of a quiet and secret relationship with the place. I shrugged my Kipling coat on. I was coming to know this valley in the way a man knows the feel of his own palms, blindfold, easily, without drama. I trespassed everywhere, ignoring paths, climbing every fence, pushing across hedges, finding the ways through that the deer had made. There's nothing like trespass. I've done it all my life, invariably alone and most excitingly at night. I've climbed into the garden of a great house in the early hours of the morning, sidling past the Renaissance pavilions, brushing past borders where the moonlight has turned the dahlias blood-purple and the lawns into Caribbean-coloured ponds. I have climbed the outside walls of a castle further south in Sussex, late one evening, thinking it an empty ruin and only found, as I topped the parapet, hauling myself over the lichened stones, that they held inside them a beautiful, tile-hung farmhouse, with a rose-garden wrapped around it. The Iceberg roses, filling the bailey with their huge white flowers, were unreal in the moonlight at the farthest, darkest corners, and apricot and peachy where the light from the windows fell on them. No daylight garden, no allowed-in garden, could have matched it.

It is an aesthetic experience, exciting, addictive even, because it is the most revealing way of being in a place that I know. It makes you slight, careful and attentive. You cannot stroll as a trespasser; it is not a breezing-about, hands-in-pockets way of being in a place. Trespass strips comfort from the mind.

I have never poached other people's game but I imagine poaching as an even tighter sharpening of the senses, screwing you into the details of the moment and the place, restoring an alertness and exposure to your presence in the landscape which centuries of pastoral urbanity – the smooth attitude to general rural effects – has clogged and obscured. To feel the immediate pulse of things, to be forced to shove yourself into a hedge when a stranger comes around the corner, the spikes of the hawthorn dug into your shoulder, the leaves against the face – that is what trespass is good for, the tangibility of the trespassed-on world.

Needless to say, being caught and ejected is horrible enough. I have had a Welsh farmer standing in front of me, arms crossed, resting his weight on the back foot in the way that Michelangelo's David does, his grey pork-pie hat tipped up off the brow, his cardigan waistcoat pouched around the stomach, while his three, circling, agile, grey-eyed dogs roared and screamed at me as I tried to make my way back off his private land on to a public path. Whenever I think of the word 'property', that is the picture that comes to mind.

The night-time wanderings here came to grip my imagination. Now and again, as it turned midnight and everyone else was going to bed, I would drink a glass of whisky, pull on a coat and go out of the back door. A moonlit night, the light so bright that it looked like a cold blue day. The sheep were coughing in the barn, kicking out their innards, hack, hack, hack, as if they'd smoked 40 cigarettes since breakfast. It was dust in the hay that did it.

I set off into the fields. The open back of the hillside was washed in blue light. The further corners of the fields, where they dropped towards the creases of the streams, were bathed in deep blue-black shadow. It was the place I knew, transformed in the way that a fall of snow can rearrange the geography. But here it was time, rather than space, that seemed oddly altered. The moonlight created what looked like a form of summer. Its light cast the same sort of shadowy patches under the trees that you get in the summer sunshine. The moon was at the same height and at the same place in the sky as the sun had been during our lunchtime picnics in June. The pattern of light was the same, only the colour had changed. It was a strange and ghostly re-enactment.

And these winter nights it wasn't warmth and chatter but cold and quiet. A car on the Burwash road spread ripples of engine noise through the night. You could hear its gears changing as it came out down the long straight towards Burwash Weald and then moaned its way on up the hill towards Broad Oak and beyond. The silence pooled back in behind it, leaving only the sound of my walking, my breathing, the crunching of my feet on the frost.

Sometimes, and I don't know why, I began to feel frightened. Once, I thought I saw the shadow of two deer grazing in the Slip Field and I went down to get a closer look but they turned out to be nothing but clumps of rushes, masquerading in this single-tone light, this bleached ultra-violet black-and-white, blue-and-white light, as animals poised over the grasses. There was a slight creeping at the back of the neck, a crawling alertness in those vestigial hackles, raised by an ancient fear.

The frost made a crust on the grass under my feet, frozen on the surface and soft underneath. Where the moon reflected off it, the ice made pinpricks of light as sharp as stars in the grey-blue grass. The whole field was the colour of eyes but spangled with these lights. I didn't want to go into the wood. If I hadn't wanted to find out what it was like in the wood in the middle of the night, I wouldn't have gone in. I looked in at the deep black shadows in there and thought, no, I won't. But that was giving up too easily. I had to know what it was like and I went in. I hated it. The inside of a wood at night is a darkened, complex, crabby place, full of the flick and twist of shadow, a place of misinterpretation, of reading the neutral and the innocent as strange and threatening. All those trees look so human. They look too like living things for comfort, they surround you and they out-number you. There is a sense that they are all at the back of you, those outstretched arms, those leaning limbs, that overarching command of the place they have. That is the sort of idea which, once it has made a bridgehead in your mind, won't be dislodged. The fear moves in and colonises you. Even as it was happening, I could not believe it was happening. Never would I have believed that these woods, our woods, could have scared me, but they did. What is it, this deep, black fear of an uncontrol-lable landscape? Modern neurosis or ancient genetic memory? Is it basic or is it acquired, something essential to our own natures or a symptom of distance from the natural world?

I wanted to be out the far side of it and I ran crouched through the moon-shadows, through the snatching bram-bles, snapping the twiggy elder branches as I passed, until I was out again in the wide, grassy, controllable ease of our far big field called Great Flemings. Panic at shadows? Surely I should be beyond that now? After-twinges gripped the back of my neck and a dog yapped somewhere down at the bottom of King's Hill, a mile away, a persistent, repetitive, dreadful barking as I caught my breath.

I sat down in the field and looked out at the farms on the far side of the valley. I knew from the hedge shapes, the dark lines of the hedgerows laid across the grey of the fields, where the farmhouses should have been, but they had merged into the dark. There were no lights on over there. A long way over to the west a jet was making its way into Gatwick and there was a sprinkling of lights further north, fewer lights on the earth than stars in the sky. It seemed as if everything local had dissolved away, leaving nothing but the dark and the calling of ewe to ewe, from points up and down the valley.

And then into that, the wholeness of that, tore the one sound in the English night which slashes bigger holes than any other: a fox, the scream-howling of the fox in the wood, a noise gash in the rest of it: *yeaow, yeaow, yeaow*, a ripping of cloth with claws, *yeaow, yeaow, yeaow*, as screamingly basic a sound as England makes. With that in my ears, it didn't seem that the wood-fear had been such an absurdity, or an anomaly, after all.

NEIGHBOURS
WITH THE DEAD

There is a small lane that runs over our land. It is, as I see it anyway, a beautiful place, with a hard stony surface where the wheels go and a grass strip between them, hedges eight feet high on either side which, at the far end, lean over to meet at the top, so that in summer it is a green and sun-splashed tunnel, full of broken shadow and leopard-skin light. Some 200 yards after it has left the road, it finally curls round a little into the wood like the warping of a plank that has been left out in the rain.

I love this lane, for the roses and honeysuckle that

hedge it in early summer, for its privacy, its following of an old line off our hill through the wood and on down to the valley at Bateman's. If I were designing a landscape, it would be full of tracks like this that can't be seen from the outside, trenched inside their own hedges, eventually curving away into apparent nothings. Landscape beauty, you might even say, consists of slight disappearances like this, not abrupt corners or sudden conclusions but turnings in as subtle as the spin on a ping-pong ball as it crosses the net. That slow, slight curve appears again and again in descriptions of landscape that are intended to catch the moment of perfection. In Philip Larkin's poem 'The Whitsun Weddings', he describes a train journey from Hull to London, and the air of warm, early summer completeness in it is set up by that one resonant word: 'A slow and stopping curve southwards we kept'.

There is a taut balance in a shallow curve which other shapes could never match. When Ben Nicholson was persuaded to discuss his own painting, he would do so, if at all, not in terms of the influences on him or the meaning of what he was doing, but of spin and dancing, the perfect execution of a turning step, the alert, controlled, coherent energy of it. Or there is Edward Thomas dedicating his book *The Icknield Way* to his friend Harry Hooton, saying that as far as walking is concerned, or even *being*, if it comes to that, 'the end is in the means – in the sight of that beautiful long straight line of the Downs in which a curve is latent . . .'

From the beginning I loved our lane because it was an unconsciously beautiful thing, in its shape and in the materials of which it was made. But there was a problem.

The lane belonged to us but was the only means of access to another house. We owned it but we hardly used it. Dave Fieldwick, who had his sheep on some of our fields that winter – I was charging him 30p a week a ewe for the winter grass – used the lane once a day to check if they were all right. Otherwise the only users were our neighbour, Shirley Ellman, the postman delivering her mail, the electricity man reading her meter, her friends coming for a dinner party or her children on a visit at the weekend, and so on.

Things became *slightly* tense between us. The potholes grew steadily worse. One particularly big one filled up with water and the children and I spent a happy afternoon trying to sail plank-and-hankie boats across it but it wasn't quite deep enough and they kept grounding. This Perch Hill Round Pond was not seen as an amenity by Shirley and she decided to do something about it. The first thing I knew, going for a walk one afternoon, was the sight of a large yellow lorry, two men and a rolling machine laying out shiny new tarmac on the surface of the lane. By the time I got there, they had covered 50 yards of the lane with the smart new blackstuff. 'No, no, no, no, no, no, no,' I shouted like a deeply deranged figure appearing on stage towards the end of a Strindberg play. I know this is what I looked like because the faces of the two innocent men doing the work became two round white blobs in front of me, with two round black holes where their mouths should have been.

The tarmac looked – was – horrible, a suburban slick, removing meaning from the place it coated, making the lane banal and ugly, no longer a place but a passageway. I had rather surprised myself by the intensity of my reaction. Could such things really matter so much?

The following evening I had a very civilised, unStrindbergian meeting with Shirley. I explained it was my lane and she shouldn't do things like that to something that wasn't hers. She said the ruts were atrocious and the suspensions of their various cars were suffering and that's why they had put the tarmac on. I said the tarmac destroyed the meaning of the place. She said what on earth did I mean. I did not mention Philip Larkin, Ben Nicholson, Edward Thomas or 'straight lines in which a curve is latent' but I did use the word 'suburbanisation.' She said she thought she was improving the lane and that I as the landlord should be grateful. I said I wasn't grateful to have what I owned altered by someone else without even so much as a by-your-leave, and that some people in my position would have had the tarmac dug up and the bill sent to her. I realised that we were getting a little Strindbergian again when the look of open-mouthed amazement came over her face too. Surely, I then said, calming, calming, we could come to some mutually satisfactory arrangement? She agreed, surely we could, but what was I proposing? I proposed that we should pay for the upkeep of the lane in proportion to the amount we used it, which we should work out, that I would get a quote from someone to bring it up to a beautiful, untarmacky, usable condition and go from there. She thought that sounded OK and that was how we left it.

It could only be an interim position. There were two irreconcilables in conflict here. I wanted the lane to look and be rural, of the place, not alien to it. My neighbours wanted it to be usable, reliable and undestructive of their cars. I wanted a stone track, which would inevitably be eroded by the sort of traffic a modern household generates; they wanted a tarmac drive, which would not. What could be done?

In part I felt, secretly, without saying so, that I was being unreasonable. Why not allow these people to make their own runway across your land? But in another way I felt, symbolically, that over this I had to dig my toes in. What else were we here for but to nurture precisely the wrinkliness in the landscape which that lane represented?

I happened at the time to be reading a book, called *The Language Instinct*, by Steven Pinker, Professor of Brain and Cognitive Sciences at the Massachusetts Institute of Technology. Pinker makes clear that language is always rich in redundancy. We don't need to say half the things we do but we get pleasure from saying them anyway. The most obvious wastage, as he points out, is in vowels. We can leave vowels out of the picture and still make our meaning clear. Yxx mxy fxnd thxs sxrprxsxng, bxt yxx cxn rxxd thxs sxntxncx xnd xndxrstxxd xt, cxn't yxx? Sntncs lk ths cn stll, n fct, b ndrstd, lthgh ths s rthr mr dffclt nd slghtl slwr thn th sntnc wth th xs whr th vwls shld b.

You can read it but it's not English and tht tght-lppd, clppd wy of tlkng sounds a little mad. It's not human. The natural human manner is voluble, assertive, open-mouthed, vowelly and fuzzily over-supplied with signals. That communicative generosity is a sign of humanity itself and the ever-present but strictly unnecessary vowels are, it turns out, symptoms of a much more general phenomenon. We surround each other with a meaning fog and we are comforted by that. We are not spitting little pellets of pre-digested information at each other like sharp-beaked, defensive-aggressive owls. We are lounging together in the same meaning-bath. Redundancy, an over-supply of meaning and a certain inefficiency are some of the most indispensable aspects of human life.

This is an intriguing idea. For something to be fully communicated, something more has to be communicated at the same time. The stripped-down meaning, the thing reduced to essentials, loses something essential in the process. Fuzz is more accurate than core. There is no such thing as a core meaning. Meaning is spread throughout what appears to be contingent or nearly irrelevant. A blunderbuss will hit more targets, or more of a target, than a rifle. Imprecision is the first requirement of under-standing. Clarity obscures the nature of what it clarifies.

The landscape is also a language and when it comes to anything in the landscape, if you don't want change to involve loss of meaning, the key question to ask is: What about the vowels? What about the soft, subtle, pervasive, apparently inessential things which constitute so much that is so important to so many people but which can't be measured, or anyway not easily? What about the darkness of the sky at night? The bendiness of the lanes near you? The tastiness of local food? The hereness of any particular here? What about the difference between Pxrch Hxll Fxrm, a location whose meaning can be easily understood but reads as though it were somewhere in the northern hemi-sphere of Venus, and Perch Hill Farm, that fully rounded, warmly syllabled, richly vowelled description of home?

If we only attend to the serious consonants and ignore the apparently unnecessary vowels, if we tarmac the crustiness of lanes, good environments – that is, good places in which to live – will have been damaged. You might even say that the more unimportant something seems, the more important it actually is. Redundancy is all. Compare a place you love with somewhere no one could possibly love, perhaps one of those stretches of mown and scalloped grass on the outside of a roundabout, an elegant region of curved turf which looked nice on the road engineer's plan but in reality is the essence of vacuity. What is the difference between them? Why does one seem like a place and the other no more than the place where a place should be? Isn't it a certain unnecessary complexity, a bobbled scurf of things, the trace of past events, the embedded quirk, the wrinkle in the face, the burble of a particular family's or particular person's multiple existence, the lack of clarity?

The poetry is in the particularity, and the particularities of particular places are not single elements dropped on a desert floor, but webbed, interfolded with each other, making a multi-dimensional grid over the extent of place and the depth of time. Anything with clarity will be clumsy in the face of that and, when dealing with webs, clumsiness is the one thing that has to be avoided.

I didn't put it quite like that to Shirley. We could come to no agreement. The untended lane remained there for months on end, rutty, their cars lurching down it, the 50 yards or so of tarmac at one end pristine, the rest in decay.

The situation was made worse by another problem. Our water system was arranged so that I had to pay her water bill and she would reimburse me for it. This became entangled with the lane issue. She refused to pay her share of the bill. We threatened to take her to court. Only months and months later did we discover that there was a leak in the pipe between her meter and her house. She had never seen the bulk of the water the meter said she was using. These were the ingredients of a bitter relationship between us. We passed each other in our cars on the way to and from the village: stiff smiles or bleak indifference through the windscreens. Occasional curt phone calls. I started to exclude her presence from my own picture of the place. She was the scab I didn't want to scratch.

It was not as though the rest of Perch Hill was in a very good state that winter. Sarah and I, as people do in these situations, had embarked on radical reconstruction of house and garden. As if deep in analysis, things at the farm were still on the downward slide. We were still deconstructing its personality, aiming steadily for the black chaotic pit from which, and only from which, the rebuilding could begin. If there were mental hospitals for landscapes, Perch Hill would have been sectioned that February. Poor, broken, misused, fragile thing.

When people, usually of the older generation, came to lunch here on a Sunday there was always a moment of awkwardness, a rather uncomfortable hiatus in the social flow, when they would usually have said how beautiful the house/garden/surroundings were, how exquisitely lucky/clever we were to have found such a perfect hideaway and how on earth did we ever stumble on it in the first place?

I started getting used to the approach of this pre-lunch crisis and could see our guests silently struggling with the problem. I pushed peanuts and cheese straws at them but it wouldn't go away. What possible compliment could they make when half of one of the kitchen walls was missing, awaiting a replacement fireplace and held up by a rusty old acro prop? When the terrace outside the kitchen was a mixture of a trench dug by mistake for a wall we would never build, incipient weeds and a zig-zag brick pattern which looked nice from an upstairs window but twisted your ankle if you walked on it? When, on the other side of the building, the groundworks for a new septic tank and reed-bed sewage system – very green, very Highgrove – had made what used to be a perfectly acceptable lawn into a scale model of Passchendaele 1917. My sons described it as sad. ('What does sad mean, William?' 'Sad is a punky word for stupid.') When what was laughably called the scullery was a muddy mixture of plastic tree guards, sheep's veterinary equipment, un-mended hoovers and put-it-there-for-the-moment junk?

What could they say? 'I see you've taken quite a bit on,' was the usual version. 'How long have you been here?' was another, a little more sly – or perhaps shy. Only the brave could admit that 'Every time I come to this house it seems to get less built.' And only they were right. My God, were they right.

But Sarah and I had something in mind. If we were thinking of becoming high-profile management gurus, we would have called it 'The Knowledge'. The Knowledge was what kept us going through the mud, like the differential lock on a Land Rover. The Knowledge was what, with time, and the drip drip of in-dripping finances, we would make of this place. It would be whole and it would be good. It would have the air of what might be called inherent coherence.

Inherent coherence: it is something you recognise every time you come across it by chance, driving down a lane or turning a corner to a small group of buildings and trees, or often in an unmetalled track, where a sense of well-made purpose suffuses the little patch of landscape. These are places where the essentials are what give them character, where the meaning or the style of the place is not pasted on from the outside but emerges from within, where there is no sense of hypocrisy, no lying, smiling front to a cold and cynical core.

It would be good. It would have to be good. One week, later that winter, I saw a picture of what Perch Hill might one day become. I was in the University Library in Cambridge. Falling asleep over what I was meant to be reading, I decided to see if Perch Hill Farm featured in that building's vast subconscious depths. There was nothing in the computer catalogue, but that was probably too much to expect, so I went to the Map Room. Here on giant green tables a serious man, writing the history of Bechuanaland in the late 1890s, was poring over garish maps of mineral deposits and catchment areas; a woman in an Inca-style cardigan was analysing the hydrography of Scapa Flow. I asked for Perch Hill Farm. 'Certainly,' the map librarian said. 'Just fill in the form.' She disappeared for a minute or two while I kicked my heels and she returned with one heavily and precisely folded piece of paper.

She left me to it and carefully I unfolded the sheet. It was large, perhaps three feet by two, and had a clean and precise air to it, as if freshly laundered. There was even the smell, in its inner sections, of newness and ink. But it was far from new. This map was part of the great 25 inches to the mile series made in the second half of the 19th century. This particular sheet was produced in 1898. I don't think anyone had ever looked at it since it was made.

At my own giant green table, I pored over the map of home. The farm just about filled the sheet. The other people may have been thinking about, or analysing, or drawing conclusions from the maps in front of them. I was not. I was in bed with my map, loving every inch of it, drinking it up, reading the reality of hedge-bend, gateway, wood-corner and stream-turn, surveyed so exactly, drawn so carefully, displayed so perfectly in front of me. This map series, which marks individual trees in hedges and names every field, which, if laid out for the whole country, would stretch 200 yards from the Lizard to the Cheviots, scarcely less from Southwold to St David's, is probably the greatest map ever made.

I looked at my sheet, one tessera of a stadium-size mosaic, and in it saw the state of perfection, described in a fortnight's work in the spring of 1898: the hop garden in Hollow Flemings, no longer there; the small wood that cut in two the big field known as Great Flemings, no longer there; the three hedges that made small compartments of the other big hay meadow, the Way Field, none

of them now there; the little wood dividing Target from
Cottage Field, marked now only by a bank and a single
oak; the orchard in the Cottage Field, of which one
fruitless plum tree remains.

Here, in the Map Room, surrounded by the nearly
audible sound of the collective Cambridge brain ticking, I
saw something else: our farm in its rich, divided wholeness, the picture a century ago, the agenda for the next 40
years. I rushed home. I shrugged on this place like an old
duffle-coat: an arm in each sleeve, a quick flick of the
shoulders and the thing thudded on, into place, as if it
had been hanging on the coat-hook pre-formed. I rolled
outside, coat on, boots on, hands in pockets against the
finger-nipping wind. The ducks were beside the old cow
shed on the pond, whose level had risen higher than at
any time since we'd been here. They remained fearful, but
that was as it should be, their own fox-proofing. The
chickens ignored me, another sign of health, busy in the
hay beside the barn door.

But all this was part of our still-to-be-sorted farmyard.
What I wanted was the fields, the eiderdown expanse of
the bed of home. I could feel myself wriggling down into it
as I entered the first of them, the yellow-green of the
sheep-nibbled grass as welcoming as any nursery ever
could have been. Was this what the fox felt when he
entered his earth, that surrounding of yourself with a
place that seems to be an extension of yourself, so that
there is no sharp transition at the skin?

As I went down through the fields, looking at the
beautiful reduced colours of the winter wood – the black-
berry purple of the hazel fronds when seen against the

sky, the yellowness of the willow in bud, the chocolate blackness of the dead bracken where it lay sodden and rotting at the field margins, the grey-eyed green of the lichen spots on the birch trunks, curling up at the edges into a sort of lettucey thickness – I could sense this whole farm webbed with the different overlying territories of the creatures that inhabit it.

It took going away to notice this, to look beyond the details of daily business. The multiple, interlocking mesh of this place became apparent to me for what felt like the first time. I realised that my own sensation of rooted, inner belonging could only be akin to the territorial sense of the foxes, the badgers, the deer, the wrens, the robins, the kestrels, the pheasants, even the bees or wasps or those chalky blue butterflies that had flickered above the surface of the summer grasses on the limy lower ground of the Slip Field, whose descendants must now be holed up somewhere nearby, waiting for the warmth to return.

There is so much said and written about biological community, but never before had I felt myself to be part of one. Nor had I recognised that what I had always thought of as a higher human faculty, this identification of self with place, was nothing more than an animal faculty for location, a means of placing oneself with precision and care in the landscape, an essential adaptive tool for survival. I couldn't actually see the other animals doing it, but I knew they were there. I sometimes caught a badger in the headlights on the lane, so much fatter and piggier than you might expect, trotting up into the brackeny laneside banks. We buried a large vixen that was lying dead and fresh on the side of the road just before

Christmas, the wind ruffling up the white hairs on her throat as she lay on the grass while I dug the hole. The deer would melt in and out of the wood in the first hours of daylight.

Seen only by chance, these animals were a constant presence. I felt no strangeness from them. They left their marks. On a dewy morning, the fields were criss-crossed with their tracks, where their bellies had dragged through the wet grass. Where the deer jumped the fences, the earth was punched away. In the Way Shaw, down on the edge of our land where the ground falls sharply towards the river, the deer had pushed out nests for themselves among the birches and bracken of the heathy woodland. The owl that sat in the giant beech at the corner of the shaw I had often looked for, often heard but never seen. It was as moulded to the place as cheese melted into the crust of a pie. But I now think, perhaps, that to want to see it, to get a visual grab on it, would only be trophy-hunting. The truer knowledge of it is to hear its unseen presence in the trees. You don't have to open up some-one's chest to know they have a heart.

My walk around the fields slowed down. I had started off briskly enough, seeing that this gate was working properly now, that stile needed replacing, checking the sheep were all right, noticing that one was limping, but as the walk went on, the progress was tripped up by the details. A woodcock suddenly flipped up and twisted away in front of me. I noticed an oak tree still covered in its brown autumn leaves, a blackthorn still laden with sloes that were burst and crusted as though cooked under a slow grill, the way the red hawthorn berries, seen against the blue blackness of the woodland, merged the two colours so that the landscape itself turned purple. Slower and slower, I noticed the ear-like fungi growing out of the elder trunks quivering in the breeze like blown flesh, the spindle berries the colour of a liquorice allsort, just going over, a wren, incredibly, not hopping but flying through the branches of a hawthorn hedge. Perhaps the slowing down was this: the reassertion in me of animal life, the reading of familiar signals, triangulating the map of the known.

Above all, I poked around our streams, but to call them that is to flatter them. One drops westwards from the house and one east, but they are trickly, weedy things, dry all summer, with a proper gush only after heavy rain. You could never have a boat-race with sticks on them. But then, saying that, I'm aware only of disloyalty. They are, in their tiny way, beautiful things. The slight winter flows make small waterfalls where the stream exposes a bed of the underlying stone, followed by small pebbly pools no more than eighteen inches or two feet across. Hart's tongue ferns fringe these places. Come the spring, one stream will be bedded in garlic, the other in bluebells. Both of them are deep in trees, one in the edge of the wood, Dallington Forest, which stretches westwards without a break for three miles from here, the other in its own little strip of trees, somewhere between a massively overgrown hedge and a sliver of wood.

There was a hidden aspect to these streams which only stole up on me very slowly. We had been here for months before I realised. They seemed in themselves such inconsiderable things, transitory, unimportant parts of a land-

scape dominated by field and tree. But as I realised late
that winter, they were, to use the phrase of a French
historian, Alfred du Cayla, describing the streams and
rivers in the landscape, '*les lignes maîtresses du terroir*', the
mistress lines of the territory. I love that phrase. Our little
streams embody it. They are a governing presence.
Whenever it was that the boundary between the parishes
of Brightling and Burwash was drawn here, certainly
before the Norman Conquest, perhaps centuries before
that because the first *written* reference to Brightling was
made in AD 732, they used these two streams as their line,
climbing up their beds from the valley to the high ground
where the farmhouse now is and then down the other side
dropping steeply to the river, 300 feet below us.

The hedges that run along them, as you would hope for
from a parish boundary, are enormously rich in tree
species, 12 of them: crab-apple, spindle, hawthorn, hazel,
blackthorn, oak, ash, field maple, rose, alder, willow and
elder all grow there. There is a widely accepted but
slightly unreliable rule that for every woody species
you can find in a hedge, you can add a century to its
age. The large amount of surrounding wood probably
boosts the number of species in all hedges here. Nevertheless, if the rule is at least some indication, then those
hedges, that acknowledgement of the tiny stream as a
mark in the landscape, are at least a thousand years old,
maybe more. The hedge date would just about match the
date of the first written record.

The history hunger built inside me. Nothing of any
detail could be rescued from the Dark Ages, but later,
when this farm was cut from the wood, there should be

something there. What was it like, when this place first emerged as a place and what, above all, was the man like who first made it? I looked for hints of what he did, the marks he left, sifting through them in the landscape here in a strangely possessive and jealous way. I wanted to know it all, in detail. It felt at times like digging through the waste-paper baskets for someone's leavings, their inadvertent signs, the give-away gestures.

But he had covered his tracks, or had his tracks covered for him, well enough. What evidence there was in this microdot of England is slight and fragmentary. You could not say that silence hangs over the beginnings of this farm, about 400 years ago. More, the fuzz of what has happened since then obscures the shapes and muffles the signals. That is what makes those beginnings seem present but inaccessible, a voice in another room of which you can't quite catch the words.

Even so, there is something about this searching for another, this listening out for the lingering presence of someone else's acts and motivations, which is curiously intimate. I am not saying that this is a haunted place, only that understanding can persist across time, that sometimes, perhaps because I have come to know the wrinkle of field and wood here as closely as he would have known them, I can imagine, at least, that there is a sense of understanding between me and the man who made this farm. Knowledge is access and his person is in the fine grain of here. In some ways, this place is his mind.

The written documents run out too early and are no good anyway, a list of men and, from time to time, the tax they paid. 1832: Edmund Goldsmith is the tenant of John

Fuller, known to history as Mad Jack, a rabid Tory, Member of Parliament, sugar-and-iron millionaire, folly-building eccentric, patron of Turner, buried in Brightling churchyard in a pyramid where he is said, erroneously, to be sitting down to a final gargantuan dinner at a cast-iron table. That's what we know about Jack Fuller. We don't know anything about Edmund Goldsmith. In the late 1770s, there's a Mr Carter, in 1771 a Mr Harrison, in 1724 a Thomas Noakes, in 1719 a John Baker. In 1711 a John Taylor lives at 'Pearchill'; in 1694 he is already there, the earliest name that can be tied to these fields. The farm is then valued at £9, on which he pays tax of £1 16s. It is the poorest farm in the parish. Perryman's, the Wrenns' farm on the other side of Leggett's Wood, is valued at £19 and Park Farm, down by Bateman's on the good land, at £24.

At least the figures confirm something. This farm is right out on the edge, the worst land where the border between the parishes runs, which no one would have bothered with unless forced to, no more than marginalia, the periphery not the main. One of our fields is called, rather enigmatically, Toyland, and the little wood next to it the Toyland Shaw. But that, I came to realise, is a mishearing of something said in widish Sussex. It wasn't Toyland but Tyeland, part of the tye land, an Old English word meaning a common, of so little intrinsic value that it could be left to supply the common needs. And that too lies at the heart of the farm's name. Perch Hill has nothing to do with fish, nor being perched up high, but simply the hill where you would go to cut your perches, the old word for a good stout stick or pole. A parrot's perch and a perch as a unit of measurement are both more specialised derivatives of that older and more general meaning. 'The tame Hoppe,' Henry Lyte wrote in his *Niewe herball or historie of plantes*, published in 1578 as this farm was coming into being, 'windeth it selfe about poles and perches.' So this is where we live: Stick Hill, part of the medieval commons, out on the edge and stuck away, well and truly in the sticks.

All this was inching us towards my man. Knowing this edginess of the place, you could start to smell the quality of whoever it was that first decided that this was where he wanted to be. He was not part of the establishment, nor in line for some major inheritance which he only had to outlive his father to receive. He was, perhaps, a younger son who needed to make his way. There would have been those dissuading him but he wouldn't listen. What other choice did he have? The lottery of the cities where you were more likely to die young than do well? Or paid employment somewhere, a ceiling imposed on your prospects and your life? Neither would do. Here, on the boundaries of the parish, there is rough, poor land which could, with work, be turned to use. It had not been wildwood for a long time but no one had ever called it home. There were more people about than anyone could remember. It was time to do something new and here in a small way was a new world to conquer. That was Perch Hill: a fragment of America embedded in the wood. Its creator was a colonist.

Who knows how it went to start with? You can only look to the fields. Certainly those around the house, including the Toyland, have the wriggliest of boundaries.

They can only have been quickly cut, fitting around existing lumps or immovably big trees and then ossifying in position. The Long Field, which slivers down between the stream and the Middle Shaw, is not now as long as some of the others and so its name must record an earlier state, when it was indeed the long field in a group of tiny wood-cut enclosures. The Target Field beyond it is almost as round as the name might suggest and that too makes it feel early. Where they meet the wood on all sides, an old bank and ditch, dug by our man, still marks the boundary between them, the crucial separation of stock from growing trees. Only on the good corn ground on Beech Meadow would he have planted his first crops and there, in fact, is the mark of many centuries of ploughing: a thick belt of soil built up against the downhill hedge.

It was all here. All the ingredients of a self-contained world were here – shelter, wood, grass, water and corn. For almost a year I had been reading these things nearly every day, scanning them for the hints they might offer, the way they might whisper of the lives that had shaped them and the lives they had shaped in return. There was a community here of another kind. We had become neighbours with the dead.

But what about the life of those first men here? Search as you might, there is no autobiographical account in English of a farmer's life in sixteenth-century England. Diaries were not kept and destinies went unrecorded. But I came across someone else that winter who, for the time, had created a miracle of self-description. He was a Frenchman, a Norman, and not quite of the right class – he might have lived in Bateman's rather than Perch Hill – but his mentality seemed to match these fields and woods.

Gilles Picot de Gouberville was the *seigneur* of the small village of Mesnil au Val in Normandy in the middle of the sixteenth century. In every aspect of his life, except one, he was completely ordinary, conducting an existence which in its enclosure and untroubled stability was utterly typical of his time. One thing only marks him out. Between 1549 and 1562 – that is between the ages of 28 and 41 – Gilles de Gouberville kept a journal every day, writing between 10 and 30 lines, usually in the evening. He never missed a day, whether ill, tired or busy, and he never revised what he wrote. His diary, of which a couple of studies have been published, is the only surviving, non-literary, unsentimentalised and undistorted depiction of the life of a rural village in 16th-century Europe. Nothing in English can match it for the pristine, unmythologised quality of the life it depicts. This is rural existence in Europe before the urban began to distort it, a written portrait of an unwritten world.

Again and again, Gilles says simply 'Spent all day at home,' 'Here at home,' 'Here in the house.' His French editor doggedly counted the phrase 'I did not leave the house' 3,310 times in the 13 years, or on more than two-thirds of the days he records.

Gouberville has only an approximate idea of time. Things happen 'at some time in the morning', 'towards the end of the day', 'a little later on'. The clock had yet to become the master of the working life. Gilles had one, but he kept it upstairs so few people saw it. When someone asked him for it, he gave it away.

Gilles plods on day by day in the long rhythm of rural existence. The hay has to be in before the rain, the wolves driven from the flocks, the boars from the oats, the herons and woodpigeons into the nets. Everything is externalised, as though the conception of an internal private existence has not yet been invented. There is no intimacy, no self-consciousness beyond the fact of the journal itself, no feelings expressed, no sorrow or pain. The account is consistently modest and opaque. Although Gilles's life is surrounded and enmeshed with those in the village, he has no wife and no legitimate children. There are hints that he has an affair and possibly a child with a woman in the village, but that is not clear, and few women appear by name.

There is, however, a profound social fluidity to the way he lives. The farmhouse door is no barrier, but a thoroughly permeable membrane through which the village ebbs and flows. The people of Mesnil could visit Gilles even in his bedroom and he, with no great ceremony, sometimes came down to meet them still wearing his nightshirt, standing at the kitchen door or sitting at the kitchen table with them in front of the fire. On occasions, he wakes up to find villagers standing patiently by his curtained bedside, waiting for him to open his eyes so that he can tell them what he wants done. One day, in the summer of 1556, before he gets up, he buys a couple of pigs from a neighbour while still in bed.

His stone-flagged kitchen is the focus of village life. It is the only constantly warm room. In winter he gets dressed in front of the fire. That is also where he makes and receives any payments that are due. He occasionally sleeps there too and when convalescing, after several days in bed upstairs, he does so wrapped up in the warmth of the kitchen, where his neighbours come in for hot drinks or dinner.

If you read general histories of sixteenth-century Europe, the air is agonised, fraught with crisis, tensed with growing shortages of food and land, with the sense of repression and the expanding state, focused on the terrors and adrenaline of religious war and imperial ventures. But here, in the virtually pre-literate world of the Cotentin peninsula, some sense of wholeness prevails. This small-scale gentleman lives embedded in the milieu of his everyday companions. His half-brother and sister live in the house with him, his father's illegitimate children, occupying a lesser but still intimate place in his life. Alongside them are his right-hand man, Cantepye, from whom Gilles is rarely separated, Arnoul, the secretary of the *manoir* and La Joye, the lackey.

Outside this central knot, a wider circle revolves. The men who work on the tasks of farming life, the agricultural labourers, are named over and over again in the journal. They are not an undifferentiated mass, but individuals, known for who they are. Every summer the same reapers return for the harvest when more hands are needed, the same roofers, carpenters and masons return when repairs are needed to the mill or the roof of the *manoir* itself. A cooper lives and works in Mesnil and a blacksmith, Henri Feullie, who shoes the horses, puts bolts on the doors and makes hooks and sickles. When a new cart is needed it has to be ordered from further away, from the cartmaker Clément Ingouf who lives in the village of Montaigu. Every year for a few days, Thomas Girard, the travelling tailor, comes to stay at Mesnil, equipped with his cloth, his tape, his scissors, his needle and thread, to measure up Gilles and his household for suits of new clothes.

Gilles is clearly friends with people from a wide social background. There is no stiffness or formality in the way he deals with them. He is a particular intimate of a peasant farmer, Thomas Drouet, the sort of man who might have lived where I live now. Gilles is godfather to one of Drouet's daughters. Gilles and Drouet often work together in the tree nursery, the most treasured part of the estate, where the *seigneur* carefully tends and grafts his young fruit trees. When Gilles is ill, Drouet spends the night in his lord's bedroom to look after him; when Drouet himself has an attack of gout, Gilles visits him regularly at home.

Of course, Gouberville's odd and inexplicable journal marks the ending of the world it describes. On the cusp of self-consciousness, it hints, for all its descriptions of social cohesion, at the profound isolation of the individual, the diarist alone with his diary, which is the defining mark of the urban civilisation that was to come. People moan about suburbanisation of the countryside now; its first tendrils were already apparent in the Cotentin in the 1550s.

Could I translate Gilles to the Sussex Weald? Or perhaps Drouet? Would my Drouet here have spent time with the *seigneur* up in Brightling, tending to him, easy with him, living that webbed life of which I too had discovered the remnants here now in the late twentieth century? It is impossible to say, too much of a guess. But at least in the feel of grass, hedge, wood and stream, something of the same relationships to place must be there and repeatable, discoverable.

I knew, in particular, that in laying a hedge I might get somewhere near the people who had made this place. I signed up for a course run by the local Farming and Wildlife people. Book early, their flyer said, because places are limited, so I did, before Christmas, and eagerly acquired the necessary kit: leather gloves with gauntlet-type cuffs that run back up the arm, a bill-hook, amazingly £24 for what must once have been the commonest of tools, some long-handled loppers and a smallish axe.

I imagined the others coming on the course preparing themselves all over East Sussex. Then I rang the organiser to check the details. 'Oh, yes, Mr Nicolson,' he said ominously. 'The hedging course. Yes. You must have been reading my mind. I was just on the point of ringing. It's been cancelled. You're the only person who has applied.'

So much for the great revival of rural crafts. You spend your life thinking you are part of some widespread socio-cultural phenomenon only to find that everyone else has decided to pack up early and go inside for a cup of coffee. So I got in touch with a hedger off my own bat. Could he come here for a day? No problem. A gentle, definite voice. He'd come Sunday and he'd be there at 8.30.

In a cartoon version of these things, Boots, as he asked me to call him, would be a gnarled old oak-bole of a man, solitary as hedgers are meant to be, reluctant to make much of a speech out of things, more articulate with his hands than his words. Not Boots, despite the nickname. He is a words man, endlessly weaving talk into the practicalities of what he is doing, about his life as a smallholder and now a teacher at an agricultural college at the other end of Sussex, where he tells students how to drive tractors, use chainsaws, keep bees, grow vines, lay hedges.

He is one version, anyway, of the modern countryside: for many years before joining the college he lived off a six-acre smallholding (net income £10,000 p.a.) raising calves, growing courgettes for the Brighton wholesale market, producing the parsley whose final destination was along-side the sandwiches prepared at Gatwick Airport for first-class passengers. He used to harvest the parsley with an electric hedge-trimmer.

What a wonderful man! The day I spent with him laying a stretch of one of our hedges here was one of the best I have ever had. It was a frozen, exhausting day in the bitterest of east winds, with two coats on, two thick shirts, two T-shirts, hats down over our ears and Boots talking and talking away about the hedge and the plants and the way to do it and not to do it and the way other people did it and the way to put a point on a stake so that it enters the ground and is not split in the process. Over to the east the distant prospect of the fields towards Rye was a stepped succession of bleached-out greys. Above it, the crows from the wood tossed themselves up in the wind.

The hedge we chose was a length of overgrown black-thorn with a couple of hawthorns in it, full of mess and old grasses in the foot, threaded with the ropy cables of honeysuckle and and a big old briar poking up through the middle. 'That'll do,' Boots said, businesslike, with an air of straightforward competence. The whole day flowed like that. It is a gift that good teachers have, to make the arcane seem obvious, the delicate accessible and the skilled no more than a matter of carefully looking and then carefully doing what you have understood needs to be done. I remember Enoch Powell writing once that the greatest pleasure in life is the process, simply, of getting to know, the sense that your mind, even the whole of your life, is in a small way at that very moment enlarging, like an amoeba putting out a foot and flowing its whole body into and through that extension of itself. Here now with Boots, on the edge of the little field where we had grown our potatoes the previous summer, I felt myself getting to know how to lay a hedge. It was a ratchet clicking up, a stage which, once passed, could never be abandoned. We chose first some thick-stubbed hazels for the stakes and some thin whippy ones for the binders. There was nothing precious about the way he did it. Chainsaw in, sticks on to the field, sawn to a length, tied in a bundle. 'I'm not a traditionalist,' he said. 'I just want to get the thing done, get the light into the hedge, get it growing again at the bottom, make it a living stock-proof barrier. If it's easier to use modern tools that's what I'll do and that's what I'll teach you. If it's done right, it'll look right. You want to get it looking right. People always have. In the old days, that was nearly all they had. You could look at what you'd done and say "Yes, that's well done." It was a way of preserving your dignity when there wasn't very much else that was very dignified in a poor man's life.'

A neglected hedge is a chaos of competing plantlife, a tangle of thorn and deadwood whose energy and focus is at the top end. These are imprisoned trees. Their trunks are stretching out, aiming for the treehood their genes are demanding of them, but leaving the hedge gappy at ground level. A lamb could push between the little trunks and so that genetic destiny is what the hedger has to subvert. A laid hedge is nature slapped back into use.

It is a ruthless business, the precise opposite of the disengaged view that sees a hedged landscape as a comfortable duvet of rural contentment. Laying a hedge is, in vegetable terms, a form of organised savagery. 'You take two-thirds of the hedge out,' Boots said, and so we started to do exactly that, him cutting, me pulling the thorny, twisted shapes that emerged from the tangle. What had looked a reasonable and substantial thing in the early morning by lunchtime was thin and hopeless, neat enough but spindly. Then we started to attack what was left, cutting three-quarters of the way through each of the remaining stems. 'Leave just the bark and a little bit more,' Boots said, and one by one the blackthorns were folded over, laid low, constrained and contained. We staked them, each stake the distance from elbow to fingertip apart, and bound their tops with the hazel wands so that, in the end, in the Siberian cold of the early evening, what was left was a neat, twiggy basket line of living plants, stock-proof, resilient and with a future.

'You should be able to go on from there,' Boots said, packing up. 'I'll come next year and see how you've done.' So that's the challenge, deliberately and carefully thrown down: get the work done and do it right. The ancient folds over into a possible future.

SPRING BIRTHS, FELLED OAKS

At the petrol station in the village one day, just as that long first winter felt, perhaps, that it might be on the verge of turning into spring, I happened to look up at a mirror on the wall. It was a moment of self-revelation. A slightly unshaven man in his late 30s was standing beside the pumps, a rather old young man who, in common with many men of his age, was both a little bald and in need of a haircut. The hair that he had was so dirty that it stood up in peaks like whipped egg whites. He imagined, I suppose, that it looked romantically informal, a little windswept, perhaps even Byronic. It didn't.

He was wearing a pair of Argyll gumboots, which were muddy around the tops. The trousers of a baggy green corduroy suit were tucked into them. He seemed to be holding them up by putting his hands in his pockets. Under the jacket was what looked like a thick blue workman's shirt. He was putting diesel in a large green Land Rover, which did not, thank goodness, have a bull-bar encrusted with rally-lamps across the radiator but was coated in the splashed mud of which he was obviously proud and had not washed off since he had first bought the thing eight months previously. He must have thought that splash-on mud was the car equivalent of those aftershaves advertised by a picture of a man in a desert with the slogan: 'Adam Nicolson. Philosopher. Vulcanologist. *L'homme est rare . . .*' Pitiable. In the front passenger seat was a nice-looking but rather fat yellow Labrador staring out of the window like a son watching his daddy going off to war.

What on earth did this man think he was playing at? He looked like a farmer in a village pageant. No, worse. He looked like a man in a pageant who was pretending to be a farmer. There was nothing to be done about the Labrador or the Land Rover, but as soon as I got home I smoothed down my hair and changed into the jeans, jersey and brown dubbined shoes that more honestly identified me as the yuppy I am. I looked into the mirror, saw Nick Leeson and was happy.

Of course I was a yuppy, or perhaps an ex-yuppy, now redefined as a marshie (middle-aged rural-suburban hack) or landie (languorous attitudinising never delivers). An urban escapee in cords, I was, a lady from Radio 4's *On Your Farm* programme told me later that week, 'part of a general phenomenon'. The words she in fact used were:

'what sounds like the pantomimic quality of life at Perch Hill'. She claimed that our form of rural self-delusion was something that was happening all over the country, 'at least in the pretty parts'.

She threatened to come down and interview us here about our style of farming. I tried to put her off. 'We're not really farmers at all,' I told her, knowing that to be the truth. She took it for the most charming sort of false modesty. 'Oh come on,' she said, burbling slightly as only producers can. 'Why don't you simply let us come down, have a chat, look around a little and take it from there?' 'I don't think there'll really be enough to talk about for half an hour,' I said desperately, thinking in fact of the dreadful mess everywhere, the chickens in their slum conditions, the ducks in their state of permanent fox-induced anxiety, the ewe that was hobbling about with a bad foot that we couldn't clear up, the chaos of most of the woods, the mud, the mud, the mud. Did I want Radio 4 to see all this? No. It would be like an entire crew of inspecting mothers-in-law coming to stay for a week. Her laugh in response was the nearest to an aural tea-cosy that I have ever heard. 'Oh, really Adam, don't be silly.'

So she was coming. I felt sick and bogus. Sarah was furious. 'I'm not cooking them breakfast,' she said when I gave her the news. 'But they need breakfast for the background sound effects. It's got to sound like a farmhouse kitchen at 6.30 in the morning before we go out to milk the cows and survey the land or whatever it is real farmers do.' 'But you haven't been outside for the last three days.' 'I have. I went to the fish and chip shop.' She snorted and left the room. I had the dreadful premonition that when the day came, Sarah would remain sulking in bed while I was interviewed by Oliver Walston. I'd have to hiss and spit during his questions so that it would sound as if the bacon was cooking in the background. It was going to be hell.

I was in a quandary. What *was* my own view of what we were doing? Part of the time, I knew we were here to recreate a beautiful, traditional landscape, rich with the polycultural detail of orchard, coppice-wood, hop-garden, pasture and hay meadow that it would have had, say, in the 1870s. And part of the time I realised that was somehow absurd, a meaningless gesture towards a bogus historical accuracy. Why not do what you want to do? Why not make it what you want it to be?

Take, for example, our latest innovation, which had been met with hilarity and disbelief among the neighbouring farmers: sheep bells for the sheep. I found them in a perfectly straightforward agricultural supplies shop in the suburbs of Palma in Majorca, where they form an everyday part of a sheep farmer's equipment. We got three different sizes for three different notes and could now listen to our small flock as they prepared to lamb at the end of March, their bells rocking gently at the far end of the Target Field. It was beautiful but absurd, pure yupsville, Petit Trianon for the 1990s. Carolyn Fieldwick, the shepherd, looked at the sky when I mentioned them. I had yet to tell her that we were also thinking of dyeing the sheep multi-colours so that they would make a broken rainbow across the pastures, pointillist dots on the spread of green. Pretty country, not very 1870s.

There was a paradox I found it difficult to accommo-

date here. The recreated landscape, the landscape which
in some ways seems truest to the place, was in a sense the
most bogus of all options, the biggest lie. And the most
flippant and superficial of games, the parti-coloured sheep
and their bell music from the Mediterranean, were most
honestly representative of our own place here now, of our
distant, disengaged and in some ways voyeuristic relationship to the land. How honest was I going to be with the
people from the radio?

The day came. Oliver Walston, the most famous farmer
in England, arrived in his enormous grey Mercedes. The
jeans-and-tweed-jacketed, rumbustious, Old Etonian con-
troversialist, who stood with his shoulders back and his
chest out like a model of John Bull in a pub, treated Sarah
and me gently, even sweetly. It was captivating. His trick
was a sort of faux-aggressive manner which allowed him
to get away with murder. Where most people say charming things full of buried hate, he said things that should
have been hateful but were overflowing with care and
attention. Sarah and I both thought him wonderful.

'What are you?' he asked me over the radio breakfast –
the usual packet of Tesco's muesli had been hidden out of
sight and plates of agricultural plenty lay there between us
– 'a lily-livered, namby-pamby, dilettante aesthete floating about in a violet-tinted world of your own where you
want your sheep to be pretty colours and your hedges
fluffy? What have I got here, Marie Antoinette?'

'Yes,' I said and went off on to a long blague about the
beauty of beauty, how this farm's main crop now was
what it looked like, that there was nothing ignoble or
contemptible in that, that if this society were not inter-

ested in the making or saving of beautiful places, then there was little hope for it. The picture that emerged was of Sarah and me as ignorant amateurs bumbling around 90 acres of the Sussex Weald pontificating about what should and shouldn't be done to the landscape. In other words, a highly accurate portrayal.

Were we consistently inane? Probably. There was a bad moment when I embarked on a lecture discussing the rights and wrongs of nitrogen applied to grassland and all the virtues of no-input management systems. Did I know about soil structure? No. Did I know about the calorie intake required by a grazing cow? No. The biochemical relationship of clover and rye-grass under conditions of climatic stress? No. Nevertheless, I decided to inform a million Radio 4 listeners about those highly fascinating topics. It was the radio equivalent of an undrained bog.

Walston was like the helmsman of an ocean-going yacht watching someone repeatedly capsizing in a dinghy far below. The more I drowned, the more benign his face became. You had to admire the man. After he had gone, the late winter drear seemed even drearier than before: our moment of exposure and then the privacy folding back in.

'It's eight months of winter here,' Will Clark said to me on a dreadful day that February as we stood staring out of a window together at a garden that looked as if it belonged in the outskirts of Chernobyl. 'Yep,' he went on, when he saw from my face that I agreed too much. 'But it won't be long before we're making hay!' He said it smiling, knowing that neither he nor I believed a word of it.

It was March before the sun shone. When it appeared, I felt like bellowing hello at it, slapping it on the back and shoving a large glass of sherry into its hand, saying 'Come on, make yourself at home! Where the hell have you been all this time?' The first days of spring turn one into a brigadier in the East Sussex Yeomanry.

There's a story I always think of in the springtime that comes from one of the deep beech-lined valleys of the Béarnais Pyrenees. A young farmer lived right in the pit of the valley where, all winter long, the mountains above him cast their shadow. It was a place of mist and frost. One autumn he married his sweetheart from another village in another valley and brought her to his cold and shadowed house. They were poor and they struggled through the winter, seeing almost no one and eating no meat. Then, one March day, as he was pulling on his coat in the morning to go out to work, he told her to kill one of their rabbits and cook it, because a good friend was coming to dinner. She duly killed it and cooked it but was surprised to see him coming home at midday alone. 'Where is your friend then?' she asked rather shortly. He took her by the arm, and showed her the sunlight which just at that moment was touching their threshold for the first time since the autumn before.

It is the light that does it, that wash of light, as bleached in reality as the appearance of a midsummer landscape when you've been lying asleep with the sun on your closed lids and you open them to an oddly washed-out world, like a photograph that has been sitting too long on a windowsill. Even in its weakness, spring sunshine is so greedily drunk up. Why is that? I can't quite believe the craving for spring we all feel, so animal an instinct! Nor do I understand how it is that each year the winter seems to grow longer and deeper, the spring more hungered for and, when it comes, richer, more interesting, more of a stimulus, more dominant in the way one feels than it has ever been in your life before. It's as though, as you approach middle age, you become more seasonal, more wafted to and fro on these annual rhythms, less continuous in your life, more susceptible than ever to the conflicting claims of memory and desire. Can that really be the case?

For weeks we had been hunting about, looking for signs of spring. I found a primrose leaf in February the size of a fingernail but crinkled like a Savoy cabbage still half-underground. The grains of soil had folded the tip a little backwards. The hard emergent dagger leaves of the bluebells were pushing through the leaf-litter as if from individual silos. The cow parsley was already there in low, soft-edged pouffes about the size of a dinner plate at the foot of the hedges. Dog's mercury was everywhere in the woods, as well as lords and ladies, and the wild garlic already smelled culinary in the edge of Coombe Wood. One or two of its leaves, bright green, striped dark green, were up and out above the brown wood floor like the blades of soft-bodied assegais.

'That bloody garlic,' Ken Weekes called it. One year, after a winter like this one, when there was no grass left on the fields, the cows had pushed their way out of Target Field and into Coombe Wood, where they saw the alluring bright greenness of the garlic in the shadows. For half a day the cattle had grazed on the stinking shoots and had then come in to be milked. 'You couldn't even put your face in a churn,' Ken said. 'Phwaw. We had to chuck the lot for three days in a row.'

Apart from that, nothing. There were some leaves out on the honeysuckles and one or two on the elders, but the other trees remained tight and bound in. The hazels and the alders had their catkins dangling in the sunlight and as the breeze blew across them you could see the pollen stream against the light blowing away downwind. But the leaf buds were still hard and inscrutable, genetically wary of late frosts.

Each has its different manner. An oak bud is a heavily armoured thing, protected behind layer on layer of scales like a pangolin's tail. If you flake them off one by one, they come away dry and brown. Only in the very centre do you find the living green, smelling sappy, the minuscule point of protected life. A hornbeam bud surrenders more easily. A couple of flicks at the protective shell, it falls apart and inside you find the cluster of leaves each no more than a sixteenth of an inch long and covered in silky white hairs like a Labrador's ear. The shape of the future leaf is there. All that is missing is the material. Style precedes substance.

It is the ash, still months away from revealing itself, that is the most defended of all. Its black buds are shielded in points like a deer's hoofs. The outer scales are thick, pointed, firmly anchored and leathery. Pull them away and you find a little capsule of brown fluffy fuzz inside, exactly like rock wool. It is an insulation blanket wrapped around the growing point. Pull that off and you will reach an ash-frond in miniature, the whole frond half the size of a single in-bud hornbeam leaf, still clogged with bits of the rock wool. It is tentacled like a sea-anemone and looks as if it should belong on a coral reef. Such care, such details! Perhaps amazement isn't really enough of a reaction. But if not sufficient, it is at least necessary. That is what springtime is: gratitude married to amazement.

A double crisis, long predicted, and even longed for, started to close around our lives. That March, Sarah and the sheep were all, in a miraculous piece of synchronicity, on the point of giving birth at home. I was waking up with my teeth clenched. I was yo-yoing between between cow shed and sitting-room, sitting-room and cow shed, in a stew of vastly enlarged paternal concern. Twenty mothers in my care! Sarah and I had erected a six-foot-wide, four-foot-deep swimming pool in front of the fire in the sitting-room. All furniture had been pushed to the walls as though for a dance. One of her advisers on natural, anaesthesia-free childbirth had started talking in January about the benefits of placenta-soup. It was enough to turn a man vegetarian. By March 1st, Sarah had already had two full-blown 'It's coming' crises and those were some-how worse than the real thing. I felt in those Phoney War days as though I were a Battle of Britain pilot sitting on an armchair arranged next to the runway, my Mae West around my neck, nonchalantly smoking, while my insides were doing the can-can. Rosie, our two-year-old daughter, woke me up one morning to ask if I minded if she cut off my head with a carving knife. I said that would be fine.

Then there were the sheep. They were due to lamb in a couple of weeks but some were bound to be early. Luckily they were unable to say when they were having an 'I think it's coming' crisis. Or if that was what they meant by their bleating and shuffling at six in the morning, I just ignored it, gave them some more hay and told them to shut up.

It was vital that no hint of pregnant sheep came anywhere near pregnant wife for fear of disease spreading from one to the other. I have never washed so much in my life. Sitting in the kitchen, I had lessons from Carolyn Fieldwick, the shepherdess in boiler suit and woolly socks, telling me in precise and careful detail what I had to do. There would be the three-hourly, 24-hour-a-day inspections of the ewes from the beginning of March until mid-April. If I found one whose womb was prolapsing ('you'll see a very red, pinkish blob the size of a fist coming out'), I had to turn the ewe over, wind baler twine round her middle, 'push everything back in' and then tie it there with a special bit of kit I had to buy.

What if the lambs were coming out head but not feet first? Reach in to get the feet out but check that the feet belong to the lamb whose head you can see. Twins get muddled up together. Didn't Ted Hughes write a dreadful poem about pulling on a lamb so hard that its head came off in the womb? What if it was coming out backwards? What if the second lamb was all muddled up with the 'bag'? What do you do about the navel? What about triplets? How do you get triplets all to suckle? What if the mother dies? I was in a state of tense, exhausted paralysis.

The weather made it worse. March, it has to be said, is the most vindictive month. There is a catty, cold-blooded compassionlessness about the way it promises you everything and never delivers. March, in fact, is a liar. It lets you pretend for a while that England is a northern limb of that benign southern Europe where apricots coat the walls and life is lush and generous:

> Again and again we sigh for an ancient South,
> For the warm nude ages of instinctive poise,
> For the taste of joy in the innocent mouth . . .
>   (W.H. Auden, *In Time of War*, XXVII, 1938)

But March comes back, old and deceiving, turns the heat and benignity off, replacing Provence with Spitzbergen, and prunes away at the loose-limbed hopes the warmth had engendered. Spring had come, with its usual severity.

Three in the morning, two weeks later. I'm in the cow shed to see that the sheep are all right. The south-east wind is cruising in like a shark off the English Channel, ten miles away. It's coming in through the spaces at the top of the barn doors and out the far side. The water is frozen in the buckets.

The ewes are in here, 19 of them, as pregnant as a fleet of East Indiamen, laden to the gunwales, bulging with themselves. Some of them look as though they had a pair of saddlebags strapped around their middles and when they lie down, as they are now, their vast, filled midriffs pool out on either side in an ocean of motherhood and fecundity.

Their time is due. Roger, our Suffolk ram, now grazing with two young ram lambs in the field on the far side of the road, did well in the autumn. Only one old black ewe, well past her prime and possibly barren, is not in lamb. She's in the bull pen now and she looks out past the hurdle at the door with an air of abandonment and age. Her black wool is grizzled; she won't last the spring.

That's not what it's like in here. Despite the cold, despite their laden condition, the ewes are lying out across their thick bed of straw in pure horizontal contentment. We've fed them well, for weeks now, on quantities of ewe nuts. Half a ton has disappeared down their gullets, not to speak of two acres-worth of the hay we made last July in Beech Meadow, good 'blue' hay, meaning there is still a certain greenness to it even at the tail end of the winter. The sheep have had nothing but the best and they look marvellous on it. There is something about them which reminds me of a plateful of gnocchi, a rounded warmness, comfort made flesh. Their chins are lifted in the attitude of sheep at ease and a low snorting sort of snoring is coming from their nostrils. The expectant mothers are happy.

One has already done what she needs to do and is over the other side in an individual pen with her lamb. It was Sunday lunchtime. She had been shuffling about all morning, looking, as Peter Clark so precisely described it, 'a little sheepish', and then during lunch must have delivered.

We found her with the lamb still smeary with the membranes at her feet and the afterbirth still hanging from her. It was all so normal, so griefless, so prosaic in its way, so without agony that it now seems absurd that I should have gone in for so much apprehension. This was as it should be: ewes in good condition deliver easily and have the appearance afterwards of nothing having happened.

I picked up the lamb to put her in the pen. The little thing felt just as if someone had broken eggs all over the wool. The ewe followed us. They licked and nosed each other. A lamb is a survival machine: a big head, a big mouth and four stocky black legs way out of proportion to the sack of a body which joins these standing and eating parts together. The ewe had a full udder, and the lamb soon found its way to suck, wriggling its tail, the instinctive drive at work, the vital colostrum running into the gut. Survival.

A sheep has no face, no screen on which its mental state can be read as ours can in such detail and with such immediacy. You look at a sheep and see a certain blankness: no pleasure, no pain, no grief, no anger, no delight, no regret. But if there's no face, you can at least read its body and, unlike the sisters still waiting for their birthing moment so relaxedly in their communal pre-crèche, the mother with its lamb was obviously in a state of acute anxiety. For 24 hours after the birth, whenever I came in to see how the lamb was doing – my own anxiety, needing this thing to survive, not to die on me, not this first one – I found the mother standing alert, eyes big, defensive, stamping her front feet as I approached the pen or picked up the lamb to look at the navel and the shrivelling cord or to feel its, gratifyingly, filling belly. The ewe is tensed to protect her own. She is a servant of her genetic destiny. Her life can only be dedicated to these fragile, transitional moments on which so much hinges. So this instant, in the pen with the hours-old lamb, with the tautened presence of the protective mother, this is one of those moments when you come close to 'the blood of the world', to the essential juices running under the everyday surface of things, when the curtain is drawn back and you find yourself face to face with how things are.

A day afterwards, Sarah gave birth to our second daughter. The contractions began the evening before. I half-slept, waking, stoking the fire, sleeping again, refilling the pool with warm water, and Sarah bathed there throughout the night, calm and easy. The midwife came at about six. By nine in the morning the whole process had steepened and deepened. In quite a sudden way, with the growing contractions, it reached a huge and passionate intensity. She looked in this extremis like one of the Sibyls on the Sistine Chapel ceiling, a vast being in pain. I could hardly recognise her. I was amazed by it. The sheer hurt of the delivery seemed at times to balloon out from her to fill the whole room, the whole house, the whole of here. She was shouting louder than I had heard anyone shout before. Human birth, when seen at home, when suffered by someone you know and love, when not dulled or interfered with by the dislocations of hospital and its comprehensive anaesthesia, is a vast and violent thing. A husband, an observer, can do little but stand and watch, gormless in his irrelevance, awed by the sort of instinctive courage this moment summons, bewildered by the sheer scale of an experience which little else in life can match and finally swept away and dissolved in the relief of its ending, its happy ending in a daughter who was well and who would survive. Sarah and Molly were well. But why should it be like this? Why should human birth take such a toll? Why can't a woman give birth like a ewe? At just after ten in the morning, Molly was born into the water of the pool, scooped up and out on to Sarah's breast and I wept with the relief of it. An hour later they were both in our bed and I put flowers all round them and branches of hazel cut from the wood, a bower for my family.

This of course was how it should be, an unbroken transition from womb to life, and as I looked at Molly that morning, still blinking in the shock of her extra-uterine existence, I realised that in some ways she was still being born.

Only one Molly, but endless lambs. By the time she was a week old, ten of the ewes had given birth and they had delivered 18 lambs. Most had been twins, but there had been a set of triplets and one or two singletons. Only one lamb, one of a pair of black twins, had died, a week after Molly's birthday, at breakfast. It had been born the afternoon before and looked all right to start with, if very small, and I didn't notice anything the matter when I checked at about midnight and again at five the next morning. But at eight o'clock I found the poor black thing suddenly crashed out and hopeless, lying all wrong on the straw, its body too heavy for itself. When I picked it up, the head hung down at the end of a muscleless neck and its body slumped in my arms like a little Pietà.

We brought it into the kitchen to warm it up and bottle-feed it. The milk went in and it seemed to be swallowing but that can only have been an involuntary impulse; the animal was already virtually dead. It had probably gone too far by the time I found it, for some reason neglected by its mother overnight, even though it had been feeding well enough in the evening. Its heart was still fluttering when I first picked it up in the morning but within half an hour the pulse had gone and its whole body had moved across the unnoticed line between 'ill' and 'dead'. We buried it near a ewe that had died the previous autumn. The dribbled bottle-milk was still coating its chin in a veined white slick as the lumps of clay fell and bounced on the body.

Death at lambing is only to be expected. In fact, we got away lightly. The ewes were all fine and the rest of the lambs well and lusty. The Fieldwicks, with 400 ewes, which were not meant to have started lambing until April, had already lost four of them. They had simply been found dead in the field. The year before, for no reason they could tell, they had 60 barren out of the 400 and trailerloads of dead lambs carted away to the tip. This for them was the anxious time. The week before, a ewe had been delivered of triplets prematurely. One of them had died almost straight away. The second needed bottle-feeding, the third was sucking well from its mother. Two nights later Carolyn found the ewe herself dead in the field. She had rolled over and crushed the one lamb that was making a go of it. The prospect of exhaustion and failure hung around the whole business. I could only thank God that this was not the way I earned my living. I knew young farmers around here, struggling in the grip of this, man and wife working all hours, crucified on the cost of the grass keep, with quota only for a small proportion of their flock, their young teenage children dragooned into helping when they would otherwise be at school, the strain telling on everyone's face. I was always amazed at how young these old-looking people were. People I thought of as ten years older than me turned out to be

ten years younger. I felt coddled by comparison, padded
by the softness of a sort of life which their whole life's
work might in the end bring them as a reward, if it went
well, if they stuck at it, if disaster did not pick away at
their sliver-thin margins.

The survival rate of lambs, the cost of rations for the
pregnant mothers, the condition of ewes after lambing:
these things are the determining factors in what their lives
would be like this year, next year and for ever. To be so
dependent on the uterine workings of another species! I
said to one of them one day, his face taut with exhaustion,
what hell the life of a small, under-capitalised sheep farmer
must be. It was a mistake. He sat up, flicked his head half
sideways in the way a cockerel might, and said 'Why?
What's wrong with it? I like my life. I like it a damn sight
more than I'd like yours.' We are all tender in the same way.

For us, though, it was the sweetest of times. Rosie
played among the lambs. They danced and pranced
together in the orchard outside the house. Molly peeked
like a mouse from her swaddlings. Tom, William and Ben
cradled their sister in turn and the lemon-yellow sun
shone on our lives.

A few weeks before Molly and all those first lambs were
coming to life, I had 40 oak trees cut down. We wanted
them for a building, to restore the oast, the other side of
the yard from the house. Forty oak trees! I could imagine
them growing in the sort of open circular grove the
Greeks would have admired, gradually filling out over
the course of this century, swept by the wind, a grassy
lawn beneath them. And I had them cut down.

In fact, I never saw them standing. They had been growing in a wood at Ashburnham, a few miles south of here, and I could imagine the rawness their removal left, a stretch of land looking like a gum feels after a tooth has been drawn: the awful, shocked absence at the site, a ragged-edged nothing where something should be, a place whose gruesome softnesses your tongue can only tentatively explore.

I first saw our trees in the timber yard belonging to Zak Soudain a few miles away from here near Broad Oak. The wood was still wet and very green, as the word is, although the real colour of sodden, recently felled oak is an orangey yellow that verges on pink. Where a chisel hacks at it, flaking the fibres of the wood, the nearest thing to green oak that I've ever seen is the raw flesh of a salmon. The lichen was still growing on the bark of the enormous, horizontal trees as they lay in Zak's yard, so you could still tell which had been the sunny southern side and which the northern when they had been standing in the wood. Despite that, though, the oaks had already moved over from one side of the equation – the handsome shape of the living tree – to the other, a dignified after-life as timber.

I didn't feel a trace of regret about having the trees felled at the time, and still don't, only excitement at what was to become of them. The new building was to have a green oak frame and be clothed in oak weatherboards. The structural techniques, the joints used and the material of which the building was made were all identical to those used to put up the farmhouse 400 years ago, the hay barn about 180 years ago and the original oast-house about 130 years ago. Every one of these buildings has used the local oaks for their main structural members. Our new building would be the fourth time in four centuries that someone at Perch Hill Farm would have had a fair stand of oak trees felled and put to use. And each time the woodland has not been lost but cropped.

There is rationale to those time intervals. They are governed by the market. Each of the moments that one of these buildings was put up marks a period of optimism and expansion in the farms of the Sussex Weald. In the sixteenth century, as prices rose under population pressure, it became profitable to farm even the more marginal lands like our wet, woody clays: time for a new farmhouse at Perch Hill. In the Napoleonic Wars, blockades created shortages and shortages created cash for suppliers: time for a new barn. In the 1860s, booming populations demanded oceans of beer, railways allowed national distribution and hops became the new cash crop: time for an oast-house at Perch Hill.

And now? The market is no longer in such obvious commodities. Hops, corn and milk can now only be produced commercially on a scale to which this landscape has been unable to adapt. Ten years ago there were five active dairy farms on our lane. Now there is none. The only crop this landscape can viably produce is beauty and the only thing it can sell is itself. It is doing that very well. New money from the cities has arrived and once again, in a green-oak building, Perch Hill is getting the reward it deserves. Ever since this farm was first cut from the forest, the market for its produce has been urban. There is no radical break with the past in what we are doing. This is the Perch Hill way: an influx of urban money means green oak buildings, built to last for centuries. The 1590s, the 1810s, the 1860s, the 1990s: these are the blips on the graph, the moments Perch Hill takes another step forward.

To begin with – doesn't everybody begin the story of a building project with that phrase? – all was marvellous. The trees were cut into the shapes required for the giant frame. Others were sliced by a cheese-paring saw into the long, feather-edged weatherboards that were to clad the walls. The money we had would be enough. We saw the building changing day by day, the holes for windows opened, the brickwork growing for the new upper storey to the roundel. But then, creepingly, apparently unawares, delays began to appear. People wouldn't turn up. Alterations turned out to cost much more than expected. An air of catastrophe hung above the scheme. Its noise and disturbance began to eat at our sense of well-being.

One day that summer, a minibus full of semi-antique ladies from Bexhill, most of them wearing the kind of maroon felt hats that look as if they should be the central structural element in one of Delia's Light Afternoon Sponges, pulled up outside our farm gate. The bus had parked just opposite the chaos of our building site. The job was now many, many weeks late. Mess lay everywhere. No one was at work.

The tour leader on the bus, microphone in hand, pointed out of the window at our building and said, 'There you have one of the old oast-houses of Sussex and Kent in which, in the old days, they used to dry the old hops. Lovely things, you could always smell the drying

hops for miles away downwind.' The bus aahed. 'But
many farmers,' he went on, 'are now finding oast-houses
rather inconvenient and, as you can see here, are dis-
mantling them to make way for more suitable buildings.
It's a shame but many farmers are struggling to make a
living in this part of the country and after all it is a free
world.'

I stood there in my gumboots and my rather stylish
leather jerkin, listening to this open-gobbed. The Fruit
Compôtes in the bus in front of me all turned their
attention from the building – which was costing as much
as a Ferrari Testarossa to put up, entirely funded by some
particularly acute investments I had made in the 1980s,
the farsightedness of Barclays Bank, Hammersmith and
the blessed generosity of my own father – and, in a single,
coordinated gesture of patronising benevolence, directed
14 pairs of twinkling glacé cherry eyes on me. I had to
turn away.

What was done of the building was, on the whole,
beautifully done. If you could ignore the fact that, six
months after it was due to be complete, it was still
unfinished, that the pointing of the new brickwork
seemed to have been done by someone who had only
ever previously worked with play-dough, that there were
no doors, that the windows had no catches, that there
was no floor upstairs, that four of the seven lights they
installed one week were not working the next and that my
brother-in-law thought the whole pitch of the roof was
wrong, it was really very good indeed.

There was the slight problem that the two charming
men who were meant to be the main contractors on the

job, and whom we engaged only because they were so attractive (one in a rather saturnine, agonised, Über-mensch-under-strain way, one a fresh-faced male version of the freckled English rose), had fallen out with each other so badly that they were on the brink of a vicious legalo-financio-emotional-hurt-and-betrayal dispute which might or might not have ended up in court. The saturnine one of the pair, who had a Heathcliff-goes-clubbing look to him, and wore a sort of silver anorak that seemed to have been cut from the fuselage of a 1952 USAF strato-cruiser, had arrived on site with a new black eye on two different eyes in two consecutive weeks and had said both times that he had walked into his car door the previous evening.

All that aside, the job went rather well. The blips and hiccups, the overruns and punch-ups, the walkings-off the job, the mysterious disappearance of a septic tank one night or the discovery that the oak floorboards we had already paid for were so wet that if they had been nailed down in that condition they would all have buckled into a model of the North Dakota badlands within a couple of months, all that was nothing more than what you might expect. That was what life should be like – a little spurty, free enough to go wrong.

No one else could understand this point of view, particularly Sarah and the bank manager. Mainly to satisfy them, I did, on a couple of occasions, lose my temper with Heathcliff-in-clubland. It was cynically done. I was at the end of my tether anyway and it seemed to me that screaming at the poor man down the phone was better than kicking the dogs/cats/sheep/ducks/chick-

ens/walls/children and would go down well with the wife.
It didn't have the right effect at all. Heathcliff came
round, explained the problem away perfectly and looked
hunkier than ever. Sarah ended up admiring him more
than me and I thought for an alienated minute they were
going to go out together that evening to a fantastic place
he knew in Croydon – 'brilliant, it's a warehouse which
has been lined inside with the façade of a Renaissance
château'. The job continued to progress at an inch a
week.

There was one little thing about the building which
remained a niggle, which ran against the lovely freedom-
is-beauty gospel to which the whole of the farm had
become dedicated. The new building had two bathrooms
in it, one upstairs and one down. Both had large windows
opening on to a view of a grassy bank and, over to one
side, the chicken slum where the three survivors out of
our original flock of 20 hens and one cockerel were
scratching out their tragic lives. Both these windows
opened fully. This is one of the breeziest places in Sussex
and there is never any shortage of fresh air. If you had
your priorities upside down, and if things ever turned
financially disastrous, this would be a prime spot for a
wind farm.

Despite the natural gush of air past our fully opening
windows, despite the fact that we would probably like to
open those windows to enjoy the sort of air that we had
come here for, we were obliged to install in each bathroom an electric extractor fan. They are ugly little things,
plastic, louvred squares which turn on when the light
turns on. I hated everything about these fans: the look of

them, their noise, their enforced presence, their waste of
money – £40 each – their attitude, above all, of tidying up
our lives for us. I could imagine lying in the bath in the
future looking up at the fan whirring its little whir above
me and thinking 'Go away, I hate you.'

It was the 1991 Building Regulations (1995 Edition)
Part F (i) which required me to install these little things. It
was all to do with 'interstitial condensation' – or damp in
the rafters. I couldn't, first of all, be trusted to open the
windows myself, which was irritating in itself. But from
talking to the Rother District Council Building Control
Officer, it became clear that this little plastic imposition
was symptomatic of a much larger phenomenon. Houses
used to breathe. Surfaces and materials were in some ways
permeable to the wet, there was more of a flow between
inside and outside. Then came central heating, then the
requirement to preserve more of the heat so expensively
created, then thick insulating materials, then what the
R.D.C.B.C.O. called 'the house like a kettle', all the hot
wetness from kitchens and bathrooms held within this
sealed container. Then came the requirement for the
electric fans because people could no longer be trusted
to open their windows and break the precious seal.

It was the classic example of the way in which people
had removed themselves from their natural environment.
Every step follows logically from the one before until you
suddenly look round and find you are halfway up a cliff
and don't like the feeling at all.

It is not that it is ugly; a light switch or a plug is ugly
and I don't mind them. The fan was horrible because it
was the mark of alienation, of a sterilised, cut-off tight-

ness, of a ludicrously unnatural way of regulating your life, of over-prescription, of denying yourself the feeling, that wonderful summer feeling, of the breeze against the skin, which is one of the reasons you are alive in the first place. So once the fans were in, I took them out and I felt the building, the beautiful, creaking, appallingly expensive, debt-creating, naturally sweet-smelling, oaky heaven of a building, sigh with relief.

It is in that fan-free place that I have written this book. I live with the wood day by day. The timber dries and as it dries it shifts. As it shifts it splits and as it splits it creaks, as though the whole thing were springing apart. From time to time, unexpectedly, at a quiet moment, the whole frame creaks, not in an old or easy way but with a sudden, high-pitched jerking under stress, a shriek of wood, a spasmodic movement, in the way that earthquakes happen. Over many months or even years, the tension builds and then, bang, catastrophe theory at work, it becomes too much. The pieces move not with an easy, oiled constancy, but in a little convulsion, a twitch.

That moment sounds not wooden at all, but polystyrene. You might hear in that agonised squeal the sound of all the torture that preceded it, a final, desperate outburst of the wood under strain, its elasticity stretched quite literally to breaking. Every time it happens, I look up at the jowl-posts and tie-beams, at the scissor brace in the apex of each truss, and see nothing. The building, an invisibly clenched and tense thing, where the fibres in the timbers are tightening and stretching against the pegs that hold them together, remains inscrutable. It looks stiff, solid, immobile, as reliable as buildings are meant to be. 'What, me?' those impassive beams ask, as I interrogate them about the noise they've just made. 'Can't you see, we are what we always were?'

IN DEEPEST ARCADIA

As spring thickened into summer, and both the hay and the corn started to coat the country in a deep green pelt, sex – or at least sexiness – began to leak and seep out into the fields and their hidden corners. The height of early summer turned into the most lustful moment of the year. Driving down Willingford Lane in those lush green weeks, dropping from Burwash Weald to the bridge over the Dudwell and then up through the outer patches of Dallington Forest, moving from sun to shade and back again, past our farm and on towards Brightling, you would find cars parked in the evening in the tucked-in gateways, reversed half out of sight among the cow parsley, an air of privacy and closure about them.

They were always young men's cars, the sets of wheels that could be afforded rather than desired: a rusting Escort estate, a brown Capri, and never anyone visible in them. Each one was a strange prefiguring of the way those old men's cars, the brown Granada, the 'Autumn Gold' Austin Vanden Plas with walnut trim, were always parked on similarly beautiful evenings, not in the quiet corners but at the viewpoints, on the Downs and the higher places in the Weald, the bonnets aimed at the landscape, the old man and his wife sitting calmly in the two front seats watching Sussex as though it were an intermission in Thursday night TV. They pass the thermos, the wife worries about the children, the dog farts silently on the back seat and the husband thinks his lustful thoughts about his youth and all those never-confessed-to lovers. 'Men are April when they woo, December when they wed: maids are May when they are maids, but the sky changes when they are wives.' *As You Like It*, the route-map to the pastoral idea.

June is the month for outdoor lust, now as it always has been. The famous song sung by the two pages in *As You Like It* is a precise description of the sexual habits of the rural working class in early modern England:

> It was a lover and his lass,
> With a hey and a ho, and a hey nonino,
> That o'er the green cornfield did pass . . .
> Between the acres of the rye,
> With a hey and a ho, and a hey nonino,
> These pretty country folks would lie.

Everything about this is accurate: they make their way right to the other side of the growing cornfield, away from the invigilating police state of the sixteenth-century village, and there find the privacy they crave. You hardly ever see rye growing in England now, but it is the lovers' crop *par excellence*, six feet tall by the middle of June, a wall of protective green. 'With a hey and a ho, and a hey nonino' sounds innocent but it isn't. 'Nonino' is sixteenth-century for 'a bit of the other' and even 'hey' has a lustful tinge to it. In Shakespeare, the word 'country' is always enriched by the pun it contains. The whole movement of the song, through the fluffy acres of the fields and on into the safe and private lying place, is sexual. It is a hymn to sex as summer heaven.

It is easy to forget how thick with all this the landscape still is. I was looking that year into the history of the woods that surround our farm, the woods that formed the rich and numinous background to all Kipling's *Puck of Pook's Hill* stories. That was my idea of them, the source of a psychic magic in which Kipling revelled, until I began to ask in the village about what the woods had been like before the war. The old men I spoke to would begin politely enough, mention their work in the wood, the trees that had once grown there, but their eyes would light up, narrowing and brightening at the same time, when they talked about 'going courting' in High Wood, no better place in the summer than High Wood or Leggett's Wood, the mossy banks in the old sunk roads, the open ground beneath the beeches where you could spread your coat on a bed of bracken, the beech mast being too crinkly and spiky if it's under a person's back, and you don't want them to feel uncomfortable, do you, you don't want them distracted by the prickles . . .

Those beech trees remain the poignant memorials, standing huge and isolated among the twiggy birches. One of the beech trees, in particular, is an incredible being, a balloon, in the newness of summer, of fresh lime-juice-green leaves, with two tennis courts of shade beneath its branches. The muscled limbs are clothed in elephant hide and the dress of windblown leaves acts the feminine to that massive masculinity. Of course it is the place for seduction.

The trunk is carved with the initials of forgotten lovers. The bark is cracked and pitted inside the rough-cut serifs and the places where an O or a C have thickened with time. Here and there, moss inhabits the carved-in words. Hearts enclosing girls' initials have been stretched so wide by the swelling of the tree that they look like one of those grinning grimaces made by five-year-olds, fingers hooked in the corners of the mouth and dragged out sideways across the width of the face. Inside that gruesome cartouche, the initials are now illegible, pulled beyond understanding, no more than a smeared-out mark which the tree has done its best to erase.

It all brought back memories of outdoor love affairs decades ago, that odd sensation of the breeze in unexpected places, the disaster with my first-ever girlfriend, on a hillside in northern Spain. She was an Argentine; I hardly knew her. She had no English to speak of and so we scarcely spoke except in inadequate French. 'Don't hurt me,' she said that afternoon as I was looking over at the view and I thought she meant I must not treat her badly, as all the signs were surely pointing in that way. 'I won't,' I said solicitously. 'No, don't hurt me,' she said with a little more emphasis and I equally fiercely said I wouldn't, of course. 'No, NOW,' she screamed in my ear and pushed me away. It turned out that the way I was leaning on her was pressing her far shoulder into a small, invisible but obviously rather prickly thistle. We never really recovered from that moment of miscomprehension.

At Perch Hill, the thistles were well into their wild annual career and I didn't like it. From my desk, I could look out across the rising bulk of the Cottage Field towards Coombe Wood. The field looked wonderful, a perfect sward, next winter's hay in the making, as invitingly edible as a plate of rocket and watercress salad. But the appearance was a lie; its reality was a nightmare of weeds. Walk across it and the luxurious softness disappeared. Your boots crunched at each step as if on shingle but what you were treading were thistles, many thousands of them, still little more than horizontal rosettes at this stage, nestling invisibly in the grass but soon to start their growth upwards. Where there were no thistles there were docks, and where there were no docks there were nettles; where there were no nettles there were brambles, and where there were no brambles, there were dande-lions.

Before we came here, I had a supremely haughty attitude to grassland. If, walking around England, I came across fields like ours, I would have one of two remarks to pass. It was usually: 'Poor management, *very* poor manage-ment. They don't really know what they are doing.' The fact that I didn't know what they were doing, or what they were meant to be doing, or what I would have done in the circumstances, or what sort of management history would lead to this sort of weed problem, did not stop me from passing judgement. I now realised why farmers hated people like me.

At other times I would say, 'Of course a weed is just a frame of mind.' That saying exists in the same sort of sententious mental lay-by as those notices at the entrances to US National Parks: 'Take nothing but memories, leave nothing but silence, speak nothing but peace.' I once picked up a sandstone pebble in the titanic desert emptinesses of the Utah Canyonlands – it was beautiful, with the ripples of a red Jurassic beach on its surface – only to have it confiscated by a National Park Service Ranger, a woman with brown curly hair and a revolver, on the basis that I was 'disinheriting the generations that come after'. Forget *objets trouvés*; they have slipped beyond the bounds of the acceptable.

There is an idea that at one time, when the people of this country were still at home with the ways of nature, the plants we now see as weeds, of which we know nothing, were seen in their true light, useful as food or medicine. Nettles cured stomach upsets and made excellent cloth; the fruit of the bramble has been found in the stomachs of Stone Age men preserved in Irish bogs; young thistle stems, blanched and peeled, were eaten like the heart of an artichoke and were said in the sixteenth century to be 'sovereign for melancholy'.

That is the side you always hear about nowadays, yet another measure of our fall from grace. But it is no more than half of it. Anyone who has read that wonderfully encyclopaedic treasure-house, *The Englishman's Flora* by Geoffrey Grigson, a work of love and scholarship from which everyone else has always cribbed whatever knowledge they pretend to have, will get the fuller picture. It provides a strange enlightenment.

Every year parts of the Middle Shaw are dominated by the dreary, tiny-flowered, big-leaved plant called dog's mercury. It looks boring, it's not useful, it's a weed and it seems to outcompete bluebells. But what about that elegant, alluring name? Until I read Grigson I always thought I must be missing something about this plant. Not at all. This woodland mercury is a perennial, highly poisonous, both emetic and purgative, one of the lowest of the low, good only for dogs. Dog's mercury means 'rubbish mercury', 'weed mercury'. What a liberating recognition that is! The name reveals that pre-modern people hated weeds too. Grigson lists 70-odd names of wildflowers which have this dismissive 'dog' element in them: dog jobs, dog-cock, dog's mouth, dog stalk and so on. As for cow parsley, which was then appearing on the banks of the lane and which everyone loves, that too is a historically despised thing, its tauntingly full but useless growth associated with the devil. It's the devil's parsley in Cheshire, dog parsley in Hertfordshire, gipsy's parsley in Somerset, hare's parsley in Wiltshire.

From admiration to contempt, from exploitation to at least local extermination, the historical attitude to wild plants covered the full range. Po-faced piety about the natural order didn't get a look in. So, I said to Ken Weekes one morning, what shall I do about the thistles?

'Hammer them,' he said. 'Hammer them as hard as you like.' So that's exactly what we did. Will Clark drove the tractor, I bought a giant flail topper with a nine-foot cut and Will, in sweep after sweep, beheaded every one in every field. It felt as good as doing the washing-up.

One morning that summer a man knocked on the back door. He wore a sort of yellowish canvas coat with a corduroy collar and took his muddy shoes off with deliberation before coming to sit down in the kitchen. He had something of an ex-naval air: affable, polite, attentive.

He too, he told us, looking at the half-wreck of the oast-house outside, had gone in for building works. Oh the headaches! He had discovered terrible subsidence and had been forced to pour money into a hole in the ground, far more money than he had. That was the reason he was now working for Orange, for Hutchison Telecom. Eyebrows up. His job was to find sites for the masts that would give the Orange network the coverage it had to provide. Would we be interested?

'Tell me about it,' I said, thinking, 'No, not here, never.' He showed us a series of photos of the masts, 50 feet high, surrounded by things that look like giant chest freezers around the base, enclosed within a chain-link anti-vandal fence and surmounted by the aerials: big, dominant and ugly.

The poor man made no attempt to pretend they were anything other than dreadful. His word, in fact, was 'beastly'. He was charming, disarming even. I wondered, but didn't ask, if this was the trained technique: spit the worst out early on, show them you understand what they are frightened of and then offer the blandishments. So what would the deal be?

'We'd make an agreement for ten years,' he said. 'We'd rent a patch of ground ten metres by ten metres from you, and we usually offer £1,250 a year for that.' My face looked like a slot machine as the dollar signs rolled. £12,500 for a patch of Beech Meadow 30 feet square? Oh yes.

'We had the Mercury man round here last year,' I said, lying, repeating something someone else had said to me about a visit to their farm months ago. 'He offered £2,000 a year.' 'I thought that might be the case,' our Orange rep said, 'and obviously, as an annual tariff, we'd have to match that. Yup. And we could say that it should rise with inflation.' Already £20,000. And he might go up a little more if I dug my heels in. But I was mucking him about. I never had the slightest intention of having such a monstrosity looming over our fields. It would be like putting callipers on the leg of a child.

'Now this is the bit I don't like,' the rep said, smiling like an old friend. 'It always sounds threatening but it's not meant to be. If you don't agree to have the base station on your land, I'll have to go to your neighbours and see what they make of it. And obviously, if they think it's a good idea, I'll be going ahead with it with them. You do understand, don't you?'

Oh Jesus. There is a thin sliver of land that runs through the middle of the farm which we don't own. Its owner lives miles away. The prospect lurched up of a 50-foot hideosity on the bank above the farm and no compensation.

We both allowed the talk to burble on around this aching pothole. He mentioned 'statutory obligation to establish a national network'. I mentioned that this was statutorily an Area of Outstanding Natural Beauty. He knew that and said about planning applications being granted on appeal by the Secretary of State. I said that if we didn't want it, we'd do everything in our power to stop it happening, and I meant everything. He said he understood and I said, smiling, shaking hands, opening the door, that I'd be in touch.

I wasn't. He rang, but I wasn't in. He wrote, offering 'to sugar the pill with some modest improvement on the annual fee of £2,000 I suggested and possibly throw in an Orange, with a year's basic tariff (15 free minutes a month). At least it should work well!' I didn't reply but I guessed that his other options were somehow closing and that waiting was working. Then, months later, the letter we wanted. The radio engineers, with their 'computer modelling tools' had decided that somewhere 'further west' would better suit their purposes. Cheers at breakfast. The future's bright? The future's Orange? Not here it wasn't.

While dreading the irruption of Orange into our lives, seeing wherever I went the spectacular unregulated ugliness of the mobile phone towers (and enjoying for the first time all the pleasure of having a mobile phone myself), I had been looking forward to something else, not the disruption of the local by the national but in many ways its opposite: the 49th Annual Heathfield and District Agricultural Show. I had been asked to be one of the judges. The invitation had arrived months before from the charming Mrs Berger, Hon. Trade Stand Secretary, and as soon as I opened the envelope, I knew that, as far as the Weald of Sussex was concerned, I had arrived. A Heathfield Show Judge! It was the OM, the CH and the DBE of Wealden life all rolled into one.

For weeks, I was modest about it at parties but privately triumphant. The badge, a hexagon of stiff, burgundy-coloured cardboard with the word 'JUDGE' stamped on it in gold, came through the post and I tried it out in front of the long bathroom mirror with a variety of different suits and ties. Dark blue was obviously wrong. Hairy Harris tweed was absurd for early summer. It could only be the cowpat-green corduroy. Come the day, I immediately realised that my fellow judges were more impressive – I want to say realistic-looking – than me. John Bines Esq. was once a government expert on the feeding of dairy cattle and then Chief Executive and Secretary of Newbury and District Agricultural Society. Mrs Valerie Chidson was Chairman of the Wealden District Council. She had, of course, unrivalled local knowledge and wore a great badge around her neck like a mayor, with a long flamboyant apricot and orange silk scarf floating above it. I was described in the programme as 'A. Nicolson Esq., Journalist' which looked disreputable. Why not 'landowner, landscape theorist and visionary?' That word 'journalist', it's no good. I was told by an insurance agent once that I should never, ever mention what I do. Only 'fairground booth operator', he told me, was considered a more dangerous risk.

Anyway, Mr Bines, Mrs Chidson and I, in a couple of

hours, were walked around the 200-odd stands of the
show. They were laid out in broad, muddy streets across a
hillside outside Heathfield. The setting-up day had been
rainy and the trucks had turned the field into a quagmire.
But now the sun was shining on the stands and tents; on
the enormously fat horses being trotted up and down by
enormously fat men in suits; on the Side Saddle Concours
d'Elégance where double chins wobbled beneath antique
veils; and on the Heavyweight Hunter class, capable of
carrying 14 stone and over, which Miss S. Waddilove had
come down from Newmarket to judge, along with the
other Ridden Hunters.

In the cattle rings, the junior handlers, the boys and
girls, were struggling with their recalcitrant calves. 'Will
you bloody well come on!' one tiny boy in his pristine
white coat said out of the corner of his mouth to his even
tinier black and white Friesian calf, which was going all
sideways in the way that calves will. Mr Vick, the cattle
judge and famous breeder from Steyning in West Sussex,
gave the tiny calf's tiny bottom a tiny pat, it walked on
and all was well. 'There we are then,' he said, and pulled
his cap at an even sharper angle to the horizontal.
Wonderful Heathfield Show!

We trade-stand judges were shepherded around by
Peter Salter, an elegant man and our steward. He wore
a pin-striped suit, a bowler hat and gumboots. For years,
he had run the South of England Show at Ardingly. To
begin with, we judges were exaggeratedly courteous about
each other's likes and dislikes. Mr Bines liked the way one
agricultural equipment merchant had managed to get a
combine harvester on to his stand. 'Always some plus

marks for a combine,' he said. I said nothing. I liked the way a tent full of little food stalls had the air of 1948 about it, one step up from a village fête. It had that delicious smell of a field inside a canvas hall but Mr Bines did not comment. Mrs Chidson liked the verve of the Sussex Express stand, its honest vulgarity, but neither Mr Bines nor I said very much about that either.

We realised, I think, that we were interested in rather different things and by the time we arrived back at the judges' tent we all, I am sure, had a pretty good idea where the others stood. We sat down at a small round table in the tent, Peter Salter got us each a drink and the horse-trading began. There was the E. Watson & Sons Trophy for agricultural stands of 40 feet and over. No problem there. We all agreed the Young Farmers were outstanding, Agrifactors (Southern) Ltd had made a charming effort and Harper & Eede, who had parked their tractors very smartly in front of their tent, deserved a Highly Commended. We proceeded smoothly to the Percy Meakins Perpetual Challenge Trophy for small agricultural stands. Wealden Smallholdings won hands down, manfully overcoming the local outbreak of Fowl Pest which had meant they had to replace their poultry display with a Wealden cottage garden at the very last minute. Plumpton Agricultural College came a well-deserved second after they had given us a welcome glass of wine on the way round. Peasridge Livestock Equipment, with a fine display of Equine Dental Chisels, One Step Sheep Shampoo and The Original Bull Shine, enjoyed a Highly Commended in the Percy Meakins.

The judges then turned their attention to the John

Harper Memorial Trophy for non-agricultural stands. Some awkwardness set in. Mr Bines was in favour of Parker Building Supplies, which had a small self-contained sewage treatment unit in operation on its stand. I was keen on the food tent that had such a charmingly *ad hoc* 1948 quality to it. Mrs Chidson liked the Hugo Oliver sausages stand. Peter Salter the steward asked us, at least, to exclude some from the long list. We did, cutting out both Shell Oil and a man who turned bowls. There we reached an impasse. All we could agree on was the excellence of Hailsham Roadstone's driveway display. I couldn't even remember the sewage unit Mr Bines liked so much and he didn't like my food tent suggestion at all. A slight crackle entered the air. Peter Salter suggested Mrs Chidson and I should have another look at the sewage works. We walked to the other side of the show, had a good look and on the way back to the judges' tent agreed: we couldn't possibly call that the winning stand. The food tent, on the other hand, was precisely the sort of small local enterprise that should be encouraged. Absolutely not, Mr Bines still thought on our return. The impasse remained. 'We're not having Parker Building Supplies,' I said, looking at Mrs Chidson. 'Well, I'm not having Taste of the South-East,' Mr Bines said. We all looked at the tablecloth while onlookers raised their eyebrows and took another drag at the B&H. It was time for statesmanship.

What about, I suggested, giving the prize to Hailsham Roadstone, second to Hugo Oliver sausages and Highly Commended to both Parker Building Supplies and Taste of the South East? Two Highly Commendeds? Highly unorthodox but in the circumstances the only option.

Judicious nods all round. Thank God for that. We could all, at last, get stuck into the G&Ts and the white wines, safe in the knowledge that compromise is always best.

Things were not so well regulated at home. The week after the show has gone down in memory as Chaos Week. My sister arrived at the end of it. She was wandering into the tail end of a disaster sequence out of hell. First, I am afraid, it was the sheep. In the intense and frozen days of mid-March, perhaps a little romantically, I had decided that our lambs didn't need their tails docking. Why should they, poor little things? If God had given them a tail, and so on and so on. So all summer long they had been whisking and flicking their tails, increasingly woolly on the outside and increasingly shit-encrusted on the inside, around the pastures. It was a recipe for disaster, as everyone now tells me. They had until recently done quite well. They were almost as big as their mothers, fat and a little lumbering, but they still gambolled about from time to time, which looked ridiculous, as if Nicholas Soames were playing leap-frog in Parliament Square. You expect a degree of dignity from a sheep and doing hop-skips with a final twisting pirouette of the hind leg, when they should, by rights, already be in someone's freezer, looks as grotesque as synchronised swimming.

On the other hand, one could perhaps see it as the last tragically gay flicker of childhood before they sank into the perpetually morose condition of adult sheepness. Why are grown-up sheep so morose? Why don't they play with each other? It's easy to imagine endless games of British Bulldog, up and down, up and down the fields, until they finally collapse in the evening, exhausted but happy. Why weren't sheep like that?

As it was, at the beginning of that week, four of the lambs suddenly developed the most gruesome condition I have ever seen. It was a case of maggoty bums, and we had to do urgent, heavy remedial work to save the poor things, dressing up in nuclear-warfare-standard protective gear to administer the dip to their unhappy bottoms, spraying them and anointing them with a flamboyant pharmacopoeia of sheep treatments.

Sheep, let me tell you, are not low-maintenance farming. This has to be understood. You don't get a flock of perfectly whole and lovely-looking sheep on perfectly lovely short-cropped green grass just by putting one on top of the other. That's what I imagined, but it's not true. So, having gone down the wrong track, my sheep now looked as if they'd just come back from a fashion shoot for Versace. They all had blue blobs here and there to identify them as mine, except for those which had green blobs to identify them as Peter Clark's. Those which were nicked in the shearing had patches of intense violet wool where we had sprayed them with antiseptic. One which knocked its horn off against a gate-post had a half-yellow head where I had smeared it with a yellow paint-cream which keeps the flies off. The lambs with sore bottoms were now, from behind, a slightly disorientating mixture of Cadbury's-chocolate-wrapper violet and vanilla-ice-cream yellow. I looked at them and felt overwhelmed by a sense of guilt and failure. Perhaps the only thing to do was to dip them all in shocking pink and pretend it was on purpose. I had to do better, I had to do better.

Against this background of three-o'clock-in-the-morn-
ing remorse and anxiety, there had been a burbling stream
of other hopelessnesses. British Telecom wanted to put a
giant new telegraph pole right at the end of the garden,
dominating Sarah's carefully orchestrated harmonies. So
that had to be negotiated away and underground but once
it had, I realised the new duct for the telephone wires had
been laid wrongly. The reeds in the new sewage system
seemed to have died and the smell predicted by Ken Weekes
from such a newfangled thing had started to waft up
towards the house. A lorry delivering stone had smashed
a manhole over the sewage pipe, which didn't help. Then I
found the children playing on the gravel among the dead
reeds, popping the little pebbles into their mouths in a game
which involved getting as many of the sewage-encrusted
stones as possible in their mouths at the same time. 'Never,
ever let me see you doing that again,' I said, and as I walked
away I saw them out of the corner of my eye hunching their
shoulders and putting their hands over their mouths in the
time-honoured signal of: Uncontrollable Giggles Brought
On By Expostulation From Old Fart.

Meanwhile, as the farm and the fields and the stock
and I all looked increasingly decrepit and, at times,
beyond redemption, Sarah's garden was entering its glory
phase. There was a time when, unkindly, I referred to that
80- by 40-foot patch of walled, trim-hedged, pathed,
manured, sanded, worked-over, reworked-over, planted,
replanted, deplanted, weedkilled, re-replanted, rema-
nured and cosseted piece of ground simply as 'The Expensive Garden'. I realised now that was a tautology;
gardens were £20 notes on stalks.

Even so, the garden had become, in its first real moment of completion, an incredibly beautiful thing, floating free of all that had gone into making it. It was brimming with intense colour, as concentrated as flowers in a vase. It was so full, you had to push your way through its paths, getting a soaking in the early morning from the dew, brushing up against things which the sheer height and thickness of the other plants had obscured until you were right on top of them, a small colony of sunflowers in one corner, wafting drifts of white and pink cosmos in another, like a hillside in Bhutan.

All week long a stream of internationally famous garden photographers had been trooping in and out of it for their various magazines. A lady from *Gardeners' World* came to video Sarah talking about the propagation of annuals. Desperate and intense tidying up had gone on between each of these visits, but the process had been dogged by something which came to symbolise the difference between garden and farm, Sarah and me.

There was a rogue chicken. It would not go back in the run but instead, just as Sarah had finished her last sweep and survey before Andrew Lawson or Howard Sooley arrived, would wander into the garden and begin to shuffle its way deliberately and unbelievably messily through the meticulously applied mulch. That was the pattern of the week: chicken, Lawson, chicken, Sooley, chicken, BBC, like some monstrous club sandwich. 'What is it with your animals?' Sarah asked. 'Can't you get anything organised?'

That's when we hit our big sheep crisis. But when wasn't there a sheep crisis? Sheep *are* crisis. The ewes had been having their problems. One of the poor things somehow cut a tendon in her back leg. It would not mend and so she had to be put down and buried. Then another ewe started to behave in a way that was most unsheeplike and, for a while anyway, I thought it rather impressive. She would wander off to be on her own, often choosing a place in the field just on the brow of the hill, from which in a dreamy and rather poetic way she would gaze at the radiant colours of the life-burgeoning Weald. This was exciting: a Romantic sheep, clear evidence of the appreciation of beauty in the lower orders of creation. One evening, the sheep and I even spent some moments together, side by side, looking at the folded view of wood and valley before us.

But I was mistaken. The ewe was growing mad, not wise. I described the symptoms to Carolyn Fieldwick. 'No, Adam,' she said. 'I don't think the ewe is gazing at the Sussex landscape.' The ewe's problem, it turned out, was a magnesium deficiency which induces a state of dignified but eventually fatal calm. She, too, had to be put down and buried in the corner of a field.

Sheep, contrary to what one might expect, are incredibly choosy eaters. They won't touch nettles, thistles, ragwort or dock. What is more difficult to accept is that they will not eat grass – perfectly good, organic, herb-rich, Sussex meadow grass – if it's even slightly too long. This is frustrating. You put them in a field of what looks like the most delicious of mixed salads, and they stand about disconsolately, staring at you with a look of slightly wrinkled contempt, like an aunt who has just stepped in some dog mess. The whole flock reminded me of the faces one sees through the rain-smeared windows of a bus tour of the Scottish Highlands. We didn't have enough sheep to keep the grass short. We needed more sheep.

This was when the crisis began. Our neighbour, Shirley, who had the cottage and a couple of acres on the edge of the Big Wood, was an accountant who worked in the village. She had a few sheep of her own, but they were eating her grass to nothing and one or two had broken out and got into our hay. We wanted more sheep, she wanted to be rid of hers. It was obvious that they should become ours. Here the waters started to become a little murky. I maintained that we had been unable to agree a price; she maintained that we did agree a price, £35 a ewe. Anyway, the sheep were transferred to our fields. The money business, as I thought anyway, was left pending, but we were in dispute about that.

Three of the sheep weren't all that happy about the transfer. They had been fed ewe nuts at home and, unenthused about the grass-only diet we were offering, decided to go back, breaking their way through our slightly gappy fencing in their bid for freedom. We took them back but they broke for home again and we left them to it.

This would have been all right, but disaster struck. Our neighbour's boyfriend, Dick, a director of a very important national car business of immense standing, decided to store a superbly luxurious car – a bottle-green Lexus (or was it Plexus? or Nexus?) worth £35,000 – at her house to prevent it being vandalised in Heathfield. What safer place could one think of than out here in the Arcadian idyll?

Only days later the poor man arrived at the back door, his face as long as a Blue Leicester tup faced with the chop. 'Your sheep,' he said, 'have been headbutting my car. They were spotted attacking the doors.'

Have you ever had a phone call mid-morning from your children's headmaster, telling you that there has been an unfortunate incident at break and do you think you could come over and talk to the parties involved because it is best to sort these things out straightaway? Sick in the pit of the stomach, I went to inspect the damage. The four doors of the Sexus were indeed neatly dented at about sheep-head height. The paintwork was beautifully buffed up and dust-free at that level too, as if by a fleece still attached to its owner. I thought of suggesting that he might like to keep a sheep in his showroom in Heathfield to maintain his cars in a perfectly shiny condition. I refrained. It was not the right time.

I had no insurance against any damage any sheep on my land might do to anyone else's property. That extra clause to our insurance policy would have cost £30.50 a year. I thought the idea ridiculous. What would any sheep living here do to anyone else's property? Go and attack it? A night raid on their ewe nuts? It was just another insurance scam. But I pay that premium now.

The sheep/neighbour/limousine/solicitor/insurance company crisis dogged our lives for years. Shirley's son, Jonny, had seen 'my' sheep (whose they actually were remained in dispute for month after month, the meter ticking away in various well-appointed legal offices) attacking the car from an upper window. He wrote a graphic account of how the sheep, in a beautifully orchestrated manoeuvre, approached the glossy flanks of the limousine. The synchronised animals then attacked the car. They kicked and headbutted both sides, Jonny told the insurance company. Nothing if not systematic. You had to laugh. But then the bill came in. It was £2,300 for repairing the damage to the doors and another £2,000-odd for the loss of income Dick would have had from hiring out the car in the meantime.

Shirley had been away when the incident occurred. Only Jonny had witnessed it, although Dick did admit to having moved some sheep into an ungated field not long before it was said to have happened. We maintained that ewes didn't do that kind of thing. We even paid a professor of animal behaviour from Cambridge University to trawl through the literature on sheep. There was not a single example in the long annals of biological science of ewes attacking cars. Rams have, but never ewes. And ewes have never been seen to kick anything at all.

Despite the power of that evidence, there was no movement on the other side. Their solicitor came down here in his red Audi estate. I walked him around the fields. We followed the presumed route the sheep must have taken. I referred at one point while talking to him, charmingly, smilingly, the sun on our backs, not to 'the sheep' but to 'our sheep.' It was a slip of the tongue. I should have said "our sheep", or made that little sign with fingers in the air to show quote marks in the way of American academics discussing "perception" or "reality". But I didn't and the solicitor, with the keys to his Audi bulging in his pocket, and his meter ticking, said, all bright and sharp, ' "Our sheep"? You mean they were your sheep, were they? You consider that you owned these sheep at the time do you?' For God's sake, I thought. Imagine living your life like that.

On it roiled. Relations with Shirley were not good but our lives were painfully enmeshed. We were already in dispute about her water supply and the track to her house. We were like a pair of sumo wrestlers, podgily shoving and clutching at each other. Attempts at settlement and compromise never seemed to work. She became ill. Just when I hoped one of the issues might have faded away, another solicitor's letter or another angry note or dark remark about the track or the water would appear. I offered to pay a third of the track repair costs. That got nowhere. There was some mutual berating. The place where we lived was beautiful but it felt as though it had an abscess in its gum.

On one particularly bad corner in the lane, Anna Cheney collided with a car coming the other way, driven by Shirley. Anna, who looks after our children, had both our daughters in the back of her car. I had a phone call from the woman who lives in the nearest farm and rushed down there. No one was hurt but the girls were in tears, the cars looked mangled and everyone was feeling fluttery and shaken. Except for one of the policemen, who was all smiles and hands-in-pockets, seen-it-all-before, get-this-every-day-of-the-week, what's-the-fuss. I very nearly had a stand-up row with him until Anna physically restrained me, telling me I would get arrested. I realise now it was Shirley I was boilingly angry with.

Two extraordinary events finally propelled our relationship into the most bizarre dimensions. Sarah and I
were sitting at home after dinner on a Friday night. The
children were all in bed and the dog was lying in front of
the fire. Then, as mothers do, even through the chat,
Sarah heard Molly crying. 'Sssh,' she said, listening. Then
we heard the sound again, but it wasn't Molly. It was a
siren coming up the lane. First one and then another fire
engine came up to our garden gate, paused and then went
on towards Ken Weekes's house, paused there, saw
nothing, and then on again, up towards Barn Farm
and Mount Farm, up at the top of the lane.

We sat down again. Some poor family or other had
obviously set fire to a chimney. We had done it once a
couple of years before. But on that Friday night the fire
engines weren't for us. The sirens faded away. After a few
minutes, though, we heard them coming back. I went out.
'Where do you want?' I bellowed. The first driver shouted
the name of a house. It was Shirley's. I told them how to
get there, found a torch in the house and ran over there
myself.

It was about 11 at night. A fierce west wind which had
been blowing all day was still spitting the rain horizontally
on to the back of my head. I was only a few minutes
behind the fire engines but by the time I got to the house
the fire brigade's whole system was up and running: arc
lights providing a wash of white light like a film set; hoses
unreeled around the house, charged with water and with
a junior fireman on the end of each one; a white-board on
a tripod where a fireman with a black marker was
recording the sequence of events. Two teams with breath-

ing apparatus had gone straight into the building and were fighting the fire in the kitchen. Shirley, still in her nightdress but with a blue anorak over it, was sitting in one of the fire engines, shocked and shaky. She had been watching TV in bed when the electricity had suddenly gone off. She had opened the door to go downstairs to the fusebox, only to be met by a solid wall of smoke, poisonous-tasting, gagging in her throat. The phone was still working and, even though she had to dial in the dark, she had called 999 and then got herself out of the building into the wet night.

The worry was her animals. She had three dogs and three cats. The cats could probably look after themselves but two of the dogs had slipped back inside the house after she had got out herself. They were now trapped in the scullery, between the fire and the locked back door, and she couldn't get at them. She was terrified that they would be burnt or were suffocating in the black smoke.

The first thing the firemen did was to break open a pane in the back door, unlock it, release the animals, all unharmed, and shut them in the stable. The boiler had burst into flames and was still burning in the kitchen. Two teams of firemen in breathing apparatus went in to the heat and smoke. Within a few minutes, though, the crisis was already over and the tension winding down. One crew was coming out of the house, tearing off their oxygen masks, their heads and faces running with sweat. The seat of the fire was out. The other crew was still in there, checking for flames in other parts.

Suddenly, from between the tiles of the roof, and snatched away by the wind, smoke poured into the night air. Firemen shone their torches up at the gables and ran extra hoses round the downwind side of the house. Smoke was crowding out of the roof. The firemen had opened a hatch to the attic, air had poured in there, and fire had suddenly erupted, soon taking hold. New urgency gripped the firemen. The fire controller got on the radio and the men in breathing apparatus went back in. Shirley sat in the fire engine. I watched aghast from outside.

The conventional wisdom is that once a fire takes hold in the roof space of a building, it is extremely difficult to prevent the whole roof going or, in some cases, to save the building itself. If no one had been at home that evening, or if it had been a little later and Shirley had been fast asleep and not noticed the electricity going off, then the chances are that the house would have burned down. For a while no one was certain if this roof fire was going to be contained. There was talk of calling in extra tenders. For perhaps ten minutes there was uncertainty until, quite abruptly, the smoke pouring from between the tiles diminished. They had extinguished it. It was 'a good stop'.

I took Shirley and her three dogs home with me that night. We drank most of a bottle of whisky in our kitchen, waiting for the firemen to finish clearing up, checking no embers remained. At about one o'clock in the morning I went back up there. Half the contents of the attic, old suitcases, boxes of books, the sort of baggage we all have stuck away in the uninspected corners of our lives, had been hauled out on to the drive in front of the house. It was all now scorched and sodden. The boiler itself looked as if it had been bombed, the kitchen black, wrecked, unusable.

It was the sight of the attic that was most alarming: the rafters charred, all the implications there of what might have happened, how near a real catastrophe might have been. A few minutes' more burning and the end would have been quite different. As it is, or so Ken Weekes says, who had a fire a few years before, 'the smell won't go away. Sometimes you just catch it, just a whiff of it. It brings it back, I can tell you.'

Shirley stayed with us for a few days, the awkward subjects untouched, a sort of grinning distance between us. None of us had any idea what was really going on in her life. There had been whispers but we had ignored them. She went off to stay somewhere else, leaving behind a pair of shoes. By chance, just then, quite suddenly, resolutions: the car insurance company graciously accepted £3,000 to go away. There had been costs of more than £1,000 on top of that. I know that £4,000 may seem like a monstrous amount to get someone off your back but we were dealing with one of the biggest insurance companies, a rich and powerful organisation, prepared to go to court and spend who knows how much, to batter us into submission, to extend and amplify the arguments, to explore the niceties of blame and responsibility, knowing that our funds would run out before theirs did. So we paid. Around the same time, Shirley's ex-husband, a beautifully reasonable man, brokered a deal about the track; and the discovery of the leak in the water pipe explained the many months of problems over the water bills.

Then came the greatest shock of all. A reporter from the local paper turned up. Shirley had been convicted of

stealing from her own clients at Lewes Crown Court and
sent to jail for nine months. The reporter also said that
over the time we had known her she had attempted
suicide twice. There had been murmurings but I had
understood nothing. What I had seen as awkwardness
and recalcitrance were only the surface symptoms of a life
in almost terminal crisis. She had never divulged the
reality. Just a quarter of a mile away across the fields had
been someone breaking down, and we had not had the
faintest idea. Her house was burnt and empty. The ivy
began to grow across the windows. Her two fields turned
ragged with thistles and docks.

Despite it all, Perch Hill itself was resilient. It provided
resilience. It was in its heart what we wanted it to be. One
morning in particular that summer (it was June 2nd) felt
as if it were the day for which the whole of the rest of the
year had been a preparation. The long grind of the winter
and its sense of enclosure and endlessness; the seeping
way its dankness enters every aspect of your life; the delay
of spring, the long poking about looking for spring, many
weeks before it has any intention of showing itself – all of
the waiting had gone. The day that we had been waiting
for was today.

    I was up early, having to get some work into the
newspaper before people arrived at the office there. As
I walked over to my workroom across the yard at a few
minutes past five, the tangerine sun had just cleared the
upper tips of the oak trees in the Middle Shaw. The ducks
and chickens were scratching about on the compost by
the old cow shed, there was a big lamb bleating for no

reason I could see down in the Long Field, there was dew in the grass and the whole place was suffused with that orange-grey, cold-warm, utterly private light of sunrise.

By mid-morning, the work was done, I'd had breakfast, and I'd got the day free. I don't understand how sunshine works but everything that morning looked as if it had acquired another dimension. Far to the east, for 12 miles or so to the hills above Rye, it was so clear that I felt I could see individual trees. Westwards I could surely make out the slats in the sails of the Punnett's Town mill, which is a good hour and a half's walk from here. Was all this simply the sharpness and clarity of rain-washed air? Whatever it was, the whole place looked like a glass of white wine tastes.

I went down to the Slip Field. It is the one field on the farm that we all love best here, and that day it was wearing its midsummer clothes. It is a south-facing bank of about two and a half acres surrounded on all sides by wood, the oak and hazel of the Middle Shaw to the right, the long frondy arms of the ashes in the Ashwood Shaw to the left and, in front of me, at the foot of the hillside, the two acres of garlic flowering then in the hazelwood shade of Coombe Wood, a stinking, lush and frothy garden which squeaked as you walked through it at that time of year with the big, rubberised, smelly leaves rubbing up against your shins.

It was the field itself which was the zone of heaven that day. Its slippy soil meant that it had never been reseeded with commercial grass mixtures and so here, between the garlic and the bluebell woods, hidden from the world but open to the sun, was our field of flowers. There were sheets and sheets of the yellow vetch with blood-red tips called eggs and bacon. Here the common blue butterflies flitted in pairs, their blue backs just greying to silver along the outer margins of the wing. Curiously, those precise colours, and their relationship, a silvery lining to an eye-blue wing, was exactly repeated in the speedwells that grew in mats among the yellow vetches. Beyond these beds of eggs and bacon, with a scatter of blue among and above them, where the dog and I were both warmly lying, the buttercups and the daisies, with pink fringes to their flowers, spread out to the margins of the woods where the pyramidal bugles clustered a darker blue against the one or two bluebells that had leaked out into the field. The dyer's greenweed was not yet in flower and only some tiny forget-me-nots and the taller spiky speedwells added to the picture. A holly tree on the edge of the wood had turned pale with its clusters of white flowers.

A slight wind started the field nodding and other butterflies cruised and flickered in. A pale tortoiseshell hung for a minute on the vetches, followed by a bumblebee which pushed its entire body inside the blooms. A big cabbage white flirted with the nettles and the balsam at the top of the field and then two brown moths, each the size of a fingernail, came dancing in a woven spiral across the hillside, as close in with each other, as bound to and as mobile with each other as the different parts of a guttering flame. The whole wood was needled with birdsong, a clustered shrieking sharpness, interrupted only by the jays' coarse squawking, the sudden dropping-off *dwaark* of pheasants and, behind it all, the continuous, laid-back strumming of the woodland bassists, the pigeons in their five-part, broken-backed rhythm, two rising, a pause, two falling, doo-doo, doo, doo-doo, the only soundtrack you need for an English summer.

I was sinking into sleep. The dog already had, and his nostrils were twitching as he snored. There was a drone of light planes. One of Ken Weekes's grandchildren must have been playing football up by the cottage and that snatched-at, childish shouting came in scraps and patches across the fields. A thin but unending river of feathery willow-seeds was blowing from out of the wood, on past me and down towards Bateman's and Burwash. Here and there a thistle standing in the field was covered in the willow fluff it had picked from the passing air.

All this was nothing compared to the soporific warmth of the sun, on the field and on my back. My shirt itself felt hot from the warmth it had absorbed. Even the hot dog next to me smelled nice, but then perhaps I only thought that because he was my dog and I thought him wonderful anyway. I rolled over, turned my face away and down into the grass, buried my nose in the sun-warmed turf, breathed it in, smelled how good it was, its hot vegetable dryness, and knew that coming to live here was the best thing I had ever done.

PEACHES ON
THE COW SHED WALL

Nothing is more calculated to turn one into a pork pie than the arrival of a poet on the doorstep. We had one staying that August and the experience changed me into a no-nonsense member of the Rother Weald Branch of the NFU. 'Don't you realise,' I heard myself saying towards the end of his time, 'that the country is where *food* is produced?' Jason, who was 22, looked back at me with the comfortless gaze of a man who had yet to suffer. He was the son of some people from whom I had shamelessly cadged accommodation and food a decade previously when touring the western half of the United

States. Reasonably enough, they had now sent Jason over to do the same to me. We had ten days of him and then he went off walking somewhere in southern Spain.

Jason was into haiku. It was quite charming to start with and I encouraged him to produce some pieces about the farm here. He gave me his first little Japanese creation on the second day at breakfast:

Hawk
twitch of long grass –
elegance of ambush.

'Thank you, Jason,' I said and felt, at least, that here was someone who was on my wavelength. But I wasn't totally at ease. Jason's wanness, his silences, the way he never said anything unless it came out perfectly rolled and made like a sushi – that was difficult. I longed for him to burp or knock something over, or spill gravy on his shirt. Surely a little lack of control might be considered Zen too, mightn't it? One morning when I came down to breakfast, he said 'Hi Adam. How are you?'

'Fine thanks.'

'Good, well done,' Jason said. 'I think it's a great thing for someone to be able to say that about themselves.'

Just as exasperation was setting in, he would come out with something beautiful. I took him to see our sheep. Roger the ram was still in a field of his own, with a couple of ram lambs for company, and the ewes and ewe lambs were all together on the other side of the lane. The mothers were wearing the sheep bells I had bought for them in Majorca. Peter Clark had said the bells were stupid and cruel. 'How would you like it?' had been his unanswerable question.

All the same, as I explained to Jason, I loved listening to them. If you heard them from a field or two away, they sounded like snatches of a conversation which you couldn't quite pick up. I don't know how many times I have sat on a mountain in southern Europe, listening to their hollow, half-carried half-notes. Jason said nothing but that evening he gave me this:

Sheep bells:
toc toc –
olives in the oakwood.

Ken Weekes came to lunch and told his stories all the way through it, beaming away at the gnomic Jason, and Jason played his part to the full, economical in his courtesies and self-contained in his stillness. Ken's performance culminated in his favourite story about the hunt – the one that ends with 'why don't you fucking well bugger off out of there.' Jason's silence was a little black hole at one end of the table. That evening he gave me this:

Farmers:
tang
of horseradish.

Even though I have since learned that those three lines are a fairly direct adaptation of a famous haiku about samurai, that was the high point of the ten days. For some reason, Jason's offerings became increasingly dark and more obscurely critical, as though we, and by extension this place, somehow embodied everything he most hated. Sarah and I would sit up after the others had gone to bed, wondering what were the implications of one or two of them:

Perfected garden:
the end
of youth.

which did nothing but fill us with gloom. Or there was:

August sunshine:
old brocade
hanging from the trees.

That sort of thing was alarmingly exact, identifying precisely the upholstered, claustral thickness that gathers around this time of year, a sort of outdoor stuffiness, which on the worst of days affects everyone's mood. I came to think that a general air of discontent was being spread through the entire household by this man. He came to seem more and more like a parasite, indifferent to the difficulties of getting on in the world and with one's life. And there he was, eating my food and drinking my drink. I saw in him, I now realise, what some of the serious farmers round here have said they see in me: an exaggerated aestheticism, an ignorance and even arrogance about the facts of life. He was the kind of fantasist who is so bound up in his fantasy that he doesn't know that it is one.

But he couldn't be so casually dismissed. What he said did have an odd and unnerving access to the truth.

The morning he left, he gave me his final verdict:

Sheep bells:
toc toc –
empty gestures.

I folded the piece of paper twice, into a little square, and put it in the bin, feeling hollow and old. Everything felt absurd.

There were peaches that September growing against our cow shed wall. By the middle of the month most of them were ripe if still rather small, the size of apricots. Those autumn mornings, their skins were wet with dew. One day, Rosie and I ate them for an autumn breakfast, standing in the cold morning sun just after eight o'clock, me with two jerseys on and her in her school uniform, side by side in the vegetable garden. The sun was coming over Coombe Wood and the juice dribbled down our chins. It reminded me of the story of James Thompson, the luxurious eighteenth-century poet of *The Seasons*, who was found one morning in the fruit garden of some large country house, nibbling at a peach that was still hanging from the tree. He had his hands in his pockets. What a sight: those lips and teeth gobbling to catch the mousy skin, the fat poet, his unbuttoned stance, his casual acceptance of paradise dangled by his nose.

On the way back from school, driving down the long ridgeway lane that runs for four miles through woods between Brightling and Robertsbridge, I got stuck behind a tractor and empty trailer. It was going slowly, and a little irritably I wound down the window.

An unforgettable smell blew in: sweet, acrid, vegetable, mineral, woody, flowery, odd, heavy, heady, alluring, druggy, earthy and sharp, a taste more than a smell, its acidy resins catching at the back of the throat. It was not one smell but a crowd of them and I knew instantly what it was: hops. I was driving along in a hoppy breeze. Half a bine or so of the plant was hanging off the side of the bouncing trailer and you could see the wooden boards were dark and sticky with the oils that had seeped from the flower-heads.

I knew this smell. At home in Kent when I was a boy we had a hop garden but the ground became infected with the hop fungus known as wilt, and the garden was turned over to more dependable wheat. That must have happened when I was six or seven. Even so, the smell of hops, once smelt, takes up permanent occupancy in the hypothalamus, always there, waiting to be summoned. There is something alien about it, not the sort of thing you might expect from a plant that is native to England. It is more outlandish than that. The hop is a relative of cannabis, one of the Cannabaceae, and the air that hangs about it is smokily dopy in the same way, a subtle and combined smell, a blended soporific in the autumn lanes of Kent and East Sussex that would be more at home, or so it seemed that morning, away on the other side of the Mediterranean, hidden somewhere in the souks of Aleppo or Isfahan.

I felt like a Bisto kid behind the trailer, nostril-led, that airborne zig-zag drawing me to its source. The tractor turned off down a concrete farm track and I followed. In the hop garden by the road, they were just starting on the last acre of the crop. One man walking ahead was slashing at the foot of the bines, another on a trailer-mounted ladder cutting away the head and a third stacking them in the trailer as they fell. Beyond the pickers, the dark alleys of the growing plants stretched away in a thick, geometrical jungle.

The loaded trailers bumped across the field and down towards the farm and its oast-houses. Hops flipped out of the trailers and lay on the track in an intermittent carpet. As you drove over them, the air turned green with the smell of the crushed flowers. On the ground floor of the oast-house, an antiquated machine was stripping the flowers from the bines, jiggering and sifting them from the leaves and string and stalks, and then feeding them through to the gantry where they were taken in sacks to the kilns.

Upstairs, some were being taken out, dry, and the men were shovelling them out on to a wood floor that was sheeny with a century of hop resin gelled into place. It was dark up here. These upper storeys of oast-houses have small windows because hops last better in the dark. The only light came sharply in at one side. I stood and looked: the lime green of the hops, the worn and darkened wood of the room, the family to whom this farm belonged, five of them, brushing the dried hops into steep piles with birch brooms and then shovelling them into the mouths of the deep sacks, the pockets, on which the name of the farm was printed. Labour-in-

tensive, beautiful, local, a high-quality product, a culti-
vated tradition, nothing fake about the relationship of
crop and its market: was this scene not a picture of what
the rural world might be?

The autumn storms came bulling into our lives. One
night in mid-September, I felt as if the house had been at
sea all night, the frame of the wooden roof above our bed
adrift in a wrestling wind. I thought I must have been
dreaming it, this manhandling of the building by the air,
but I wasn't. In the morning, the frame had clearly
shifted. Hairline cracks in the plaster had opened a hair
or two wider. Everywhere you looked you saw them: dark,
roughly drawn graphs up in the corners of the rooms or
where the roof met the walls, little jagged longitudinal lips
that had opened and only half closed, like the caulked
seams of a ship that had worked in a storm. If you put
your cheek next to one of them in the bathroom, you
could feel the air whistling in. This was what these
wooden houses did. All our rooms upstairs had the marks
of old cracks that had opened and been sealed, opened
and been sealed, over and over again ever since the frame
was put up 400 years or so before. Ken Weekes said it was
in the wood. 'That's one thing you can be sure of,' he told
me. 'Oak never dies.'

The wind was still careering around the farm. I was
dealing with my agonised tax affairs and no weather could
have been better suited than those equinoctial gales. It
went without saying, of course, that the staff of the Inland
Revenue South East office in Cavendish House, Castle
St, Hastings were some of the most charming and helpful

on the planet, and were preternaturally understanding about cash flow difficulties and revenue stream bottlenecks (my ref: 057 D 58979/NCP). Nevertheless, those 'Dear Mr Nicolson' letters did have something of the reality dose about them. It was all the oast-house's fault, its massive budget overrun, knocking out cold any chance we might have had of staying out of a debt even deeper than the one we were in already.

The tax demand sitting on the desk in front of me that morning was a fat, slapping, smacking squall of reality coming snorting into our lives. All those balmy midsummer ideas for this and that change, this fencing and hedging scheme, that alteration to the back of the house, the new roof to the barn, the new tractor and cart shed: the whole lot was blown heedlessly away. I could stand at the window of the oast-house and watch our plans being tumbled and driven far out to the other side of the millennium, those distant, sunny, cash-filled fields, from which the burden of backlog tax, a pernicious weed, would at last have been removed.

There was an exhilaration to this moment. At least the thing had been faced and we were still there. I had been walking around the farm that morning, in the wind, the real wind I mean, trying to chew over schemes for generating some money and delaying the payment of bills, but I could hardly concentrate. My whole field of vision was taken up with the excitement of the wind's sudden, savage blanching of the trees. Summer was over; here was the gateway to a whole new way of seeing things.

I'd never looked at wind the way I saw it that morning. It

articulates the landscape it disturbs. All still things are alike in their stillness but every windy thing is windy in its own way. That's the stripping pleasure of a wind. It breaks the landscape apart; each element becomes itself. Perhaps this was no more than a mechanical thing, the angles at which branches join the trunk, the inherent strength of twig and leaf, but the effect is that the wind makes the landscape talk.

Outside the garden gate the willows were driven by the wind, their bright and glaucous underleaves exposed as the wind blew down on to them. They were like girls with blown hair. I looked at them and saw an actress, a long-haired blonde, was it Julie Christie? her hair blown hopelessly all over her face. She picks at strands of it but the wind plasters them back across her cheeks and eyes. She shakes her head to free herself from them but they won't leave her.

In the garden, the Victoria plum was overladen. We should have unburdened the tree of the fruit but we hadn't and the top branch had snapped with the weight. Poor old thing, bowed down with her trappings, not Julie Christie but a jewelled duchess, somehow, tragically, or at least pathetically, broken down mid-ball.

There was a general cowering of the trees. The whole roof of the wood, as I looked out across the five miles of the Dudwell valley below us, was glossed and whitened in the wind. The blasts were humpbacked as they arrived at us: a low and slow building to a peak in which the big oaks suddenly seemed much bigger, out of phase with themselves, a broken swell stirring about in their branches, with different winds in different parts of the tree and then, quite suddenly, the gust dropping sharply away and we were waiting for the next.

The clouds cruised past the tiled ridges, a frame a second, and in the distance a deeper grumbling note marked the passage of a gust through the big wood. Down in there, sheltered by itself, the wood was still. The upper branches were waving among themselves and it was like standing as a child in a giant football crowd, with a crowd of waving men far above you, that sweeping-dying roar, but hoarser than a roar, almost a whispered roaring, heard far above you where, in manic circular motion, the trees were waving at events you could not see.

Out on the other side of the wood, the blades of new grass, after hay, twitched and flickered, the antennae-whiskers of the meadow. Along the edge of the Way Field, the hollies clicked like the quills of an anxious bird. The seed-cases of the hornbeams beside them made the high, dry chatter of rattled maracas. The ashes were all blown to pieces, their fronds offering no more resistance than a palm in a hurricane. The beeches, hammered by the summer, were now hammered again by the first of the autumn wind. They looked more bruised than anything else but at least the lower, sheltered branches were all right, dark but still fresh. It was up in the windy fringes of the beech that the leaves suffered, blackened in the wind, desiccated and made useless. No tree travels a greater distance from bright to dark in the course of a summer, from maidenly to matronly, the spring's most brilliant debby green to this heavy darkness, a whole life in a year. Beneath them, on the small birches colonising High Wood, every little leaf was struggling on its imprisoning stem.

There was a sort of bustling, a boxer's movement, to all
the big trees here, the oaks especially, working at the
wind, weaving away from its advances, a knitted, dod-
ging, evasive dislike in the movement. The wind was
unkind, the end of summer: we'd had the cheque; here
was the bill.

Some money had to be raised and so we decided to take
some of the old ewes to market. I went through the flock
with Fred and Margaret Groombridge, picking out the
ones that were past their best and, as Margaret said,
'would only be trouble if you kept them.' The ones to go,
13 of them, were marked with a squirt of green spray paint
on the back of their necks.

The Groombridges brought their trailer, we hitched it
on to my Land Rover, loaded up the old things and drove
them into Hailsham. The sun dabbed at the green-
tunnelled lanes. I drove at 40, with gradual stops and
cautious starts, conscious of the animals packed in behind
me. Margaret filled in the Sheep Movement Declaration
Form: Holding number 41/019/0216; total number of
animals: 13; identification mark: green 'A' on flank.

We unloaded the sheep into holding pens in the market
and they were sorted into three lots: half good, not so good
and unspeakably bad. Other sheep from other trailers were
going through the same process and, once sorted, were all
then driven through the maze of hurdles and gated
corridors into the selling pens.

I have heard that markets put heavy stress on the
animals that go through them and that cattle, for example, cannot be expected to grow for a month after they

have been to market, but it did not seem too bad for the sheep. All the men who handled them talked to them as they did so, 'Come on old girl, come on then, this way then,' and it wasn't rough.

Even so, to my own surprise, I felt a little cheerless about it all. Some of these old sheep were from the first lot that I'd had, and looking at them now, in these market pens, I couldn't help but think of that day when they had first arrived here and we had led them all out of the trailer and into the Long Field. Everyone had felt that day to be a step forward here. 'Well, well,' Ken Weekes had said, 'livestock back on Perch Hill Farm.'

Memory summoned other times: lying out one night that summer in their field and in the dark finding, amazingly, that the sheep luminesced – round, moonlit bundles scattered across the grass; this spring's lambing, the anxiety, the acid cold of the March nights and the strange, casual passion of it; one or two of their sisters dying, for no known reason, in the middle of an otherwise eventless summer day. 'Animals are the soul of a landscape,' Rudolf Steiner said, and in Hailsham Market that was the phrase that came to mind.

There were other things there too. I didn't want these creatures to go for nothing. I wanted a good price. The auctioneer and his cluster of buyers were starting on the fat lambs down at the other end of the market and the rhythmic, lulling-aggressive banter of the auctioneer came drifting up over the pens. The old ewes, the cull ewes, were the last category to be sold and it so happened that my three pens were the last of all.

There were three big buyers there, one a wholesale

butcher from Essex who buys 140,000 cull ewes a year for what is called 'the ethnic trade' – Moslem retail butchers and Indian restaurants, mostly in London, doner kebabs, that sort of thing – and a couple of Sussex farmers, who will pick the good from the bad and make their profit that way. The three were all physically big men. The Essex butcher was shaven-headed, had two pipes in his back pocket, a mobile phone attached to his waist and drove a shiny new Discovery. The joshing between them was tough, commercial, competitive, no more than half-funny.

I stood and watched as the noisy cluster came near our pens. 'Straight off the Downs, they are,' the auctioneer said of one lot, the ends of his tie tucked in between the buttons of his shirt. 'Real good sort of big things, they are. Don't be stupid. Has she got teeth? She's got more teeth than Hannibal Lecter.' The sheepdogs were nosing about the alley-ways. The auctioneer described one of the buyers as 'the only 55-year-old bachelor in Sussex still living with his Mum. Aaaaah.' The man flicked him a V-sign and everyone laughed. Prices were running high. There was a sort of savage buoyancy in the air.

The group arrived at our pens. 'From Brightling,' the auctioneer said curiously, 'Mr Nicolson.' I put my hand in the air and the small group turned to look. 'Some big Suffolks,' the auctioneer said and the serious buyers, with their sleeves rolled up over hairy arms, climbed into the pen and felt the backs of my sheep. A muddle of protective-defensive thoughts went through my head. 'Twenty eight, eighty fifty, nine, nine-fifty, thirty I have.' The price climbed, quickly, dispassionately. 'Are you bidding or are you having an itch?' He was bidding and the sheep went in the end to the Essex butcher for £35 each. The second-best three also went to him for £33 each. We came to the remaining seven, the truly bad, end-of-their-lives animals, and the Essex butcher turned away. They were not worth the bother, and he pulled some tobacco from his pocket. The auctioneer squeezed a bid of £12 out of one of the Sussex farmers. There was no energy in it, the lot was an embarrassment but somehow, still, the price crept up and these old scrags were finally knocked down for £18.50 each. 'Stupid,' Fred Groombridge said. 'I wouldn't give a fiver for one of them.' So it had been a great morning: £333.50 (minus commission) for 13 end-of-the-road sheep, all thanks to BSE and the flight from beef. Watching them walk up with the others into the big red, multi-tiered Essex lorry, the green As still there on their sides, I felt as if my children had done well at school. The money would pay for something; not much, but something.

At seven o'clock the following evening, I was feeding the dog when Ken Weekes's burglar alarm went off. Sarah and I knew what it was: the manic oscillations of the alarm, its unworldly wailings, shrieking and booming across the orchard and the Cottage Field. The early night was already solid black, it was raining slightly and I didn't think twice. I shouted at the dog to come, grabbed our giant Dragon torch, a sort of portable headlamp, and ran out of the door.

I had to hurry. Ken had been burgled in the daytime a few weeks previously and on that occasion I was up at his house within about five minutes of the alarm going off, to find the front door kicked in, the jambs smashed to pieces and a drawer in a bedroom upstairs hanging half open and rifled, like the lolling tongue on an exhausted dog. I then crept around the house, banging open the door of each room as I came to it – this felt absurd, cop showy – anxious not to find a person inside, but the burglar had gone. Later that day, Ken's wife Brenda found one or two of her things scattered along the lane to Burwash: an old bundle of tissues, a pendant, treasured but not valuable, thrown from the burglar's car window like the discarded wrappers from a box of chocolates.

So I knew I had to hurry if I was going to find anything more substantial this time than a broken pane of glass and an empty house. The beam from the torch was jagging and veering all over the lane and the wood as I ran uphill. I had passed the gate into the Cottage Field and was opposite the entrance to Blackbrooks Wood when I saw the man coming down the road towards me. His whole body was white in the beam of the torch. The white drops of rain were flicking everywhere around him. He was coming definitely and deliberately towards me.

That was frightening; there was no fear or reluctance in his movement, just a steady walk down the lane towards me. I had stopped as soon as I saw him and, as he kept moving towards me, my own fear grew. I kept the bright beam of the torch on his face, still 80 yards away, and screamed 'Who are you? Who the fuck are you?' He didn't answer but kept on towards me. I shouted at the dog to get near me and began involuntarily to walk backwards, the torch still on the man, keeping the distance between us unchanged. He was holding something in his right hand. 'What's that in your hand?' I screamed at him. 'A bottle,' he said. 'A water-bottle. I know this looks bad.'

I felt tight in my neck. This stupid situation, this chance of a fight in the lane at night in the rain. I heard my own voice coming out desperate and violent. 'What the fucking hell are you doing here? Don't get fucking nearer me. Stay there. Stay there. Stay where you fucking well are, will you.' I understand now how much of a realist, at least on one level, Quentin Tarantino is. This is simply how fear makes one talk.

All he was getting was the beam of the torch and the strangulated, wildly aggressive voice in the dark. He was now 20 yards away. He had an empty plastic Evian bottle in his hand and he was holding his head away from the light in his eyes. He had trainers on and an anorak. 'I know this looks bad,' he said again.

'Get down there,' I said. 'Walk in front of me. Get down the fucking lane.'

I let him pass me on the far side of the lane and we started walking back down towards our house. I kept ten yards behind him and as he walked in the beam of the torch in front of me, he put his hands in the air, surrendering, his right hand still holding the empty water bottle, dangling up there in the light of the torch like a lit and rather blurry lantern. I hadn't asked him to do this. He was treating the torch as though it were a gun and I can only suppose that my own terrified voice had in some way terrified him in return.

Of course, I hadn't worked out what would happen next. What if this man had been violent? What if he had been armed? What if he had tried to knife me? Not a single moment's reflection or calculation had been given to those questions.

Still shaking, I marched him into the kitchen and told him to sit down. I saw then that he was shaking too. Sarah called the police. I offered him a cup of tea, which he refused, and I then wrote down his name and address. He said he'd been out jogging. He had a whole string of emotional and financial crises in his life at home. He knew this looked bad. It was the last thing he needed. He looked at the floor and rubbed his head and eyes. I didn't ask him any questions, I didn't search him and I didn't feel, once he was sitting here at the kitchen table, that he was any threat.

The police arrived, in two cars, a policewoman and two men. They had taken 20 minutes from Hastings, 15 miles away on small country roads. Two of them searched Ken's house for signs of break-in and one sat in our kitchen talking to my man. 'You look nervous,' the policeman said. 'Frightened of what they're going to find?' He said he wasn't, and he was right. The searching police returned: no hint of a break-in. It was a false alarm. 'There has never been a false alarm with that system in two years,' I said. 'Must have been freak weather conditions,' the policewoman said. They drove the man home and I comforted Rosie who had been crying with the commotion. Next morning Ken came over and told me that the detectors on the windows were sensitively set. 'You've only got to tap the glass and they'll go off,' he said.

Sometimes in the summer Sarah and I have lain awake at three or four in the morning listening to the poachers in Blackbrooks Wood, on the other side of the lane from our house. The stinging smack of a rifle shot in the middle of the night is a strange thing. You feel as alert as the deer for which it is intended. You listen, so awake, for the sound of movement or even voices over there in the wood. There is silence and you wonder . . . That silence lasts and then, from nowhere, the noise of an engine pulls out into the night, the headlights stream across the dark, the smoke of the diesel exhaust is picked up in their beam, and then the van turns away, its lights throwing the hedgerow trees into silhouette, and you listen as it moves off towards the village.

It is the sort of thing that makes you wary, much warier than either of us would like to be. Ours was the only house in the lane that was not burgled in the first two years of our being there. In the past, this has been classic thieving ground. As Roger Wells quotes in *Victorian Village*, his study of nineteenth-century Burwash, it was said of this parish in the early years of the century that the 'labouring Class had become very dissatisfied, disrespectful and insolent to their superiors, riotous and turbulent, ready for extreme acts of depredation, prone to Robbery, violence, and lawlessness.'

Only the truly rabid would think of describing Burwash now in quite such fruity terms. There is no more than a little burglary here and there. Nevertheless, there is no need to be starry-eyed about the facts. Despite the apparent slosh of money, we live on the edge of an area of high unemployment (11 per cent, compared with 6 per cent further north and west around Tunbridge Wells or East Grinstead), which has been given special economic status as a Rural Development Area. Poverty is an every-day reality. So, here on the boundary of rich and poor, with what looks like disposable wealth lying about un-protected outside, theft seems an inevitability.

There is one form of wealth readily to hand and it is regularly taken: roofs. Roof theft is one of the signs of our attachment to a hand-made past. You are driving along a lane. It's one you know well. Just around the corner, as you come to a rise from which you get a sudden view over the Weald, there is an old farmhouse with a huge pitched tent of a roof.

The roof is a wonderfully crinkled micro-landscape of its own, covered in clay peg-tiles, many of them crusted in yellow lichen. Some of the tiles are bowed slightly out of true so that the tiny shadows thrown by their lips vary as your eye runs along the length of them. These Wealden roofs are beautiful things, pegging the houses down into the landscape. They are often, in this steep up-and-down country, the first part you see of a house or its assembled barns.

But one day you turn the corner and the roof isn't there. Or at least the roof structure is, the timbers, the felting and the laths for the tiles, but the tiles themselves have gone, ripped off and removed. The house looks odd, top-light, so to speak, like a guardsman with his bearskin off. Usually the tile thieves don't manage to get every last tile and the roof is left with quadrants of its old surface in the uppermost corners. The arc of what remains is a measure of the thief's final reach as he stood on the roof-battens before a car in the lane panicked him or his co-burglar thought they'd got enough and to risk any more would be dumb.

Roof-thievery is profitable enough. You can't exactly

lock a roof up, and for a thief it will represent a good
night's haul. A fair to middling roof might have 12,000
tiles on it. If you were to buy them from a builders'
merchant, they would cost 65–70p each. The merchant
puts on a hefty mark-up; anyone selling tiles ('from a little
barn this friend of mine in Hampshire wanted getting rid
of – he wanted to put a nice garage up') will be lucky to sell
them at 45p each, £450 a thousand, which would be
£5,400 for the load.

I am told that if there were a pair of you, and if you
really went for it, you could get a thousand off in half an
hour, that's six hours for the roof, in the depth of the
night, 11p.m. to 5a.m., and then you are away, the yield
as anonymous as you like. One tile looks pretty much like
another. There are, of course, colour variations between
tiles made within a few miles of each other, depending on
the clay, but that makes passing the goods on even easier.
Identifying the area from which tiles have come is nearly
impossible. It's a sure-fire theft. Someone somewhere will,
soon enough, be happy to pay the owner of an antique
architectural materials showroom something like £8,000
for your night's harvest.

So the wheel goes round: demand for old-looking roofs
means, inevitably, the destruction of old-looking roofs. I
know one new roof on a building a few miles from here
that was completed on a Friday and had disappeared by
the Monday. Everyone around here now has insurance
against tile theft and you could look on the whole
business as quite a contribution to the local economy.
I've heard it said that roofers, short of work, have stolen
the tiles, sold them, advertised their services to the

recently deroofed and then been paid to replace the tiles they had so recently removed.

As winter came on, we lived in dread of waking up to find, so to speak, the duvet whisked away and the whole household lying shivering under a light blanket of snow. You come to appreciate the enclosure of a house, its protective envelope, at the approach of winter when the world prepares for closure and withdrawal into itself. This was the time for shutting down, for the dumping of excess and the reduction of risk. Old leaves padded the sides of the lane so that you found yourself driving down a brown leaf runnel. The sodden bark of the trees and their twigs were leather-jacketed against the outside. The ponds were full to overbrimming. No insects moved, except one morning a lost butterfly, flittering inside my work-room and dying there, so that it came to lie stiff and dusty on my desk like a fragment of an old dress too fragile to wear. The hops I had hung up in the autumn turned crisp with the heating. A bee, drunk with winter, crawled hopelessly across the window, all wrong, bemused in a nectarless world.

At night with the torch, that November, I could catch the amber eyes of the deer, grazing out in the field beyond the wood now that the leaves had fallen. The grass was the only food to be had and the deer were dining on it in secret. In the early morning, when the light was still hesitant, half there, with the arms of mist pulling back into the wood, you could see the deer's dark bodies, still grazing, the last of the night shift before they too faded back between the trees, present one minute, absent the next, as the owls hooted for the last time and the day came on hard, if somehow still dark for all the light it brought.

All day long the fox would cruise up and down the fields between us and Coombe Wood. He was furtive and cat-like, a sneak among the grass, so that at times he disappeared behind a higher tuft, a slink of reddish brown in the dew-soaked field, low-slung, white-eared, padding through his territory. It was the time to worry for our ducks and chickens, which had been wandering about all summer and autumn as though no threat existed in their lives. At least the ducks had an island in the pond. We were making a new ark for the chickens around which, no doubt, the fox would taunt them at night, round and round with the smell of fear, the brilliant killer and his stupid prey. But what would happen when the hard frosts came? What would happen to the ducks then? The pond would be no moat for them. I would have to shut them up for days on end. It was not the time for openness.

I felt some hibernating impulse at work in us too. I found myself wanting everything tidied away, as though all the looseness and excrescence of the growing time of year were inappropriate now. We had been messy all year. Old cement sacks went wafting around the yard. Piles of semi-dealt-with stones, old paving slabs, some hardcore which never went into the trench it was intended to fill, bricks for a retaining wall which had yet to be built, steaming piles of manure, bean-sticks pulled out once the beans had been picked – all this lay around like the remains of a party no one had bothered to clear up. Urns from some flower arrangement Sarah had done in July were still where she had dumped them out of the Land Rover one warm summer evening. The lobster pot I had brought back from the Hebrides in early September was still stuffed into a corner of the cow shed. None of it looked fitting any more.

At least the fields were good and tight. This year we had, for the first time, managed them in the right way: grazed them hard over the winter, right down to the bones of clay and mud, let the best of them grow away to a big hay crop which we took in mid-July, and topped them twice after that. They looked like grassland should and I didn't mind taking people round. 'This field looks nice,' they said. What better feeling could there be than that, a well-made, well-kept piece of landscape for which all the people here who had helped over the year were responsible. Will and Peter Clark, Dave and Carolyn Fieldwick, Ken Weekes, Fred and Margaret Groombridge, Ray Bowley: they all had a share in how ready the place now looked.

We had sold our ram lambs and got good prices. We had sold our old ewes and old Roger. The remaining sheep were now with the new ram, a big young Kent, and would be lambing with his progeny in April. We had remade the driveway and redug the pond, putting it back where it was marked on maps before the war. An old man came by one day and said 'I'm glad to see the pond back.' That was good. The oast-house had been finished. The trees planted in the orchard last winter seemed to be growing all right, although one or two had died and needed replacing. The financial crisis of the autumn had been weathered, eased away. I had signed a contract to write a book, some money was coming in, our heads were above water. We could look forward again. There were hedges to go back on the old lines from where they had been torn out over the last 50 years or so. I was thinking of planting a new wood to divide up our biggest field, Great Flemings, and to give us chestnut poles for future fencing and hazel for the wattle windbreaks without which gardening up here was nearly impossible.

Sarah wanted to grow organic vegetables on a commercial scale and we drew out the plot on Beech Meadow, the most fertile of the land here. As the year closed down, and as the dark began to colonise the beginning and the end of each day, the tightness which that brought seemed enabling not debilitating. Hibernation was clarifying the purpose of being here at all. The rush and tumble of the more open times of year tended to obscure the point, which now, in the growing dark, emerged quite clearly. It was this: simply to get it right, to do it properly, to make something good that integrated all the virtues of a good landscape, a good place for people to be and work in, and a good way of farming and gardening. For the first time, on these cold and sodden mornings, I was starting to think we might one day get there.

I started sowing yellow rattle seed in Beech Meadow. Because days were short and I was too busy, I had been doing it just in the dark of the evening, as the frost was coming on and the grass began to crunch underfoot.

Yellow rattle is a slight and unimportant plant, which grows in hay meadows that have not been improved with new thick grasses and clovers. It is a sign of infertility, and infertility is, on the whole, what wild flowers like. At the end of summer, in the hay, the yellow rattle develops little round dry pods, which is why the plant is known, at least round here, as yellow bollocks or rattle bollocks, the loose seeds inside the pods still rattling even when the hay has been baled up.

But there's something else about yellow rattle, which was the reason I was walking slowly up and down our fields with a bag full of the crusty seed those winter evenings. It was more than just a means of escaping from an overheated house. Yellow rattle is semi-parasitic on grass. If you can manage to establish it in the sward, it will begin to drain away some of the vigour with which the dominant grasses grow. It's a way of reducing their dominance, of beginning to provide the conditions for some kind of herbaceous democracy in which all those other flowers we want here, the dyer's greenweed, the vetches and the orchids, might begin to decorate this landscape again.

It was only a trial patch of three acres. I bought three pounds of the seed, a pound an acre, for £60. It was collected last summer as part of a pilot project to restore floweriness to the meadows of the High Weald. No one is quite sure yet whether it will work, but the large plastic bags in which the seed came looked like the promise of a diverse and beautiful future.

I walked up and down in the cold of the evening, on the grass grazed tight now by the sheep. We would keep them in there until the end of February and then shut the fields up and let everything in them grow on until the hay was cut, late in the summer. I took handfuls of the seed out of the bag as I walked along, letting it dribble out between the fingers of my hand. I didn't scatter it as I might have been tempted to, like Millet's Sower, flinging handfuls of the precious stuff into the last of the evening light. You need a far more even, as if windblown, distribution to get the maximum effect.

Up and down, up and down across my fields, I felt like a draught-horse at work, not really considering what I was doing but in a removed and contemplative frame of mind. The clear plastic bag in which the seed came was identical to the clear plastic bag – albeit inside a small copper urn – in which I and my sisters had taken our mother's ashes a few years ago to a place in Switzerland she knew, a flowery meadow above Wengen in the Bernese Oberland, where, before she died, she had asked for them to be scattered.

This sowing of gritty mixed seed was rather like that strange, half-sad, half-gauche moment. I didn't dribble my mother's ashes through my hands. I simply tipped them slowly on to the grass straight out of the bag as we walked along. The wind took the lighter stuff away but the bulk of it fell on to the Alpine meadow like a top-dressing of some kind. I wondered then what the effect would be on the plants, what the biochemistry was of human ashes on Alpine flowers. Should I aim to spread them more widely? Would too much in one place be too rich for whatever was living there, too many trace elements in one helping? I started to swing the mouth of the bag to and fro, scattering the ashes more widely and thinly in the way that the nozzle at the back of a lorry salting the road scatters the salt in even swathes across the whole width of it.

At the very end of that bag, as of this one with the yellow rattle in it, the same moment came. Some specks of grit remained stuck in the corners, somehow held there

by the plastic, so that only by holding the bag upside
down and tautening and snapping it along its base would
those few flecks of human ash, or, now, of yellow rattle
seed, drop out on to the grass.

Why was it so important to leave these bags pristine and
empty? Why must even the slightest speck be distributed
on to the ground? Because ash and seed are not to be
wasted? Surely not. There was no practical consideration
here. But the idea, then, of putting even a microscopic
fragment of my mother's body in the waste-paper basket in
a hotel room in Grindelwald – which is where the plastic
bag went eventually, along with the urn, so flimsy that it
bent like a Coke tin – was unconscionable. And perhaps,
with this seed, the memory was too strong and the parallels
too close to treat the yellow rattle in any other way. One
bag and one sowing felt, however odd this might sound,
like a continuation of the other. And when I saw Beech
Meadow washed with the pale flowers of yellow rattle the
following summer, I thought of the hillside above Wengen,
from which the hay had recently been cut and raked, and
where the tourists on the mountain railway were looking
out through their passing carriage windows, wondering
what my sisters and I were doing with that bag of something, halfway through a rather sultry morning one week-
day in July. And of course, in part at least, we were
wondering the same thing too.

THE CLOSING OF DOORS

Everywhere around us there was evidence of things coming to an end. It was clearly a world in transition, one from which the old sustaining structures were falling away. Farm after farm was being sold up. Ex-farmers were looking for other kinds of work. A huge appetite from 'the London buyer' meant that places that would struggle to produce £15,000 a year in income were going for £750,000. The social network of old Sussex was fraying and disintegrating. All you could hear was the closing of doors.

I wanted to see one of the engines of this process at work, close up, and so I spent a Saturday morning in Freeman Forman, the estate agent's in Heathfield. There was electricity in the air. The London market was hungry for the country and here were the people who had the bait. Or at least they were desperately trying to scrape the bait together. There was, in the jargon, 'a lack of instructions', a clamouring pack of Londoners hunting for rural contentment but a deep and rather mysterious reluctance of people already in possession of that rural contentment to sell it to anyone else.

Joyce Eldridge, Office Manager, was there in red blazer and grey coiffure, a colour scheme to match both the walls and the swivelling upholstered chairs from which the staff were tending to the clients. John Morrilly, a man of long experience, was on the far side of the office, a blue-blazered specialist in the weekend business, and behind the scenes was Mike Sweetman, jacketless in a button-down shirt and well-established tan, advising on mortgage and financial services. Jason Stubbs was the valuer, sharp, young and hectic. Simon Forman – 'an excellent man,' Joyce said, 'inspirational, a superb motivator' – the partner and co-founder of the firm, was out winning business in his plum-coloured Mercedes. This was the well-honed team, but it was not always quite enough. 'I've got my husband on standby,' Joyce said. 'He's a retired banker and we use him. Well, we abuse him actually.' There was more steel to Joyce than you might have thought.

It was not quite high fives, getoutahere, yo! country in the Heathfield office that morning but things were heading that way. Jason Stubbs swivelled on his chair, phone hooked into his neck, a biro flicking between the fingers, sweet-talking a potential buyer. Joyce had this client on a red card. She explained: 'Green means local; but red means hot.' Jason was doing the talk. 'Smarden Farm,' he was saying, 'yeah, that's the fella. Total area extends to over three-quarters of an acre. Yup. Three nine nine.'

'A London Buyer,' Joyce half-whispered, half-mouthed at me. 'I love it when Jason drops his voice, don't you?'

Jason was building the position. 'It's a period property with bags of character,' he said. 'Give me a buzz on Monday and I'll tell you what's going on. That's right. If the property's right, if the price is right, it'll go. A period property, anything with tiling, in the Sussex style: that's not going to hang about, is it? Look at Greenoaks – you had Greenoaks didn't you? – right, or Sandy's Nook? We're getting offers for that kind of thing the same morning they come on the market.'

Somewhere in a hideous London street, a man living a desiccated life, anxious to escape the tight dreariness of his surroundings for the soft, green, sustaining generosity of the Sussex Weald, thinking in some ways he might be returning to a slightly simpler life, finds his previous vision of the countryside unravelling before his eyes. Now he realises the territory he has entered: estate agent heaven.

All four phones in the office were exploding into life, being picked up and the stream of ruralist fantasy was finding itself running and bubbling across the gravel bed of what really was and what it actually cost.

'You'd be looking at five or six for that.'

'How about 1.5 per cent for four weeks, sole agency?'

'He was asking 995, we had one million and twenty-five offered, it was accepted, two weeks to pay, he didn't get the money in time and so the guy sold it to someone else for one and a quarter. That's the way it's going. He's moving to Guernsey. It's more a tax thing than a weather thing.'

'No, but look what happened the other day over at Etchingham. They said "We're cash." But did that mean they were cash? No it did not. It meant they had 50 cash but they had to get another 250 somewhere else. And those other people at Stonegate. "We're sold." Too right. What did it mean? It meant someone had told them they were thinking of making an offer for their house. You can't be too careful.'

'When you say you'd prefer single ladies as neighbours, would ladies living with their husbands be all right?'

'Uh-huh, something older with a little bit of character. A period property, what we call a Country House. That's over 250. No, a Character Home would be under 250.'

'I have a Mrs Perrott who would like to come and look at Hunter's Hill at 3.30 today. Would that be convenient?'

Joyce explains to me how everyone wants the same thing. It's got to be deep in the country, a period property, in need of work, with land, not too done up, somewhere with character but capable of having its character erased by the new buyer putting his own stamp on it. This was close to home. I was not a person, I was a social phenomenon. I was the London Buyer, my house conforming to Joyce's stereotype, my existence a little knob of putty in Joyce's mighty palm. 'Joyce,' I said to her, 'you know so much.'

'Yes,' she said, 'but I don't know why people don't want to sell.'

'Do you think perhaps that people are waiting to make
a killing?' I said. 'You'd have a ball if you'd got something
to sell.'

'We would, but it's dead. We put adverts in the *Courier*
and we're inundated with people wanting to buy. But now
there's greed entering the market. It's a seller's market and
the sellers know it.' There was one case in particular,
unprecedented she thought, of a man who had a nice
house to sell. He was asking a million. Freeman Forman
prepared all the particulars but the client insisted on
sending them out himself to anyone who was interested.
He didn't explain why but the agents soon discovered.
Potential buyers were ringing up, outraged at the note
that the particulars for this house contained. It said, 'If
you are earning anything less than £350,000 a year, it's
not even worth your getting in touch.' Perhaps that was
the real pointer to the top end of rural bliss today: it was
fatcat country.

Soon afterwards I went to a meeting at the Horseshoe Inn
in Windmill Hill. Everything about it dramatised the very
opposite end of this process. Farmers and their wives,
perhaps 200 of them, had come here – from the High
Weald, from the Pevensey Levels and from the Downs.
Here were the Sussex farmers, not rich men, nor in your
tailored tweeds, but in heavy jerseys drawn tight over the
shoulders, rough, kitchen haircuts, faces in which the
wind had broken the veins, and a certain tense reticence,
a lack of ease in the public forum, overlying a sense of
unfairness, of an injustice being done to them.

They were all stock men, cattle and sheep farmers, and

they all used Hailsham Market to buy and sell. I'd seen some of them there before. It was a necessary part of their business, to realise some cash when they needed it, to sell at high prices and buy at low. The nearest other markets, apart from Rye which was small, were at Ashford in east Kent or Guildford in Surrey, both possible on a big occasion but too far on a regular basis, taking up most of a day to get there and back. These small farmers needed Hailsham Market if their businesses were to work.

But Hailsham Market, like nearly everything else in their lives, was under threat. The government had banned the building of out-of-town supermarkets and so the livestock market's location, within the confines of Hailsham itself, made it an ideal candidate for development. No one was sure who wanted it, but the name on everyone's lips was Sainsbury's.

The company that owned the market was getting £24,000 a year from the site. If they could sell it, with planning permission for a supermarket, it might be worth £1.5 to £2 million. In other words, the current return was 1 per cent of the site's potential value. If the market could be closed, the site could be sold, the shareholders would have realised a huge amount of money, the supermarket chain would be happy . . . and East Sussex would have lost its only cattle and sheep market.

In a back room of the Horseshoe Inn, a grey, functional, modern space for company dinners and anniversary dances, the farmers were crammed in, standing against the walls when the chairs were full. The local press sat at a table on the side. We were addressed by the chairman of an action group and then by a solicitor who described the threat to the market and the way to lobby against it.

Already Wadhurst, Lewes, Heathfield and Haywards Heath had lost their livestock markets to the same pressures: a growth in direct sales from farm to abattoir and an increase in the value of the market sites for other purposes, such as supermarkets or housing.

The solicitor, in his beard and grey suit, his fingers interlaced on the desk in front of him, dispassionately described what was obviously felt as an emotional issue in the room. Although his purpose was to motivate the farmers, he scarcely roused them. They listened to his description of the arcane processes by which Parliament works and of the methods they could adopt to address those processes, but the very way in which he talked made it all seem unapproachably foreign, as if this were not something an ordinary farmer could have anything to do with. At one moment he said 'There are lies, damned lies and developers' promises.' The room shifted at that, but its scarcely articulated anger did not emerge.

It then turned out that sitting there, in the front row but at one side, was the developers' own representative, Martin Robeson, Chartered Surveyor, of Littman and Robeson, acting on behalf of Carter Commercial Development. In the strangely theatrical way of these things, he looked exactly as a developers' agent should, with the sort of suede and black fur car-coat a developer in a TV drama would wear, a fairish goatee beard and a soft cow-lick of hair across his forehead. Questions began to drift away from the platform and towards him. He smoothly answered anything that was thrown at him, about the viability of the market and the ultimate purpose of his involvement here. 'Just because we intend to suspend the obligation to have a market here,' he said, 'does not mean to say that we will close the market.' There were jeers at that. A farmer from Punnett's Town – I could see his fields across the valley from Perch Hill – said 'As I see it, big money and vested interests are overriding the interests of local people and that is a disgrace.' There was applause for that and Robeson took on the role of bogeyman for the meeting, so that whenever he stood up to speak a grumble of resentment accompanied his words.

I spoke to him afterwards. He was in a hurry, he had to get back to Oxfordshire, but he smiled and said they had received 'a lot of quite expensive advice about this, so we feel pretty confident we've got a good case. On a long-term trend, the market isn't viable. The graph goes down.' he angled his hand towards the floor. 'We can prove that. And if the market is not viable then something else has got to happen to that land. OK?'

As we went out to the car park, I spoke to Buster Davis, the sheep farmer from Great Worge just up the lane. 'What do you think, Buster?' I said. He smiled. 'They've got all the money, haven't they? That's the problem. How do you fight that kind of thing? How do you fight it?'

As it happened, there was a stay of execution for Hailsham Market, for a year or two anyway, but that was one small stand against the flood. Otherwise, the local integrity of local places, sustaining local ways of doing things and local economic networks, out of which grow local social habits and a sense of locality in its richest forms – all that was draining away in front of my eyes like the suds in a soapy basin from which the plug has been pulled.

The farm sales were the worst. They were all, in their different ways, the same. Prinkle Farm, over at Dallington, went one sunny day. The tenant farmers had reached retiring age and their children had no wish to take it on. The 90 acres of heavy, steep clayland, even if run together in one unit with the neighbouring Carrick's Farm on the hill above it, could scarcely support a viable business. Closure was the most rational outcome: the tenants would go, the farmhouse would be sold or let to some ex-urban incomer, who could afford the rent or sale price, and the land would be absorbed in some larger enterprise. That was what usually happened. There had been a steady stream of farm sales around us. At each one, the life and belongings of the old farmers were sold away and the new money came in, nostalgic and acquisitive in equal measure.

At the sale itself, the crowds expressed nothing but delight as they picked over the remains of an existence whose time was now up. Hay knives, brass scales, horse harrows, implements whose use few could now recognise, cast-iron pig troughs, even cast-iron foot protectors, once strapped to their boots by men digging potatoes for too many hours at a stretch, had been dragged out of the back ends of sheds and half-abandoned barns and paraded here as 'mantelpiece stuff', 'bygones', 'collectables'. That was what got people excited and there was something vulturine about the excitement, a ravening for the carrion.

It was on a beautiful morning. The sun shone on the thousands of acres of Dallington Forest, arrayed before us around the flanks of the Dudwell valley. From the one or two farms scattered among the trees you could hear in the distance the heifers bellowing.

In the banky field opposite the farmhouse, three or four hundred cars and Land Rovers, some with trailers, were parked in ragged, shiny rows. And in the other banky field, the far side of the house, those innards of the farm were on show, long ribbons of intestine streaked across the field. All week the two identical twin brothers, John and Peter Keeley, both now 64 (Peter 10 minutes the elder), who had farmed here for the last 37 years, had laid out everything they could find. The auctioneers had brought other lots in from other farms. Over 1,000 people came to the sale, some from as far as the eastern end of Kent.

The chubby auctioneer, in shirt and tie, began. 'Look at that view,' he said. 'That's worth £50.' There was a buzz around him, a swarming so thick that only if you pushed in could you see him conducting the sale, lot by lot. These redundant objects were stripped of their dignity by the appetite for them. A group of three rather corroded old spring balances, used I suppose to weigh sacks of grain, lay on the grass in the centre of the clustering swarm. The usual rigmarole. 'What will you give me? Let's have a hundred. Eighty. Give me fifty. Fifty. I have fifty. Fifty-five. Sixty.' And so it went up. These things, neglected for 20, 30 years, who could say how long, sold to someone with some kind of farm museum for £80. A hay-knife went for £40. Nostalgic money, or at least money that intended to make money out of nostalgic money – there were thought to be at least 15 dealers here – poured out into the sunshine.

At the end of the row, we came to something else. It was a large Massey-Ferguson seed-drill, in good shape, capable of sowing 15 rows of seed at a time, a relatively hi-tech tool even if not of the most modern air-pressurised kind. It was a so-called combine drill which can inject nitrogen-based artificial fertiliser into the soil at the same time as the seed. It had obviously been kept in a shed and there was no rust on it.

'A fine Massey combine drill,' the auctioneer said. 'What will we have? Three hundred? Two? A hundred pounds? Fifty? Any bids? Any bids at all?' The crowd was silent around him. Some of them were clutching the bygones they had bought already, the cracked buckets, the unidentifiable implements, the blades from a root-cutter, the wormy hay rakes, the paring spade and the trenching gouge. Nobody wanted a tractor-drawn com-bine drill. Somebody offered a fiver and there was a little flurry, £7, £10, £12, £15, and there it stuck. £15 for a £3,000 seed drill of some real use if you were a cereal farmer but rather too big, at 12 feet by 8, for a mantel-piece.

'They would have got more if they had taken the wheels off and sold them separately,' a farmer said to me. But why did no one want it? 'Because you'd have to disc-harrow the field before you could use it. No one can be bothered with that.' Some tractors went for a couple of thousand and some mowers for a few hundred. The ewes averaged less than £40 a piece and the cattle under £300 a head, less than they had been bought for in the spring. It was all upside down: the decrepit was treasured, the useful and the healthy scarcely required.

I went to see the Keeley twins the next day. We sat and talked in their garden. They had never been apart for 64 years. Even when they did their national service, they had been together as radar operators in Fighter Command. 'He'll come on to say something,' John said, 'and I'll come out with it,' Peter said. They both sat on the edges of their chairs, both picking with their fingers at the other hand.

They were disappointed with the livestock but pleased at how the dead stock had gone. 'We were amazed at some of those prices,' Peter said. 'We couldn't believe some of it,' John said.

'A pig trow, cracked, for £50 . . .'

'Those horse harrows . . .'

'. . . we didn't even know we had half of it.'

'Those were the harrows Father used.'

'During the war . . .'

'. . . three hitched together.'

'The best one went for £25 was it?'

'£30 wasn't it?' They looked only at me throughout the duet.

This was the end of something. They had never sprayed their pastures 'because Father says it kills all the vetches . . .'

'. . . all the herbs.'

'We just run the mower over it.'

What Father says remains in the present tense. The sale had been 'a terrible day, a terrible emotional day.'

'My stomach was churning over all day . . .'

'. . . turning over and over.'

'A terrible emotional day.'

John was staying in a bungalow in Dallington. Peter was moving to a house in Ninfield because he couldn't afford one in the 'village on the hill', as he described the place he had always lived. 'That's what I'm most sorry about, he said, 'leaving the district. It won't be the same.' Ninfield was just over six miles away. Something had come to an end.

The catastrophe was going on all round us, the ebbing of a tide, leaving a new and denuded geography. The Weald is a place of small farms, 100 acres on average, and more woods than anywhere else in England; of low incomes, intractable soils poor in trace elements, and of great beauty. The exigencies of the modern market have made this whole way of life virtually untenable now. The impact here falls not on farm-workers but on the small independent farmers who have always been the backbone of the place. It was always dairy country, but the Weald dairy herd had dropped by 40 per cent – 20,000 cows – in a decade. The number of full-time farm-workers had declined by a quarter in the same period.

The District Council made a study of four Wealden parishes which found that, of 75 farms in those parishes, not a single one could make enough profit to provide a market return on the land, labour and capital that were needed to run it. Low incomes meant no reinvestment, which meant lower incomes in the future, which meant no investment, which meant decline and collapse. Wealden farmers were already deeply in debt, far more than the national farming average, and there was already a danger that they would not be able to keep up with their interest payments. That year many were hanging on, hoping for something better, not wanting to give up the lives and the places that make them what they are. The general farming decline in the late 90s compounded a situation already taut and tense with strain. Failure was being staved off week by week.

Yet these beautiful and unprofitable farms were worth a fortune. A pretty, comfortable farmhouse and 100 acres or so of wood and pasture was selling to the urban rich for anything up to £750,000. 'Why not let the market take its course?' a particularly cold-brained city analyst said to me one day at a drinks party where we were leaning up against a fireplace together. 'Let the uneconomic farmers go out of business and realise their one real asset – the place. Send them off to live on the investment income and allow the commodity brokers and merchant bankers the pleasure of owning their place in the country. The real value of the Weald is now effectively as extensive suburbia. Any other outcome would be artificial.'

That was, effectively, what had happened to upstate New York or Connecticut. The farms had been abandoned, driven out of business by the massive cheapness of the prairie, and the trees had reinvaded the pastures. You could drive for miles through derelict landscapes where the old field walls net the scrubby woodland like the ghosts of a life once lived; where clapboarded family residences, occupied by Martha Stewart clones, preside over their own private, wood-hemmed clearings. Why not let the Weald become Connecticut?

I felt a big raging NO come up inside me. Why not? Because the essential quality of the place comes from the sort of farmers and woodmen who had made it. Lose them and the place would be lost, the people would be lost, the life of the meadows and the coppiced woods would be lost.

A wrinkling realist sneer crosses the lips of the city man. 'What are you going to do about it, then?' I made him a speech. The place derived its qualities from being a labour-intensive landscape. Modern farming orthodoxy had seen labour-intensiveness as the great enemy, to be eradicated at all costs. But labour-intensiveness, as some people were now coming to realise, was the essential ingredient of the good landscape. It employed more people; it attended to the needs of the landscape more closely than a system whose priorities were set by the requirements of the machinery and chemicals used to run it; it generated other jobs; and it created places that other people would want to come to, see and stay in.

Didn't this provide a clear model for the future of any agricultural subsidy? Don't pay farms to sack people and then ruin the landscape with the giant labour-saving machines the subsidies allow them to afford. Pay farmers to employ people and to look after the more close-knit kind of landscape that people love. Hedges needed hedgers. Payments should be made not per acre, as they then were, but per man employed. If there was a stimulated demand for farm labour, then farm wages would rise, the rural economy would benefit and so would rural services. Instead of money pouring into the pockets of machinery manufacturers and chemical conglomerates, it would be spent in the village shop. People made places good.

I knew one place, just along the lane the other side of Brightling, which did in some ways embody what might happen to the Weald, providing a route out of disintegration and the purely suburban. It was an inspiration, a folding over of tradition into the future. More than 20 years before, David Wenman, a graphic designer, and Karen his wife, a nurse, had visited a friend who had a dairy farm outside Battle. They helped him with the haying. 'This is nice,' they thought, and their life turned a corner.

They looked for somewhere for months. They wanted to be away from the big roads and have a well-drained, south-facing slope, sheltered but not windless, because bugs gather in windless places. It had to be remote, or anyway feel as if it were.

They found, at last, ten acres of field for sale near Brightling. There was no piped water, no electricity, no track down into the land off the lane. But the sun shone on the sloping fields, the wood beyond the Glottenham Stream provided shelter but not too much of it and, like so many of the fields in this pocket of woody England, it had an air for the Wenmans of arrival and wholeness, of being the place where they needed to be. They called their farm Scragoak, which was the old name for it, meaning an oak with great lumps and scrags on its bole.

They bought a tatty caravan and put it on one of the fields. It was not popular locally. They were too alternative, Friends of the Earth, Greenpeace, Anti-Apartheid, CND-ers, for the older locals. There were petitions and planning problems. Clearly, the Wenmans looked alarmingly subversive. They were described as gypsies by the old Wealden culture into which they had parachuted. They may have seemed alien but, as the story of the following 20 years shows, it was the Wenmans who, in some ways, were the true heirs to the traditions of Wealden smallholders, the independent-minded, self-sufficient, anti-establishment types who had occupied these wood-encompassed farms, always marginal, since they were first settled in the fifteenth century.

By the early 1980s Karen and David had set up a tiny shop on the laneside, 'a shack like a shed', in which they sold the organic potatoes and carrots they had grown, as well as local apple juice and organic flour. There were chickens, goats, Gloucester Old Spot pigs, beef steers and 70 geese which they fattened for Christmas.

The shop was repeatedly burgled, and their freezers and scales taken. The decision was made for them. They got rid of the pigs, moved the shop down into the old farrowing pens, away from the road, and concentrated on vegetables. Mountains of mushroom compost, organic straw, calcified seaweed and horse dung was ploughed into the heavy clay to lighten it. Drains were put in and the Wenmans turned decisively towards the market.

It was a significant change, part of the much larger transformation that came over the whole green movement in the mid-80s. From seeing themselves as the pioneers of a new way of living, in fierce distinction to the world that surrounded them, they turned into providers of good food for that world. They boomed. The

shop, which began to stock all sorts of organic things from
all over the world which they couldn't produce themselves, was turning over £3,000 a week. They kept it open
all year round. Other people came to work for them. The
housekeepers of the rich and famous did their shopping
there. By 1988, the Wenmans could afford, against some
local opposition, to build themselves a small house on the
farm.

Then there was the crash. By 1990, turnover had
shrunk to £600 a week. Karen was forced to return to
nursing, at least part-time, to make up the income. David
slogged on at the farm, 'docks and thistles, docks and
thistles, pulling and pulling and pulling. I've been getting
a spade to them for years and years.' The whole organic
business was collapsing. The supermarkets, which held a
whip hand over producers, wound down their organic
sections and producer after producer went bust. The
Wenmans could afford to invest nothing in the farm
and fell behind with their mortgage payments. Scragoak
was put on the market but no one wanted to buy it.

In the pit of the recession the Wenmans were faced
with bankruptcy and failure, not simply of a business but
of a whole way of being. They could do nothing but stick
it out. 'You just carry on really,' was their phlegmatic
description of this time in their lives.

Slowly the world turned back towards them. The
business ground back up to pre-crash levels. Karen could
give up nursing again. They became part of the box-
scheme phenomenon. All over the country, away from
the influence of supermarkets, organic growers began to
sell direct into people's houses, with weekly deliveries of

vegetables, a service to which the householders sub-
scribed. Scragoak was soon delivering 300 boxes a week,
all round south-east England at prices from £5 to £9 a box.
There was a new shop on the farm. You could buy organic
champagne there, wholewheat spaghetti tricolore, organic baby rice and all the rest of it. The buildings and the
polytunnels were surrounded by seas of leeks and beet-
root, Florence fennel and Swiss chard. The Wenmans
employed five other people, part- and full-time, and there
was an air of buoyancy, enterprise and success. It was a
wonderful place to go, like so many organic farms,
heroically maintained in the face of great difficulty and
many hard lessons. They were turning over £250,000 a
year on ten acres. It was a measure of what might be.

There were others in whom a real sense of the optimism
and possibilities of the future were burgeoning out of the
death of the old ways. 'Will you look at that?' Simon
Bishop said to us all one evening. Farmer, chef, agricultural lecturer, father, husband, wit and Sussex man into
the very pit of his boots, just turned 40, slightly thin on
top, smiling a gee-shucks smile like Wallace and Gromit's,
he took a wing rib from the oven and placed it on the
table in front of us. It was from a pure-bred Sussex steer he
had raised himself. Sarah, I and our two daughters,
Simon's wife Tessa, their daughters Becky and Holly
and their son James were all there around the table.
The winter night was dark outside. There were candles on
the table. 'Quiet everyone,' Simon said.
  We looked reverently on the glistening rib, its glazed
surfaces, its ruckled fat, the oozing flanks of meat. It was

beef on the bone, months after such a thing had been banned amid the BSE crisis. We gazed on its heroic naturalness, its grand status as a hunk of nature. 'Will you look at that,' Simon said. 'It's holy.'

'Get on and cut the thing,' Tessa said. 'I'm starving.'

'Wait,' Simon said, with a sudden and astonishing inrush of authority. 'We must let it rest.'

'What do you mean, rest?' Tessa said. 'It's dead.'

Simon, the priest-magician, easing and wooing with his spell-casting fingers, said that the juices had to go back into the meat. We waited as the smells wafted around the dining-room. Cooked in an oven that was fuelled by logs cut on this farm; surrounded by the leeks, carrots, potatoes, beetroots, red and white onions, marrow, to-matoes and parsnips that the Bishops had grown here, this too was a version of completeness, of how things should be.

The moment would have been less without that beef and without that bone. The primitive crudity of what was obviously a cooked part of an animal played a necessary part in the drama. It was the base-line, the level at which you could be certain that this was what it said it was. Nothing had come between us and the animal except the killing, the butchering and the roasting of it. Here was the man who brought it up, who tended it until it was ready, who invited the butcher down to have a look, awaited his verdict, which was whispered, confidential ('It does you credit, Simon'), who chose the hauliers to take the animal without fuss on the four- or five-mile journey to the abattoir, who had it back here now to eat with his family and friends. This beef was a form of certainty made flesh.

Perhaps only what is threatened needs celebration. The beef feast at Simon Bishop's farm was such a moment because so few could enjoy it. If this had been a restaurant and he were not the grower, he would have been prosecuted for that dinner and heavily fined. Any chance of BSE being present in his animals, let alone of us contracting new variant CJD from eating the beef, was literally nil. The wing rib came from Simon's single suckler herd, in which the animals, once they have weaned themselves from their mothers, are fed on nothing but the grass in the fields outside the window and the silage made on the farm. But the law applied to this beef as to any other. Beef on the bone was treated as poisonous.

It was a kind of madness, a floating away of the legal and political understanding of what was right from the shared, communal understanding of what was right. But it was also a measure of more than that: the culmination of a wrong approach to farming, a wrong vision of our relationship to farmed animals and a wrong, purely mechanistic, understanding of our relationship to the rest of creation.

Of course, one can be sentimental about the local, about the old ways of doing things, and all too easily forget what was wrong with it. One day that year in Burwash, someone put up a large placard on his house wall. It said simply: 'Keep Burwash Clean and White.' Its author wouldn't talk to me about it. 'It was only up there 12 hours,' he said. 'To tell you the truth I didn't know what I was saying and I got so much strife about it. The village, the police, the lot, they were all giving me grief . . . So I'm sorry but it's no comment. That's all I've got to say.'

There had been a plan to set up an Indian takeaway in an empty shop – it was, by chance, the building in which my neighbour Shirley Ellman had once had her accountancy business – down at one end of the High Street. It had been met with a general burbling discontent, at least from those who lived at that end of the village. Only the author of the sign had come out quite so blankly with the racial purity line. The other arguments had focused on the traffic hazard of having a takeaway on that difficult corner, the lack of car parking and the possibility of litter. They pointed out that an application for a fish-and-chip shop a couple of years previously had met with exactly the same objections and that one of the pubs had had a huge success with a Thai evening not long before, which was more than welcome. So the problem with the Indians was nothing to do with their race or colour. When you mentioned the poster, there was a slight, smiling turning away, 'disgraceful', not the right way to go about this at all. Only at the margins did the objectors move off on to hazier ground. They began with the idea that a place should be able to decide what it wants for itself. It was all about 'keeping Burwash a village, with a village atmosphere'. After a little downwind drift, this argument started to talk about 'a nice village' and then perhaps 'a nice English village, with a traditional English atmosphere' and then, if you began to ask what it was that might erode that atmosphere, the smell of the rejected alien began to waft across the Sussex fields.

Once I was attuned to the presence of this thought-

chute in the ways of rural England, I started to detect it everywhere. By chance, after seeing the white supremacist poster in Burwash, I happened to be talking on the phone to a local lady. We were discussing the most insistent pressures on the rural landscape, roads perhaps, housing certainly, when without any warning she took a swerve into dangerous territory: 'Let's be honest about it, Adam,' she said confidingly, 'we don't want fuzzy-wuzzies and nignogs, do we, and you're bound to get them unless you're careful.'

Perhaps this is everywhere, virtually unstated, or stated only in private, the hidden but governing motivation of rural England. It brought back to mind a charming and wonderful man I knew once in Somerset. He was an eel fisherman. He knew everything about those secret and magical creatures, their lying-up places in the rhynes and ditches of the Levels, the way to catch the elvers as they came in off the Atlantic, smelling their way to the sweet fresh water of the moorlands, and the excitement of the silver eel harvest when, on a stormy and moonlit night late in the year, with a big spring tide licking its way deep inland, the adult eels, their backs silvered in maturity, make a sudden rush for the ocean, in places teeming across the fields like a disease or an infestation, rustling in the night past your feet in the grasses. Everything about this man and his intimacy with the place where he lived was to be admired. But then I asked him what he did with the eels that he caught. 'I send them up to London,' he said. 'We put them in boxes with holes in so they can breathe, and when they get there it's the Jews that eat them. We don't eat them. It's only the Jews in London

that eat that sort of thing.' No description of anything
could have seemed more alien to him than 'the Jews in
London'. The phrase was shorthand for everything that
was not his and not known, not down there with him in
the wet, private world of the Somerset Levels.

I wonder now, in the light of this, if my own liberal
attitude is not in something of a muddle. There is little I
value more than the kind of local distinctiveness which
oozed from the eel-man's pores. He was the human
version of the place he lived in. He drew his sustenance
from the almost purely local and as a result had a kind of
integrity which had its roots in the closeness with which
he was moulded to the place. But it was precisely those
same qualities which led him to think about the Jews in
London in the way he did.

Can you have one without the other? Does the fluidity
and acceptance of the strange, which is central to a liberal
view of the world, always eat away at the sense of the local
which is so valuable a part of the rural landscape? Is local
distinctiveness necessarily intolerant of the foreign?

No one addresses this difficult question. We all assume
instead that one can have something that is locally vital,
of the place, distinct from other places, rich in its in-
dividuality, which is nevertheless liberally and happily
open to the other, prepared to accept all versions of the
strange without gagging on them. Of course this can't be
true. I would love to have an Indian takeaway in Burwash. I wouldn't have to go to Heathfield to get my prawn
korma. But that is only a measure of what an urban alien I
am anyway. I don't describe gypsies, or people who look
as if they might be gypsies, as 'pikey', but most of the

Sussex people round here do. 'Who was that pikey lot round here last night,' they will say, if they don't like the look of someone new. Pikey: there is something highly aggressive in the word. Its connotations are of petty thieving and travelling rootlessness, of the kind that doesn't know, or at least doesn't care, about the local rules, the well-worn ways of doing things. The two attitudes – attendance to the local, distrust of the foreign – are founded on each other. One is the other's ugly side. Is it sentimental to select one and despise the other? Perhaps it is. This landscape certainly loathes the alien. But despite that recognition, I nurture a hope, never-theless, that a new way is possible, that a new future, local but tolerant, embedded but open, conscious of tradition but not entrapped by it, able to farm in ways that sustain the environment without folding back into a park-keeper mentality, might emerge from the crisis that is afflicting this place.

I was upstairs, one spring morning, in my work-room in the oast-house, hiding. It was the first day of Sarah's courses. She was running them here at home. It was the first real attempt to make some money out of Perch Hill. She would teach people how to create a cutting garden, that is to say a garden not for looking at but for harvesting or in other words destroying. Cutting Garden, Killing Fields, what was the difference? This refined combination of nurture and vengeance had obviously appealed to the darker regions of the nation's soul. Seventy-two people, exclu-sively women, had signed up and, not of course that this was in any way important, paid up. But now Sarah had to deliver what her brochure had promised. I could hear her voice in the room below mine, telling the ladies about the need for 'a good friable soil and a warm, well-drained site.' An absorbed silence accompanied her words.

It had begun as a nightmare. The worst frost of the year had chosen the previous night to attack and we woke up to see the thousands of tulips and imperial fritillaries bowed and frozen, like ranks of collapsed ice-lollies. The euphorbia was drooping on to the path when it should have been all pert and Edwina Curriesque. Then Anna Cheney's car broke down in the village and so there was no one to look after the children. Anna was going to bring Peter Clark to help tidy the garden, so he couldn't get here either. Half an hour later, the fleet of beautiful new silver Audis and dark blue Mercs started to nose cautiously into the farmyard. We knew there was nothing to pick. Secret panic reigned. 'Keep them inside till everything warms up,' I hissed at Sarah. A look of utter despair passed across her face. I then brushed the paths rather badly, hoping the ladies might think chaos charming. Then my father turned up and insisted on pressing his nose against the lecture-room window to see what the ladies looked like inside. God knows what kind of impression we were making.

By 11.30a.m. we'd had the first session and then coffee. My sister Juliet cleaned the floor. The flowers had begun to lift in the sunshine. During the coffee break, two of the ducks decided to have sex in one of the flower-beds outside the kitchen. It was a terrifying vision of avian rape which finished only as the drake decided he'd had enough and walked away straight on up the back of his victim and then over her head, shoving it deep into the mushroom compost, as though her body was just another one of those things one has to negotiate in life. The rapee shuddered and shook herself like someone coming out of the shower in a shampoo ad. 'Do you always let the ducks into the garden?' a lady in an apricot cardigan said to me. Before I could answer, Rosie, my three-year-old daughter, in a deep Sussex accent said 'Oh yeah. They eat the slugs, donay Dad?' 'Oh really,' Mrs Apricot murmured and sipped at her coffee, smiling a little distantly with her eyes.

Just before lunch, the party was out in the garden wielding scissors. Individual characters were emerging. Those who felt they shouldn't entirely destroy Sarah's incredible, sumptuous, intense and beautiful spring garden were hesitating before snipping one or two rather small tulips that were, if they were honest about it, slightly going over. Others, it was clear, thought they'd paid their money and so they were bloody well going to make their choice. One lady in particular returned with a bunch so large that you couldn't see her head behind it. I was hoping she would trip over. She didn't, but dumped her gatherings in a bucket and then said to me, 'Are you the man who tells everyone he writes articles in the *Telegraph*?'

'Yes,' I said, a little warily.

'Well, I've never seen any. Have you ever got one published?' I could hear myself laughing and it sounded like the last drops of water draining from the bath.

Lunch was a rip-roaring success. Just before it began, Sarah had recommended that cut flowers needed one thing more than anything else: a good long drink. 'Oh yeaah,' one laconic American beauty said, 'and what about the clients?' Long drinks all round.

After lunch, the natural tendency was to wander a little among the flowers, over towards the edge of the garden from which the lovely view stretches down the Dudwell valley. That was all very well for background, but in the foreground, upwind in the prevailing breeze, was the totally failed, utterly disgusting and profoundly health-hazardous reed-bed sewage system whose accompanying pond still looked like a tureen full of mushy peas. It was of course inevitable that the entire course should end up surveying this part of the garden.

A Neapolitan smell of what are always called 'drains' blew across the ladies. I was praying they thought it something obscurely agricultural. 'Is that your wildlife pond?' one of them asked empathetically. A long and quivering moment of hesitation followed. Could I possibly get away with this lie? Which answer would be least likely to undermine Sarah's standing as a horticulturalist of genius? 'Yes,' I said resolutely. 'We think it's very important to allow the wild a place in the garden and for all sorts of natural processes to be seen for what they are . . .' Grim nods all round at the wisdom of this, and I saw one of the Japanese ladies making a note in her notebook. I knew what it said: 'English character – never less trustworthy than when claiming high moral ground.'

By 5p.m. it was over. We slumped around the kitchen table. A champagne cork lolled on the floor. Only another nine days like that one. It had been a triumph. Every one of them went away saying how much they'd enjoyed themselves. Sarah was exhausted but exultant.

Everything worked in the end. I was thinking of the money and how to get the schmooze schmoozier. 'Ladies,' perhaps I would say next lunchtime, 'I'd like to show you our wildlife pond. It's so important to let the wild into the garden, don't you think?' Or perhaps not. Sarah said it would be better if I spent the day in London.

For some reason, high stress entered our lives that third summer. Word had got out among the local ladies that I had described them in one of my articles as 'cheques on wheels'. Sarah was unable to show her face when taking Rosie to school in the morning. What I had written was passed around on the 7.42 from Stonegate, the commuting husbands sitting in judgement on the cruel descriptions of their innocent wives. Sarah was told that having a husband like me must be like driving a car with dodgy brakes.

One evening – it was actually the night the fox finally dismembered our few remaining chickens – Sarah and I went to a lovely party, Moroccan theme. I was in a sheer cotton nightie with Afghan dressing gown and borrowed fez. Sarah was in black velvet. Many of those I had recently insulted were there. The offending article had, it turned out, been passed around at Lloyd's. I tried to describe how it came out much ruder than I meant it to. I had meant the jokes to be as much on our own uselessness (smelly sewage, randy ducks, financial chaos) as on anyone who was nice enough and interested enough to come on Sarah's course. It was no good. Somehow, invisibly, as I wafted about in my nightie, I knew I carried a giant placard on front and back like a sandwich man: GUILTY.

It all contributed to the stress levels. We were running out
of money again and had terrible rows about it after a glass
or two of wine. As we were trying to work out how to
reduce our outgoings, I sometimes wondered if we had got
the recipe wrong here. To engage with things to the depth
which, for some reason, we thought we should was so
demanding that the point of doing it was in danger of
getting drowned. The simple life, or at least the version of
it which our inner psychic drives were pushing us towards, was the very opposite of simple.

What we had landed ourselves with was a maze of
commitment and complexity, an organic interlocking of
people and place and process. It was expensive, compli-
cated, ambitious, prone to disaster and failure. It could
produce moments of unassimilated, ecstatic beauty and
happiness – our daughters in the uncut hay – and times
when things had gone so well that an effortless unfolding
into the sunlit future was all that seemed to await us. But
in truth, that was not the dominant note. Our need to
improve house, garden, farm, oast, cow shed, woods,
hedges, grazing, gates and fences – and still go on holiday
– had left us overstretched, in more than just the financial
sense. It was difficult, in the end, to say whether this life
and this place that we had chosen were more sustaining or
more demanding. Were we pouring our energies into
something which would never, even in the end, reach
a contented equilibrium? Would it always niggle, a sickly
little hollow in the stomach at night?

Sometimes I was convinced that this was true, and
hankered for a place that made fewer demands, that cost
less, that was simpler, the place-equivalent of the shop-

bought rather than the fox-murdered chicken. But lingering in the back of my mind was the idea that the two things – the sustaining and the demanding – were in some way connected. Was a place, or a way of life, only sustaining to the extent that it made demands of you? That, at least, was an interesting idea. It was what everyone always says about a marriage, that horrible phrase 'working at it', which comes out of people's mouths, groaning and grinding its way into a gloomy world. I'd rather think of my marriage as Nijinski and Isadora Duncan carelessly laughing their way across the high grasslands of the steppe, but I could see that might not be an entirely realistic or comprehensive picture. Sometimes, it was rather more like a pair of oxen plodding their way across a brown, muddy field.

This was the theory then: in the same way that home-murdered chicken is tastier than the shop-bought variety, precisely because you've got down there with it in the crucial life-and-death moments; and in the same way that a marriage which chews over its own domestic cud from time to time is better than an oh-so-beautiful, windblown relationship that sashays its way from Porto Ercole to Patmos via an exquisite little Berber village in the High Atlas; so living in a place that demands total involvement, sacrifice and pain is more satisfying than somewhere that you might feel a little extraneous and *dégagé*. The condition to be avoided is to be a tourist in your own life, that awful alienated gazing you see on the faces of New Zealanders in Trafalgar Square, a kind of gravity-free looking around by people in brown trousers and white trainers, an aching on their faces for something that means anything to them, a hunger that lasts until they take photos of each other in front of Nelson's Column, the nearest thing to a familiar object they can find in this hemisphere. That, of course, would be a fate worse than over-commitment.

So the idea of a euphoric freedom was illusory. The only choice was between slogging away for 15 years to make ourselves happy, and vacuous weightlessness. Isadora Duncan was a piece of lying propaganda; the ox in harness is the only happy beast.

I wasn't sure.

The earthworks on which Sarah had embarked were eating away at me. I heard her on the phone to Frisky Fieldwick, the earth-moving contractor. 'I would have thought two or three men for a month would do it,' she said. I opened a bottle of whisky.

Frisky was one of the wildest-looking people I had ever met. He was the human equivalent of a Sussex wood. If you stood him in the undergrowth of some rather unkempt coppice, it would be impossible to tell he was there. Like those wonderful 1960s photographs of the model Veroushka, her body painted to mimic the wall or trees against which she stood, Frisky would quite naturally have melted into his background. If I had to cast Puck, he would be the man. It may largely be an effect of his hair, which looks like a hedge which has been driven through by an alcoholic with a brush-cutter, or maybe the jerseys the colour and consistency of a well-raked loam. I never saw him wearing anything except ten-gallon gumboots but Frisky was pure style. He would have looked fantastic on a cat-walk – Alan Bates meets Alexander McQueen – and he was blessed with the most spellbindingly seductive manner.

I tried to adopt something of the way in which he presented a bill. An enormous smile stole across his face, one eyebrow lifted a little, his hand moved like a gunfighter's towards his back pocket and you knew what was coming. 'You know what's coming, don't you Adam?' he would say as the brown envelope, always folded in two, began to move elegantly towards you. The ritual continued. It was the same every time. 'I suppose you'd like it paid today, Frisky?'

'Well, we've all got bills to pay.'

'Yes, but have we got money to pay them? That's the question isn't it?' I said.

'Some of us have and some of us haven't. I tell you Adam, the money doesn't stay in my pocket. It'll be gone by ten o'clock this morning.'

I would write the cheque out to 'T.A. Fieldwick.' I had no idea what either T or A stood for. Meanwhile Frisky continued with the charm offensive. 'Now what about a pony for your little girls, a nice New Forest pony? They'd love a bit of riding round here. You've got just the place for it.' Frisky, apart from being earth-mover extraordinaire, also bred and dealt in horses but thank God I managed to resist. 'Think of the memories they'll have,' he would say. I knew that he knew that I wouldn't dream of buying any horses, but we went through this little routine most weeks all the same.

'And why is it you're called Frisky, Frisky?' I then asked, going back to a favourite topic.

'Oh it's because I was pretty frisky once!' he said, pocketing the cheque.

Paying for the earth-moving was the best part of it. For some reason, I found the actual digging deeply disturbing. Frisky would turn up in his Land Rover, which was loose and baggy, like a giant gumboot. With him would come his son Jason and Jason's younger brother Ben. All three Fieldwicks had smiles like searchlights. They climbed on to the diggers and dumpers, Steve Moody, the garden contractor from up the lane, would join them, and the work began. Parts of the place, familiar not only to us but to the 20 generations of farmers who had thought of Perch Hill as their home and foundation, were sliced and eased away as if they had no permanence. This was surgery, landscape liposuction.

I couldn't bear to watch. I felt threatened and uneasy. I spent hours in my work-room reading yellowing copies of articles I had written 20 years before. Sarah was striding around like Patton in Normandy, buoyed up by change, by things happening, by the sight of the Fieldwick battalion making its all-too-definitive cuts.

I knew, in my rational self, that this work was a good idea. The area around the pond was a mess and needed improvement. I knew that and I was sure that what would emerge would be better than what was there before. But for all that, the process was troubling. The Fieldwicks were blithe, confident and skilful. And perhaps it was precisely that panache in execution which was troubling. I wanted to think that the place I saw around me was imbued with a permanence I didn't have myself. Everything we had done to Perch Hill Farm since coming here had been to enhance that sense of deepness and solidity. The buildings were now embedded in gardens that weren't here before. The house was literally surrounded by gardens and garden walls. It was as though we had pegged the place down. These new earthworks were part of that process too. When the little wood that we were planting on top of them had grown, full of hazels and hawthorns, wild cherries and one or two oaks, they too would embrace the buildings and farmyard, folding them in, diminishing the rather bruised openness we found on our arrival.

Sarah could clearly see the conclusion. I found myself stumbling over the way to get there. These machines were showing us how powerful we were in relation to the place. We could have demolished the whole lot in a couple of days. Within half a mile were the abandoned sites of two farmsteads which, until 15 years before, had everything you might have wished for: beautiful stone farmhouses, barns, yards, farm ponds, lives lived, memories treasured. They were demolished one day by the landlord, to prevent squatters occupying them. In the summer the nettles now grew there shoulder-high. It was that threat of erasure which alarmed me.

One day I was trying to show off to Steve Moody, the strapping gardener and dumper-truck driver. In Sarah's Blenheim-scale rearrangement of the local landscape, Steve had been acting as her *chef d'équipe*. Digging a couple of holes was meant to be my contribution. This was a mistake. Ever since an experience with a beautifully muscled masseur in the Andalucian quarter of Fez – I think the place was called the Hammam Ritzy-Sevilla – in the late 70s, my back had not been what it should be. The big masseur, gleaming like an aubergine, as heartless as a stone, didn't seem to have cottoned on to the modern idea that 'No means no.' He obviously thought my scream-groans were the English for 'Stop it, I love it.' Ever since, a niggle has lurked down there somewhere in my lumbar regions to remind me of the foolishness of youth.

But sometimes vanity and competitiveness get the better of me and I imagine that manual labour is something I can still do as well as the next man. That's why I walked out that day with spade and shovel to the site of the new orchard. Funded by a remortgage, a serious workforce had been on site for three weeks. A National Trust-standard car park had been installed. The ground had been cleared, what looked like blitz detritus had been spread over it, then a layer of stone precisely the colour of taramasalata, then some more blitz rubble of a finer grade, then blackish road scrapings, which might be mistaken for dead men's teeth, partly ground, and then the final Lutyensesque topping of rich, deep river stones.

Future archaeologists would scratch their heads over this centrepiece of the new works. How on earth could a hovel like Perch Hill Farm have deserved something modelled so carefully on the traffic-handling facilities at Sir Norman Foster's Stansted Airport? For the answer they would have to hire a medium to interrogate my wife's spirit. 'OBSESSION,' the Ouija board would spell out. I hoped the spirit world would understand. At least, as the debt collectors and Inland Revenue representatives turned up over the following months at our superbly enhanced back door area, they would enjoy that most opulent of English sounds, the deep, swimming, semi-liquid crunch and susurration of tyre on gravel. Don't thank me, thank the Nationwide. I took to signing off letters to them with the words 'Yours literally,' but I don't think they ever quite got the joke.

My contribution to the Wealden Versailles was to plant and stake a couple of apple trees. The first was OK: hole, tree, stake, ties, earth, water, complete. The second went hole, tree AAAAAARGGHHH, that neural, spasmodic, earth-shattering click, the moment every back-pain sufferer will recognise as the gates of hell. At least that was the sound inside. I wasn't going to show Steve anything was wrong. 'I'll think I'll go and get a glass of water,' I told him and broke for the house, stiffening, hobbling, crumbling upstairs and on to the bed, where I then stayed for a week, laid out, aged and with only my drugs and my laptop for company.

It was deep, deep agony at the time, an all-over clenching pain, but it wasn't long before I was under some really big-time medication. Sarah said I was as high as a kite but it didn't feel like that from the inside. It was the normal me in a rather good mood. Just a shot or two of morphine they gave me. Pure liquid wooze it was, straight in, happiness from a needle and I felt fantastic. At last I'd come to understand the drug culture. The world was just beautiful, beautiful. Everyone loved me and I loved everyone. The sheep were woolly and the grass was green. I was having my own private Woodstock, but the sun was shining. We were deep into hippydom here and I was wearing my Afghan dressing gown. Modern technological medicine is a remarkable and adorable thing. Who needs the Tardis when you can have such a charming low-tech visit from the Burwash GP?

It was a dreadful/lovely time. Dreadful for the hint of paralysis it brought, those shuddering spasms of pain – the condition of washing as it travels through a mangle – but lovely as the drugs came on and you started to think this was the best of all possible worlds, that warm druggy dusk of sleepiness after pain.

I could see only the sky from my bed but I could hear life going on: trucks delivering yet further tonnages from the quarries of the globe; Sarah on the phone next to the open kitchen window saying 'Of course I wanted 4,000. If I said 4,000, what do you think I meant? 400?'; Steve banging in post after post as his trees went effortlessly in; Ken Weekes's trowel clinking against the bricks of his new wall; the children screaming 'YES, YES' at the table football; the ducks on the pond; the ewes being penned up by Fred and Margaret Groombridge; the bees zzzing in the sunshine . . . Perhaps this was the kind of contentment bees felt, too, when the weather turns in the right direction. Who knows? Sarah came in. 'I've ordered the lawn,' she said. 'That's all right then,' I said. 'There'll be croquet in a matter of weeks,' and with those words fell fast asleep, dreaming of a heaven in which lilos covered the Perch Hill fields from hedge to hedge.

THE VALLEY OF ITS SAYING

Recovered in two weeks, I was back to work. I was standing on Stonegate station one morning, waiting for the 5.55 to London. I didn't want to miss a train leaving King's Cross later that morning for Leeds, and was feeling anxious. A government minister, Steve Byers, famously clever, famously on top of every conceivable brief, was going to show me around some of the problems of that city and we were travelling up together. In my mind I was rehearsing conversation after conversation with him in which we discussed the future of the world. I was coming a cropper on every one, a little tornado of neurosis, waiting for the 5.55.

Such an early train was the penalty for not living in

London. Anyone else, in a more settled relationship with his role in life, would have strolled out of his Islington house at five past eight coolly prepared for a sophisticated outing with the Minister of State. I wasn't. I had the suit and tie, briefcase, shoes polished the night before, tape-recorder, batteries in it, notebook, pen, briefing papers from the Department, cuttings; but a frantic search at 4.25 had failed to find any cufflinks. Paper-clips were all I could get hold of.

I was trying to fix them properly, screwing them round and round, twisting them round and round the ends of the shirt cuffs, and my mind was running through the sort of things I could ask the minister ('Have you got an authority problem, Adam?' he kept saying to me. 'Yes sir, yes sir, I think I have sir,' I was jittering back at him) when I suddenly realised something else was going on. I was listening to something I had never consciously heard before. The noise was loud beyond belief. It must have been there for the five minutes I had stood on the platform but I had been shutting it out with all this habitual chewing over past humiliation. Now I had clocked on to it, I could do nothing but listen. Three or maybe four nightingales were singing in the scrubby thorn trees growing around the station and its car park.

I had read about nightingales. Ken Weekes and Brian Wrenn had told me they sang in our own woods at home. I knew that the first time you heard a nightingale, or at least heard it for what it was, allowing it to advance from the background to the front of your mind, was said to be a revelatory moment, a sudden infusion of uninvited beauty on a scale which made other birdsong seem trivial.

I knew all that, and had discounted it as the usual overstatement. It's the kind of thing people say. But now it had happened to me, in the six or seven minutes before the train arrived, as the other commuters, timing their runs to perfection, paused, door open by the ticket machine, on down the car park, skid stop, reverse into the slots by the footbridge, then trotting over it, one hand holding shut the flap of the mac, the other swinging the laptop.

First a punched and a rattled rhythm, a drilled, single note but then, without warning, dropping a register. What followed was such a heavy, operatic sound, meaty, a sirloin steak for birdsong, a bird digging a trench, a big chest to it, not the thin lips-and-tongue-only of a lark or a blackbird, but a song of substance, that the whole being of this creature seems to inflate into the song it makes. What other bird could be as loud as this? And then, out of this song of sheer assertion, came the most miraculous sound I have ever heard a bird make, an absolutely pure and liquid riffling down the scale, a finger running the length of a keyboard until, just as it comes to the end, there is a quick lift to the sequence, a turning-up of the tail without which the run would seem unfinished. And then back through the whole pattern again, not repetitively, but with different combinations of these elements in constant, insistent, demanding play. Why on earth does a nightingale sing?

I didn't tell the minister about my suburban ecstasy but it somehow shaped the whole day that followed. It went like a dream.

The whole pattern of our lives was moving more into balance. I could hear the nightingale on the way to Leeds. I could see, in the great new ceiling of St George's Hall in Windsor Castle, about whose restoration I was then writing a book, the same beauty and problems with green oak as in my own shrinking, splitting oast-house roof. The rest of the world was connected to us, even beyond that local net of Weekes and Clark and Groombridge and Fieldwick and Keeley and Wenman and Bishop. That early tight circle around Perch Hill, that intense and sustaining need for it as an enclosure, which had driven us so fiercely in the early days, was becoming dilute. The urgency of the appetite for pastoral had given way to something more integrated, not so exclusive, not so painful and not so hurt. The cord had loosened and Perch Hill had performed something of its therapeutic task. Happiness could be softer now, not so bound to the private hunger for the natural.

Not that our world at Perch Hill had reached any kind of permanent or static condition. Far from it; change was ever-present here. That spring Will Clark died and was buried in Burwash churchyard. At his funeral, the sun shone and the traffic roared down the village high street. From his grave you could just make out, a little more than a mile away, the last of our fields, the Way Field, dipping down between the woods towards the river. In the afternoon sunshine, the field was like a green flag, glossy with new growth, and a beautiful colour like the polished skin of an apple. It was neither browned off like those around it that had been part-abandoned, nor the chemical blue-green of some of our neighbours, who were pushing their land hard with nitrogen top-dressings. The colour of our grass was both richer and more natural than either, and for that lovely cared-for green I had only Will to thank. He had spent hour after hour on the tractor, topping the fields, nailing the weeds, bringing the farm back to health. He had been ill a long time. We all loved him.

Ken and Brenda decided to move away. He too had looked after us. A multi-talented man, he built beautiful walls and converted sheds to greenhouses. He could install electricity and was an expert joiner. He dug trenches and designed duck-houses. But more than any of that, he gave us all access to other things: a contact with the past and with Sussex; a sense of continuity amid all the changes we had imposed; any number of introductions to the local world of Groombridges, Keeleys and Bowleys, the underlying essence of this part of the Weald; and an unending sequence of jokes and stories rolling round and round the kitchen table.

Now Ken and Brenda were leaving for a house in Robertsbridge, travelling back down the road he had come up in 1942. The trust which owned their cottage was selling it. Ken had been at Perch Hill for 56 years, Brenda for 39. I looked out of the window one evening just before they left. Ken was walking there, Gemma at his heels. Perhaps I was over-interpreting it but it looked as if his tread was heavier than before. He climbed the stile into his garden slowly and laboriously, conscious, I am sure, that this was the end of something. Gemma died the day they left and she was buried in the garden of their new house. Ken planted a rose Sarah and I had given them in the earth above her grave. People like them wouldn't live at Perch Hill again.

It wasn't all gloom. A kind of burgeoning momentum had begun to fill the place. These departures, what were they but the natural rhythm, the coming and going to which a place is always subject? I was alive late that summer with a sense of well-being. I was spending all the money I was earning. And what a wonderful sensation it was.

It was pouring into the farm: new gates, new fences, new hedges, many many thousands of pounds, in a way that was quite different from the rather careful, step-by-step approach I had adopted in the early days. Then, I would feel deeply respectful of what was here, as though my own presence was even slightly illegitimate. That whole view had been shot to pieces. I was rampant now. It was like going swimming: a little reluctance at first, a feeling perhaps that one shouldn't, the dreadful, shivery consequences looming if you did; an inner longing corseted by guilt, sobriety with a double-Boston on desire, but then – oh, for God's sake, why not? Anyway, as a friend I happened to meet in a Chelsea restaurant said to me the other day – she was en route to buying what she called 'day china' in Harvey Nichols – 'It's not spending, it's investment isn't it?' The words spread a haze of beauty across her face.

Money, it now seems to me, is our natural environment, as sustaining and happy for us as the sea for a dolphin or the breeze for a bird. I once saw a documentary on TV about swallows. The young swallows were on the verge of taking their first flight. They were fully fledged and looked, from the outside, indistinguishable from any other swallow. Only because we had followed their history did we know that these were neophytes. They had yet to leave the nesting box in which they had been hatched. Through its open window we could see the domes and towers of Oxford in the sunshine, with the terrifyingly inviting expanses of air between them. One of the young swallows edged towards the hole. Further and further it poked its head and then its shoulders outside. Curiouser and curiouser, its feet moved towards the lip. It reached the point at which clearly physics had taken over. There was no way back. The young bird was committed to its adult life. The air beckoned, the pavement loomed 60 or 80 feet below and the swallow had no choice but to let go, falling from its nest, out, terrifyingly into the thin and dangerous air. But it didn't fall. Its wings spread, its governing instinct locked on and it *flew*, an arcing down and then a curving up, perfect first time, an absolutely pure scalpel cut out through the air in which it was genetically at home, a miracle of adaptation. That is me with my Visa card: a being in his element.

No one ever talks about money like this, particularly in relation to nature. We might look to nature for uplift, as though some kind of spirituality were available there, and ignore the fact that no organism, none of the constituent parts of this spiritualised nature, has any spiritual content itself. My beautiful swallow is entirely and exclusively a materialist being. Its familiarity with the material world in which it lives is what constitutes its beauty. That limitation, that inability to choose, that pre-determined swallowness of the swallow is what is beautiful, and even enviable, about it. Can a swallow ever be brave, or fearful? Can it ever be indecisive or rash? No. A swallow can never stand apart from its swallowness and can never feel that it is less than wholly itself. It is a get, get, get, spend, spend, spend sort of creature, relishing the delights the world can give it. Its careless, unintellectual, unspiritual swoop is the bird equivalent of a girl in search of day china or me happily gathering a few extra cc or another new fence. We are animals in action.

But if we love it in swallows, why don't we love it in us? Why don't we applaud the purity of that graspingness or the grace of that extravagance? Is it perhaps that we are too aware of how destructive human beings can be? In some ways, nowadays, we fail to distinguish power from damage. But that is the crucial distinction. Unless the two remain separate, unless we can think of big actions that are good in themselves, we are condemned to a modest small-mindedness, which rates humility higher than triumph and our own achievements as nothing but pollution, in other words a nostalgic cul-de-sac. And where's the oomph in that?

I am reminded of this: in southern China, in the ninth century AD, one of the great but now anonymous masters of the T'ang dynasty painted landscapes of unparalleled grandeur by first of all getting very drunk indeed. He would then tell an orchestra to play the storm passages from contemporary symphonies and after dipping the ends of his long hair into a pool of ink, he had his assistants spread out enormous sheets of pure fresh silk. Then, in an ecstasy of laughter, the master, always with a small audience at his side, would dance backwards and forwards over the picture, dragging his inky hair after him and smearing at it with the soles of his feet, creating valleys and mountains, canyons and plains. 'At the end of the performance,' one of the spectators recorded, 'it seemed as if the sky had cleared after a storm to reveal the true essence of the thousand things.'

Later, all passion spent, this T'ang Jackson Pollock came back to his picture and, by adding a bamboo house here, a willow tree there, converted his smeared magnificence into the landscape his subconscious had always known it to be. Contemporary critics, who divided painters into three classes, the competent, the wonderful and the divine, were unable to find a place for this man in any of them. He occupied, with a few other like-minded activists, a class of his own, the 'unconfined' or 'untrammelled.'

That is precisely the category I want to belong to. Executives in the BBC, one of which, at a particularly benighted phase in my life, I wished to become, may want to work their slow and ruthless way through the ranks of established virtue; analytical geniuses in the Foreign Office can proceed calmly up their ladders from the competent (Second Secretary Commercial), to the wonderful (unchallenged expert on the internal workings of the EU) and eventually of course the divine (intimate confidant of the current favourite spin-doctor). I don't. I want to be ecstatic in the landscape, my inky hair dragging and smearing all over our fields and hedges.

I know that in certain parts of the Sussex Weald, that verdict has already been passed on 'the Mystic of Perch

Hill Farm' and his wife. Eccentric, oddball, weirdo: those are the words. The intense colours with which Sarah has planted her garden, a kind of beautiful smoky richness that sharpens in places into the brazen and the garish, have, I hear, drawn adverse comments. The garden doesn't go with the landscape. Its colours are much too strong. It's nothing like neat enough. It's untrammelled, unconfined. No one has ever done such a thing before and that is a good enough reason why no one ever should.

Of course I'm not really the Jimi Hendrix of the rural world. More's the pity. I look in the mirror: suit, neatman, not a whiff of the Byronic. Does everyone suffer from this who-you-are/who-you-think-you-are gap? I imagine they do but I realise that the deep, unequalled luxury of my situation is that the fields are there to hand as a canvas on which to make the imagined version of the self into some kind of concrete reality. Nothing is easier than envisaging my liberated Hendrix-landscape around me.

That third summer at Perch Hill, I had my 40th birthday party and it felt like a prefiguring, in an almost ritual, ceremonial way, of that future. We had the party in Great Flemings, overlooking the valley of the river Dudwell, with the stepped and wooded ridges of the Weald folding back one after another to the north and east. The field had been mown for hay and the new grass was thick with clover like a flowery lawn. One open-sided tent for supper was at the top of the hill, another smaller one for dancing half-way down it. Simon Barden, who at that time drove the tractor here, had made a giant wigwam of a bonfire 12 feet high, from a pile of well-seasoned oak, cut two years previously from a tree that had begun dropping its boughs in the drought, just at the time that Stephen Wrenn had died. A few splashes of diesel in the foot of it and the thing burnt like a torch for six long hours, still there when I last saw it at three o'clock in the morning, a hot glowing ring like a fire-disc in the grass.

About 50 people came, and we drank and drank and danced and danced, untrammelled, unconfined, and the place itself, so soft and inviting in the last greying light of the evening, played its part in that, as though to say: 'This is what life can be like, this is what the world can give you, this, if you leave those dead power-structures behind, is how happy you can be.' The words of my R.S. Thomas motto-poem had never seemed more apt:

> Life is not hurrying
> on to a receding future, nor hankering after
> an imagined past. It is the turning
> aside like Moses to the miracle
> of the lit bush, to a brightness
> that seemed as transitory as your youth
> once, but is the eternity that awaits you.
> ('The Bright Field', 1975)

That is a recognition that can come and go, be forgotten and remembered again, but on that party night the brightness seemed to be there for a while, irradiating us all, a ratchet clicked up, a point of optimism from which the whole future could be bathed in light.

I know this bit of country now. The real pleasure is not

in the management, control and decision-making that owning land involves. It is something both less and more than that. I mean the ability to roam in your mind across the surface of a place which is so well known to you that it has become in a sense indistinguishable from who you are. A deeply and properly known stretch of country clamps itself on to your existence like a second skin. It is then, I think, in that marriage of you with your surroundings, that something extraordinary happens. You can run your mental fingers over the place you know, feel the familiar grooves and hollows, the shiny, well-rubbed parts like the burnished wood on the arm of a chair, or the nicks and elbows in it, the quick-flick corners and the knobbly interruptions to a path as it makes its way down to the bottom of the valley, or the boggy, gluey places in winter where you have to teeter along the drier edges and which in summer stiffen into hard clay corrugations, preserving for three or four months the last wet footprints there.

If you lie in the bath and think of these things, the mind becomes like another eye or hand itself. These are the workings of the sensuous memory. The more I come to recognise it, the more I understand it to be the most retentive of all mental faculties. It can feel a remembered landscape like a shepherd at the market feeling along the back of a lamb for the amount of meat covering the bones. Once you know what to look for, and once that purely sensuous knowledge has registered, it enters an ineradicable section of the mind, a deep and animal layer in the consciousness from which physical shapes can be recalled far more easily than anything that is more refined or more abstracted. It puts you, almost literally, in touch with the world.

Coming back from the airport, after a week in a place of few trees and no intimacy, nothing hidden, I remembered why I love the place where I live. The oaks bulked as big as elephants in the hedgerows. I couldn't believe that something vegetable could be that fat. Everything was thick, deep-pile country, as promising as the barrel of wood-shavings in a tombola, concealing hidden things in invisible depths. The little hedgy fields, where the ashes and willows, in particular, had sprouted in high summer sometimes five or six feet above their cut winter line and were shaggy with their own vitality, were an almost unending series of interlocking, muffled, private rooms, each replete with its own private history, and each at its far gateway inviting you on to its neighbour. 'Have me,' the country said, 'I am yours, you know me but you haven't seen this part of me before.' Just at those margins, where the known evolves into the still-to-be-discovered, is where the pleasure in place reaches its peak. It is like coming back to a writer whose work you have known well for many years, and finding something that suddenly stretches out into new territory. The whole geometry of what he has done before shifts with that sudden extension to the landscape. The growth of understanding is an almost physical sensation.

Of course, everything along the main roads on the way back from the airport was hideous: too many buildings and too many signs strung along a strip of tarmac filled with too much traffic. But that is one of the defining characteristics of southern England now. The main roads through it reveal nothing of the underlying nature of the place. Whole swathes of the country are now a net of noise and ugliness laid over a background that still, in its corners, preserves a rich and hidden identity.

Some people talk irritatingly about 'real country' as though such a thing were the preserve nowadays of the far north and west and as though the octopus of London had destroyed everything within 100 miles of Trafalgar Square. Only ignorance stemming, paradoxically enough, from dependence on their cars allows them to say that. All you have to do is walk away from the tarmac and a richly layered complexity is to hand. That is the country over which my mind's eye runs. That is the place I know as Perch Hill, those creases in the skin.

All the same, there is some anxiety hanging over the edges of the picture. Ken Weekes feels that his moving is only the natural end of something that has been going on all around him for the last 10 or 20 years. 'I'm a stranger here now,' he says. 'It's all changed. There's hardly anyone I knew as a boy still here. It's sad really.' None of the five former dairy farms in our lane is now occupied by a farmer, in the strict sense of the word. We're all incomers now, deriving our living from other places: the City, the media, estate agency. Only the Moodys in the nursery at the top of the lane, a lady who grows cyclamens, and Sarah, with her cut flowers, actually get a living from the land.

So this place does, at the moment anyway, exist in a sort of limbo, where there is all this richness of meaning in the landscape but it is in an almost dormant condition.

All those resources are waiting to be mobilised, to have life injected back into them, but they are suspended, far more valuable for what they look like than for what they might produce. There is something wrong with that and something must be done to make these places work again. Beauty is not a sufficient crop.

I was given a small homily late that summer. It was in the evening. My old friend Patrick and I were camping above the shore of a small island, our boat anchored below us in the dark in a nick of sea between weed-lined rocks. Where we had stepped ashore, the bladder-wrack had phosphoresced under our feet, glowing with the pressure of each successive step. It was like that moment in the 'Billie Jean' video, when red-suited Michael Jackson, still then in his pre-Jesus-fantasy days, lit up the paving slabs of the wrecked and slummy street simply by stepping on them. But here the phosphorescence was better than that, spreading out from our feet in circular webs along the fronds of seaweed as if along the veins of an electrified eyeball. Overhead, a snipe was fluting in the dark, the Milky Way was splashed into the spaces between the islands and the waves were stirring against the pebbly shore.

What about living here? It is the question asked by everyone who ever goes on holiday. Why not plunge yourself properly into the natural envelope of something like this? You could surely survive the bad times if this sort of thing was going to be the reward. And to live here would be a truer, richer version of what you meant to do than the farm in Sussex, so easily within reach of London, so much of a half-way house, not really set apart from the city.

Patrick then told me the story he had in mind. Its hero was Georges Gurdjieff, the prophet and teacher of the early part of the century, who began life as a Greek in the Russian Caucasus and ended it, I think in obscurity, in New York. The story was set there, somewhere in Manhattan. Gurdjieff, his accent as thick as the pelt of an Abkhazian bear and his manner both obscure and intermittent, was meeting some disciples in a café on the Lower East Side. One was a rich young man who had decided to give it all up, to leave the city and everything the city represented, to abandon all that for a life far away, out in the country where, Thoreau-like, he would bury himself in the deep leaf-litter of a natural existence. 'So, Mr Gurdjieff,' he asked at the end of his speech, 'do you think that sounds like a good idea? Do you think that's the way to go?'

Gurdjieff, master of the pause, a miraculous air of authority hanging about him, delayed and delayed before making his deep and grumblingly important reply. 'It is a good life,' he said in his beard, pausing again while the American waited for his destiny to be steered and settled by the man he admired more than any other. 'Yes, it is a good life,' Gurdjieff repeated, 'for a dog.'

Pastoral – the idea that a rural existence can somehow regenerate those who give themselves over to it – carries the seeds of its own failure within it. It is, by definition, a sophisticated attitude. Only those who have abandoned the idyll, or have had the idyll withdrawn from them, are in search of it. The fact that they are searching means they cannot find what they are looking for. They are the fallen. We are all Adam and Eve, we have all been expelled from Eden and we are all taking our solitary way through the postlapsarian world. Some are apparently content to live their lives without the dream country hovering over them. Some, apparently, are content with things as they are and the gratifications that things as they are can provide. I am not one of them and never have been.

Even in the knowledge of its inadequacy, pastoral seems to me not a worthless but a necessary myth. It provides a sanctuary in which a bruised mind can rest. It puts a torque on the material concerns of the everyday, twisting them towards something else, some better state. It is a form, in that sense, of idealism, the template on which poetry, or the poetic, can be moulded.

When Yeats died, in the winter before the Second World War began, Auden wrote a great elegy:

> The brooks were frozen, the air-ports almost
>   deserted,
> And snow disfigured the public statues;

This was more than a eulogy to a dead man; it was a hymn to poetry itself, as an alternative and richer world:

> For poetry makes nothing happen: it survives
> In the valley of its saying where executives
> Would never want to tamper; it flows south
> From ranches of isolation and the busy griefs . . .
> It survives, A way of happening, a mouth.
>   ('In Memory of W.B.Yeats', 1939)

There is an almost universal need for beautiful places, not
only in our culture and not only in our time, and that
need, even if it is expressed as house-hunting or holiday-
going, can still be seen, I think, as a search for the place
where poetry has its hidden source, for 'the valley of its
saying'. We cannot help searching for metaphors, for
inner landscapes in the outer world. When we spend
all our money on a wrecked farm; when we feel threatened by changes to somewhere we love; when we hang
on to the privacy of a genuinely secluded place: the one
thing we are thinking of and aiming for then is not
physical, the actual substance, but the poetic qualities
that a place can enshrine, the valley of its saying.

The valley of its saying is a place apart, hidden from the
mundane world in the way that a hanging valley in the
Alps opens only as you arrive at its lip. There you will find
an expanse of pasture where you had expected only rock.
And there you will stroll on to the ranches of isolation
where, as Auden wrote at another time,

> The lion griefs loped from the shade
> And on our knees their muzzles laid,
> And Death put down his book.
> (*Poems 1931–1936*, 'XIV', 1933)

I could not conceive now of living somewhere that did not
have an actual physical equivalent of the valley of its
saying, of the poetic core of things, somewhere near to
hand. That phrase and that idea will always be attached
for me now to a damp and rushy place hidden, almost
surrounded by wood, down in the Slip Field, at the rough

bottom end of the farm. The ground has slipped there and, during the winter, small eyeglass pools gather among the bumps and hollows. In spring and on into the early summer it is the most flowery field we have. It is the place to go and sit at any time, to lie down, to hang out, 'For poetry makes nothing happen.'

No one else ever goes there. You never get caught in the silence. Deer wander out of the big wood without wariness and rabbits eat too much of the grass. The sheep don't like it much in that field – perhaps the grass is too acid, too sour – and we leave the whole place uncut until September when the black seed-heads of the dyer's green-weed pop like popcorn at the touch and the wood-edge brambles are heavy with blackberries.

It is a precious place, at least partly because there is nothing about it to say that it matters. I'd do almost anything to defend that field and I know if, for whatever reason, we had to leave this farm, that is the place I would remember and in some ways continue to own; not the house and all its organised appurtenances but the damp field, the source of meaning, its immediate roughness, in the valley of its saying.